RUSSELL CROWE
THE BIOGRAPHY

Dedication

Tim: To my mother Joy, Emma, Oliver and Carole Anne
Stafford: To my wife Janet, my daughters Claire and Rebecca,
and my mother Rosemary

Design copyright © 2001 Carlton Books Ltd
Text copyright © 2001 Tim Ewbank and Stafford Hildred

This edition published by Carlton Books Limited 2001
20 Mortimer Street
London
W1T 3JW

ISBN 1 84222 423 9

Design – Adam Wright
Editor – Sarah Larter
Production – Alastair Gourlay

Printed and bound in Great Britain.

RUSSELL CROWE
THE BIOGRAPHY

Tim Ewbank and Stafford Hildred

CONTENTS

PROLOGUE

*A lot of people think I've had it easy. But I've got rejection
slips that could wallpaper a suburban house twice over.*
Russell Crowe

New Zealand is a country comprised of two islands, the northern of
which – the smaller of the two – is where Russell Crowe was born.
Away from the towns, it's made up of active volcanoes, geysers and
hot bubbling springs, which flank the fertile green land upon which
many thousands of sheep graze their days away. And there are
those who have encountered the Oscar-winning actor over the
course of the thirty-seven years of his life who will swear that
Russell Crowe must have been hewn from the very land of his birth.

He is, they point out, a rugged man who threatens to erupt at any
time, an achiever who shoots relentlessly for the top, a man who
overflows with a restless, bubbling energy that proves much too
scaldingly hot for some, and a part-time farmer who is at his most
balanced when on a solitary walk through green pasture land surrounded by his own animals.

It's a basis for character assessment that Russell himself might not
entirely disagree with, although there is, of course, a very great deal
more to the man's make-up. Add in a confident self-belief, an assur-
ance, an arrogance bordering on downright rudeness, an unswerving commitment to his craft, a compact, muscular frame, a cleft chin
and a virile sex appeal underlining his huge acting talent and it's
not hard to understand why it all makes for a potently dynamic
screen presence. There's a sense of anger there, too, and the angri-
er his movie role, the better the screen performance seems to be.

Gladiator gave Russell Crowe a role in which he could harness
those talents and natural traits and it made him a movie star of global
magnitude. It also put a Best Actor Oscar on his mantelpiece and elevated him to the point where he can demand $15 million a movie.

Although he might appear to be the epitome of the Hollywood overnight sensation, in reality he's that actor who's had years of striving to get where he is today. Russell didn't make his first appearance in a film until he was twenty-five, and by then he experienced his fair share of rejections. He had also suffered abject failure as a pop recording artist under a fancifully invented new persona.

And yet, when once asked if he anticipated success in Hollywood, he gave an unequivocal "Yes", delivered with the bold stare and unnervingly direct eye contact from his grey-blue irises that is a Russell Crowe trademark. "You get accused of being arrogant by some people because I seem to – in some people's viewpoints – expect success," he said. "But it doesn't surprise me when it comes, because I know how much work I put into it." His prolific film output of twenty-one movies in ten years is testament to the effort he has expended and to his fierce commitment.

But ever since he struck out for better scripts, stronger roles and bolder acting challenges in America's movie capital, Russell has tended to get up Hollywood's nose – in more ways than one. In a health-obsessed town where cigarette smoking is taboo, the movie moguls he deals with dislike Russell's habit of lighting up without asking and their having to discuss multi-million dollar movie projects through the clouds of smoke he blows annoyingly in their direction. They begrudge, too, his unwillingness to base himself in their midst, preferring instead to retreat to his farm in Australia at any and every opportunity. Taking on Hollywood's mightiest doesn't phase him. "I'm still the same arsehole I always was," he says with characteristic bluntness. "I don't feel any pressure to live up to anybody, mate. Except myself."

But tobacco habits and his living arrangements aside, the word has long been out on the actor that if you take Russell Crowe on board, then he comes with "Attitude" with a capital A. Geoffrey Wright, the director for whom Russell created the terrifying but charismatic neo-Nazi skinhead character Hando in the Australian movie *Romper Stomper*, remarked, "Russell's the rudest actor I've ever met. He's also the most committed. So if he wants to abuse me and then give me the most sensational take of all time, I don't care."

Russell himself partly explains away his bad boy reputation as a misconception. If he's driven people crazy by his demands, he insists it's not because he's egocentric but because he's taking his job seriously and therefore applying the highest possible standards. But he's learned from dealing with his farm animals that teamwork is usually the key to a well run operation. During the making of *Gladiator* he arrived one morning after a day in which he had not held back in putting across his own views and handed out CDs of his own band, Thirty Odd Foot Of Grunts. "I laid into you all yesterday," he explained, "now it's your turn."

Russell is passionate about acting and making movies. Those who recognise that as a quality to be admired and emulated are the people he can happily work with. As for the rest: "The meek are not on the phone anymore. I just tend to be talking to people who have very strong personalities and want to make a significant piece of art when they make their film and they want to have somebody who's ready to come along and wants to work. And work on behalf of the character."

To many of the legions of first-time fans he garnered as general-turned-slave Maximus in *Gladiator*, Russell appeared to have come from nowhere to "unleash hell" on the big screen. But behind him he had a body of film work which had seen him play a gentle dish-washer, a chillingly ambitious moccasin factory sales executive, a homosexual rugby-playing plumber, a small-time criminal on the run, a virginal Welsh Baptist factory clothing supervisor, a revered horse-man, a high plains loner and an Old West outlaw turned preacher.

He has immersed himself in his roles with such chameleon-like versatility that he's been able to hold conversations in bars with people who are telling him about movies he's been in and yet have had no idea that he is the actor they are talking about. As corporate whistle-blower Dr Geoffrey Wigand in *The Insider*, Russell was almost unrecognisable, even to those familiar with his work and his normal appearance.

But it's *Gladiator* for which he has gained world-wide recognition. He's become Hollywood's hottest male star, a throwback to manly actors such as Robert Mitchum, Burt Lancaster, Kirk Douglas and Steve McQueen, actors from another age of film making. But significantly he can play the good guy as well as the bad guy and it's turned him into an international sex symbol, adored by women for his virile screen presence. Stallone's and Schwarzenegger's exaggerated air of invincibility and machismo in screen thrillers of the last decade looks to be a contrivance compared with Russell's testosterone-fuelled real-man masculinity. It's also a masculinity which stands out in an era of pretty boy idols like Brad Pitt, Johnny Depp and Keanu Reeves.

More than one recent poll has named Russell "Sexiest Man In The Movies", but there's a paradox about the female fan worship he encounters wherever he goes. His success and insatiable appetite for movie roles has come at a personal cost. Russell's attitude has always been that what he gets out of life, he gets through his job. Maybe, he concedes, that attitude is the reason he hasn't been able to sustain a relationship with a woman.

His parents have been married for forty years, and Russell yearns for a similarly loving and loyal union with a good woman one day. But the unrelenting pace and workload he has set himself has left love affairs unfinished or snuffed out prematurely. "I'm the master of unrequited love," he admits sadly in an introspective moment.

There is no question that Russell Crowe is a driven man. When he was younger he went so far as to change his name briefly to reinvent himself as a pop singer and to distance himself from two renowned sporting cousins in a bid to be his own man. When times were lean and he was out of work, he still managed to remain the consummate professional. He avoided taking jobs where he could be seen publicly, believing it might destroy the illusion for people who would go to see him in the movies.

A famous story, which every actor and actress in Australia seems to have heard, is the one about an alleged sexual encounter between Russell and a young actress who was shocked when, during the act, he began cheerleading "Go, Russ, go!". The story, which first surfaced many years ago, has transcended industry gossip to become a legend that has clung to Russell as his star has risen inexorably. Even the august British Film Institute's monthly journal *Sight And Sound* has referred to the actor as "Russell 'Go Russ' Crowe".

Those who know Russell well will say he is a man of contrasts, a complex man full of fire who is rarely happier than when he is enjoying the simple life. He's full of self belief yet superstitious. He can be affable and charming, but cross him and there's an aggressive instinct lurking just below the surface, which can explode in an outburst of four letter words and more. Again, he will deflect such accusations. It's down to holding very definite views, speaking his mind and knowing exactly where he's going and precisely what he's doing.

"Unleash hell" may have been the war cry of Maximus but it's far from unthinkable that it's Russell Crowe's as well. Tales of his boisterous partying are legendary. Then there are the hushed-up brawls and the odd *fracas* that makes the headlines, like the rollicking rampage at a hostelry in Darwin on a stop-over with his motorbiking pals. "There were a few days when we were pretty hung over, especially when we were in Darwin," he concedes.

There's even the occasional rumpus that makes for some interesting footage on a security video, as was the case outside a New South Wales nightclub in 1999 when Russell appeared to start three fights, argue heatedly with a woman and throw a punch at his own brother, Terry, before being pinned to the ground by a security guard. "Unfortunately, all it takes is one ant to ruin the picnic," said the bar's co-owner, "and he was it."

But those moments of pressure release from the burning intensity of his approach to acting seem only to add to the masculine image of Russell Crowe, one which uniquely appeals to both women and men. For women, Russell is a sexy, successful, virile, wealthy fantasy man. They adore him. But that aura around the actor is not something which men resent. They admire and envy him for it. They wish they could be like Russell Crowe, who moves effortlessly between being a superstar and the average Joe who cheerily calls everyone "mate".

It's said that persistence is an innate quality in a New Zealander – Sir Edmund Hilary, the first man to climb Mount Everest, was a Kiwi. It's said that Australians have a happy-go-lucky attitude to life. As a Kiwi who has lived much of his life in Australia, Russell has both qualities in abundance.

He has shown an extraordinary tenacity in reaching the top, first in Australia and then in Hollywood, while not forgetting to enjoy, if not the roses, then the local beers and music along the way. His is a fascinating story. He has played a wide range of interesting characters on the big screen, but the most interesting character of all is Russell Crowe.

I

EARLY LIFE

He was always flamboyant. He had that drifty
flair about him. He had a way of doing things,
over-dramatising things a little bit.
Troy Serhon, a school contemporary of Russell Crowe

Whenever New Zealand excels at the games of either rugby or cricket, it lifts the spirits of the entire nation. And, as March gave way to April in New Zealand in 1964 the sport-mad Kiwi population were still glowing from an heroic staving off of Test Match defeat by a powerful South African cricket team on their own local Auckland turf. The toast in the pubs was to a display of typically New Zealand dogged defiance and persistence and to a diminutive batsman called B.W. Sinclair, who hit 138 runs – the highest ever test match score by a New Zealander in New Zealand – to help save the game and the series.

It was into this buoyant state of general Kiwi euphoria that Russell Ira Crowe entered the world on April 7, 1964. There was much rejoicing for Alex and Jocelyne Crowe at the arrival of a second child – a brother for Terry – and they gave him his middle name Ira from his illustrious great uncle, Ira Cunningham, head of the Animal Health Division for New Zealand and a noted scientist in his time.

Russell was born in Wellington, New Zealand's capital port at the southern tip of the northern island, the island where most people live because it is warmer and less rugged than the southern. And he was born into a fast changing world. It was a time when youth was having its day, seemingly like never before. In America, Beatles records held the top five spots in the singles charts, an unprecedented feat, and Beatlemania had hit its peak. In England, a new generation of scooter-riding, fashion conscious Mods – as they called themselves – fought running battles on the south coast beaches with Rockers. In Australia, as in other countries around the world, audiences were flocking to the cinema to see a new screen idol, Sean Connery as James Bond in *Goldfinger* and *From Russia With Love*. It was a buoyant time for show business generally and the movie and television industry in particular, which suited Alex and Jocelyne Crowe as they were set caterers.

When Russell was four the family moved over to Australia and settled in Sydney. It was here, in Australia's best-known city, a thriving harbourside metropolis renowned for its great natural beauty and its magnificent bridge, which had opened in 1932, that Russell was to spend his formative years.

Russell was sent to the local primary school at Vaucluse, a smart area of Sydney not far from Australia's famous Bondi beach. Retired teacher Mrs Morgan remembers him vividly: "Oh, he was a darling child, a lovely chubby little boy with those cheeks that you could push." Not quite so darling was Russell's habit of mimicking the way people spoke. He had a keen ear for accents and would pick up on them instantly. Even now it's not unusual for Russell to call on a variety of accents and inflections in his speech each day. Some still find that maddening but back then, from a child, it could be an infuriating habit. Visitors arriving to see his parents would soon get an apology from Jocelyne or Alex for the way their younger boy appeared to be aping their speech so accurately. Years later he would look back and cringe: "I was always an annoying little bastard and an embarrassment to my parents. I'd mimic their friends and my mum would say, 'Don't worry about Russell, he's a bit mental'."

When he wasn't at school, Russell became a familiar, inquisitive figure on the locations where his parents were working. At first he was wide-eyed at the make-believe world of TV and movie-making. He found it fascinating to see a door and discover nothing behind it. He was often to be found exploring the sets. When, much later, he became a full-time actor he was able to look back and realise how lucky he was to have lost any fears he may have had about TV and film performance at such an early age because he had found out for himself that it was all fantasy.

When Russell was five his parents were working on a TV wartime drama series called *Spyforce*, directed by Jocelyne's godfather and starring a popular Aussie actor called Jack Thompson. Russell was roped in for a scene with a group of other small children. Conspicuous in a red and green hooped South Sydney "Rabbitohs" rugby jumper, the team he would so fervently come to support after watching them in action for the first time when he was five, Russell was at the forefront of the group and was allowed to deliver a single line of dialogue. It clearly struck a chord. His mother Jocelyne remembers that from then on he was always dressing up and pretending to be a pirate or a soldier, "and whatever he was, he was always the leader," she said.

That first taste of TV acting, however, gave him ideas above his station. Whenever he watched the action where his parents were working, he always imagined himself in the role. Even at the tender age of six, when he was still in short trousers and playing with toy cars, he would watch an actor playing a war veteran in a film and nag his parents as to why the director hadn't seen him in that role. He might admittedly be a bit on the short side, he'd tell them, but he was sure he could do it. It was the first sign of the remarkable self-belief that was to propel him to the top as an actor, although conversely at times he could come across as terribly shy; once he was lined up to enter for a talent contest but pulled out.

Quite apart from his own parents' movie connections, Russell was brought up with an understanding of the power of film gained through the work of his grandfather, who had worked as a film cameraman during the war. Stan Wemyss, whose family had emigrated to New Zealand from Scotland, was a pioneer in New Zealand's TV industry. He produced documentaries and then worked as a cameraman, risking his life countless times to bring back images of war while under fire himself. His bravery won him the MBE.

Stan Wemyss' films have since been hailed as masterpieces in the field of film photography during combat. With his camera he brought back graphic images of Fijian troops under fire in the jungles of Bouganiville Island, Papua New Guinea, which left no doubt that he was operating in the heart of the fighting. With death and horrific scenes of carnage all around him, he simply carried on filming to capture images for the New Zealand Film Unit showing the stark horrors of war. He was famous among his colleagues for the disregard for his own safety and at first carried only a dagger as a personal weapon until he was wounded and then resorted to carrying a gun.

Russell came to have the utmost respect for his grandfather, who always played down his own bravery. In a documentary filmed just a few years before his death, he said: "Your mind gets dulled to death and destruction. It's only really when someone you have been talking to or have been close to, something happens to them, and you see it that close that it becomes something that stops your mind and says, 'Hey!'"

It's a commonly held belief that it was grandfather Stan who first instilled in Russell a love for the movie industry. With his second wife Joy, who is English, Stan ran a little film theatre with studios in the basement and Russell spent many a happy hour following his grand-dad around watching him at work. Stan's ex-business partner Kelvin Peach has an abiding memory of when he stayed with Russell's parents and of a six-year-old Russell announcing to him, "Mr Peach, I want to make pictures like you". Significantly, Russell insisted that he wanted to be in front of the camera, not behind it.

Joy recognises in Russell several of the qualities that made up her late husband, who died aged 72 in 1988. Stan was a man who liked to win and so is Russell, as was amply illustrated when Joy found she could still beat Russell at tennis when he was about fourteen years of age – and he didn't like it one bit. He lost his temper and threw his racket about the court in a tantrum. Joy reports that he eventually calmed down and shook her hand but he didn't look forward to going home and telling his parents that granny had beaten him.

Another was an air of arrogance she noticed about Stan when they first met at a hotel in Wellington. But, as with Russell, she says, it wasn't really arrogance, it was just that he was an achiever.

Five years before Russell was to star in *Gladiator,* Joy handed over to him Stan's MBE medal together with his dagger, his camera and a selection of wartime stills. It was the medal he would wear with such pride to honour his mentor when he won the Oscar.

Time spent on his parents' TV and film sets naturally decreased as Russell grew up and school lessons became more important. But watching the "Rabbitohs", as his favourite local rugby team were known, had given him a taste for the game and while representing the school against another from Beverly Hills he had a tooth knocked out during the match. He was then ten years of age and he was not to have the tooth replaced until he had his first starring role in a movie fifteen years later.

Soon Russell moved on to become a pupil at Sydney Boys High School, some twenty minutes distance by car from the centre of Sydney. The school had as its motto *Veritate et Virtue*, meaning "truth and honour" – a variation of which Russell was to adapt as a war cry in *Gladiator* many years later. The school had a strong educational and sporting record and the main building itself, situated on a fringe of Moore Park, was just as impressive. Its grand pillared facade looked out across a large grassy expanse flanked by the outskirts of the Paddington and Surry Hills areas of Sydney, not far from the famous SCG, the Sydney Cricket Ground.

Suddenly work, not play, became the norm for Russell, although he did get the chance to appear in an episode of the TV series *The Young Doctors* when he was twelve, playing the small part of a boy who hangs around the hospital when his parents are away.

Teachers at Sydney Boys High School remember him as a lad always on the move, full of energy, always with something to say and a bit cheeky. In the school photograph of the 13As rugby team, Russell can be seen among the tough teenage scrummagers holding up a flower in his hand. Troy Serhon, a contemporary of

Russell's, remembers: "He was always flamboyant. He had that drifty flair about him. He had a way of doing things, over-dramatising things a little bit."

By the time Russell was fourteen, his parents were set on moving back to New Zealand and Russell had to bid goodbye to the friends he had made at school. At that point in time, his Sydney Boys High School contemporaries saw nothing in him that suggested he was going to become an Oscar-winning movie star. But some of them do remember Russell being involved in an incident with a stink bomb, which forced many of them to jump out of a window.

II

THE SINGING CROWE

*He was so uncool that he was actually cooler than most
of the so-called cool people. He was kind of a freak but he
used to get away with it. It was a bullshit time and Russ
was for real. He used to walk around with this jacket
that had "Russ" on the back. He had so much bottle.*
Trevor Reekie of pop group Car Crash Set on
Russell Crowe's teenage alter ego, pop singer Russ le Roq

Russell's father Alex is very much a New Zealander and he had
never intended for himself and his family to have stayed away from
the country for so long. He was pleased to be going back home.
But Russell's formative years had been spent in Australia and adapting to life once more in New Zealand after ten years away wasn't
the smooth process it might have been.

Once the Crowe family had settled back in New Zealand, with
his father running The Albion pub in the city in Auckland, Russell
was sent to Auckland Grammar School where his time was not alto-
gether happy. Ironically, in view of the film that was to win him an
Oscar, Russell hated wearing Roman sandals to school. That wasn't
the only thing he disliked about the school. He objected to what he
viewed as a pupil's value being judged by their sporting prowess –
or lack of it – rather than his creative qualities.

For the uninitiated, rugby is a religion in New Zealand and the
New Zealand All Blacks have dominated the game at international
level for long periods. But though not unathletic nor untalented at
games, Russell was not as big as some of the other rugby-loving
boys of his age. This was something of a disadvantage in a country
whose legendary All Blacks captain Colin "Pine Tree" Meads was so

powerfully built that he did his training by running up and down hills with a sheep under each arm.

Russell and the other pupils at the school had a lot to live up to in the school's sporting sphere. Russell was in the mid-low stream of 5F and one year above him, and nineteen months older than him, was his cousin. Martin Crowe, a fine rugby player, was already showing on the cricket field glimpses of the effortless timing and brilliant range of strokeplay that was to blossom into his becoming one of the world's most naturally gifted batsmen and a mainstay of the New Zealand team. Martin's brother Jeff, also a run-getter and destined to captain New Zealand at cricket with distinction, was naturally also a bit of a school hero. Jeff and Martin, whose father – Russell's uncle – had been a first class cricketer, went on to play more Test Matches together than any other brothers apart from Australia's Ian and Greg Chappell. Also in Russell's form was Mark Greatbatch, another determined and gifted batsman, who would become a national hero nine years later by hitting one hundred runs on his test match debut for New Zealand at Auckland against England.

Then there was Russell's form master, Graham Henry, better known today as the celebrated coach of the Welsh Rugby Union national side and coach of the British and Irish Lions rugby union team, which toured Australia in 2001. The school were also rightly predicting a great rugby future for one of Henry's *protégés*. He was another of Russell's contemporaries who went by the name of Grant Fox and it was no surprise when Fox progressed to become a permanent fixture for many years at fly-half in an all-conquering All Blacks rugby union team. Eventually, Fox kicked his way into the record books by becoming one of the greatest international points scorers with his boot of all time.

Under this weight of sporting expectation, it was no surprise that Russell looked to excel elsewhere. He became known as the "cousin of the cricketing Crowes". And even when he picked up a guitar and formed pop bands he couldn't shake off the spectre of his sporty cousins. He became known as the "singing cousin of the cricketing Crowes". Though he respected and even envied Martin and Jeff their achievements at the batting crease, to be linked to and compared with them continually grated upon him. Happily for their respective families, it never affected the friendship between the three boys, but it does explain why, when he eventually wanted to try and make a go of it as a singer, he changed his name.

Although Russell won his class's English prize, he and his brother Terry were both transferred the following year to Mount Roskill Grammar school. The word was that he left before he was asked to leave. Warren Seastrant, former head of English at Mount Roskill, told the *New Zealand Listener*, in its fascinating profile of Russell in his early years in Auckland: "He was unhappy at Auckland Grammar, but he wasn't expelled. It was decided that he would go into my class because he had a little bit of form."

Mr Seastrant remembers Russell as "a fairly wilful student. Into image making." He said: "He had a bit of a career of disruption. He would do enough to get by, usually at the C-plus/B-minus level. He was capable of much more." The arrogance that he would later become famed for was there even then. "There was a measure of it. The hooded eyes and the cool disengagement. He had a great deal of self-assurance – superficial self-assurance at least. A lot of the prescribed arrogance was a part of the image he was projecting."

Russell formed his first band while at Mount Roskill. Ever since he could remember, he'd been playing imaginary guitar on a tennis racket to the pop hits he heard on the radio. But now he started to show an interest in playing the real thing. The transformation occurred when he was fourteen years old and his family had only newly settled back in New Zealand.

Russell's father had now moved on from The Albion pub to another in New Lynn and Russell's eyes were opened to a much more adult life and some scary situations. He has recounted how when he was fourteen he worked security during university pub crawls: "When people drink they go to a lot of weird places emotionally. I've been in a room where fifty people are punching each other because they're drunk. I was basically a kid faced with adult fury. This is tattooed on my brain."

Because of his family's association with hotels and film, Russell had throughout his young life always been around performers and he had come to liken hotel life to working behind the scenes as a caterer, where he got to see the best and the worst of people. "In the morning all the glamour is gone, and it just smells of stale beer," he commented.

One of the performers he got to catch in action at his father's new premises was rock 'n' roll revival singer Tom Sharplin, who entertained the pub punters with his band. He was at once drawn to the whole concept of musical performance and got chatting to the band about it all. Sharplin could see this was more than a young fan wanting to tag on to a band enjoying a bit of local fame and he encouraged Russell to try writing some of his own songs if he really was that interested in music.

Russell went away and picked up enough of the rudiments of guitar to drag in school pal Mark Staufer on bass and another on drums to form a group calling themselves The Profile. They considered themselves a cut above other embryonic musical outfits in the school. When any other bands played at Mount Roskill, Russell and his group would very blatantly position themselves in the front row and superciliously turn their backs on the musicians. But their ultra-cool stance backfired. When it was the turn of Russell and The Profile to take to the stage, the seventh-formers turned up *en masse* to hog the first three rows, all with their backs to the group in retaliation. But the self-confidence as a performer, which was to be a recurring trait throughout his career, saw Russell through. He and rest of The Profile just kept playing away through the massed ranks of disdain.

Following the pop trends of the time, there was a brief excursion by Russell into the fringes of punk music as Dave Deceit And The Interrogatives before leaving school early with a head full of dreams. But his first job was with an insurance company to make ends meet while he angled for a break into the local music scene. By now Sharplin, with whom he had struck up a real mutual affinity and a friendship that was to last all his life, had begun running a club in the city called King Creole's – named after the Elvis Presley movie – and Russell eventually chucked in his insurance job to become the DJ there, much to the disappointment of his parents. He was still only seventeen and they were none too happy about their younger son whiling away his nights at a licensed club with no day job to go to.

But Russell was fairly happy with his lot. Even though DJ-ing in those days was not the art form that the likes of Fat Boy Slim have raised it to in modern times, he felt he was somebody when he was tucked away in his booth with headphones on and planting the needle in the right groove. Hanging around late at night at King Creole's also ensured that he started meeting lots of girls. And he was becoming immersed in music, listening to records for hours as well as regularly catching the performances of Tom Sharplin and his band. From his vantage point near the stage he could study the stagecraft and pick up a guitar chord or two.

His ambition was still to get his own band together and make a record and in 1982 Sharplin called up some of his own musicians to provide the backing for Russell to record a single. It was one of Russell's own compositions and its title was freakishly portentous – *I Just Want To Be Like Marlon Brando*. The legendary actor, along with Hollywood action man Steve McQueen, was one of Russell's influences when he was growing up.

Russell laid down the track at a studio in Pakuranga in Auckland and it was released on the Ode label, but not under the name of Russell Crowe. Instead, he called himself Russ le Roq. The record won airplay just twice on 1ZM radio, sold only five hundred copies and barely caused a ripple.

Russell had chosen the name Russ le Roq as a tongue-in-cheek moniker to get away from the label of the "singing cousin of the

Crowes". He also intended, rather as David Bowie had created his alter ego Ziggy Stardust, to invent a new persona for himself as a cool rock singer. The difference with Russell was that unlike Bowie, who shed Ziggy and all his trappings the minute he stepped off-stage, Russell intended to be cool Russ le Roq outside of the recording studio and the music venues as well as in. So successful was the alter ego that there were quite a few who made his acquaintance around this period who did not realise until years afterward that Russ le Roq was a member of the Crowe family. In retrospect, the invention of Russ le Roq can be considered as Russell's first convincing piece of acting.

He followed it through with the release the following year of another Russ le Roq single, called *Pier 13*. This was issued as one hundred limited edition copies with a photograph on the back of the record sleeve of Russell trying to look stylishly smooth in a white jacket, a black shirt, white tie and sunglasses, while smoking a cigarette. There is an air of affluence about Monsieur le Roq because the photo was taken outside a hotel and in the background is a bell-boy with luggage following him through some sliding doors. The nonchalant pose belies the story behind the picture, which was taken by photographer Trevor Coppock. Russell had hung around nervously outside the hotel waiting for just the right moment when the bellboy would appear in shot laden with luggage so that he himself would look suitably superior and successful in the foreground. Then he quickly took up the pose and shouted "Now!" to Coppock.

Soon he recruited Graham Silcock, a former guitarist in Tom Sharplin's band, and a couple of other musicians to form his own three-piece backing group, calling the band Russ le Roq And The Romantics. Russell then geared up for some serious image-building. He decked the boys out in a uniform he designed himself, with each of their names emblazoned brightly on the back of their jackets.

The bright pink record sleeve of the next single, *Never Let Ya Slide*, throws light on Russ le Roq's approach. In the top left and bottom right corners are hearts with an arrow slicing through them accompanied by kisses. In the centre is a photo of Russ Le Roq looking casually and moodily cool standing with one hand in his pocket and the other by his side holding a cigarette while the Romantics pose in the background in bow ties.

The back of the sleeve continues Russ le Roq's mythical French mode by listing the three songs – *Never Let Ya Slide*, *Fire*, and *St. Kilda* – as "Le Music". The musicians are also introduced and listed as "Le Playerz", and there is even a jokey "Le Warning" spelled out in capital letters, which reads: "This is 'Roq & Roll' music. It is <u>not</u> a rock 'n' roll revival disc. Anyone caught saying it is will be murdered by death, or shot by hanging or…forced to play session on my next record!!!" Russell finishes off with, "Signed, Moi" in his own handwriting and adds two kisses.

Also printed on the sleeve is an address for the Russ le Roq fan club, although history does not record whether anybody joined or what sort of newsletters or merchandise anyone might have received.

Never Let Ya Slide, recorded at Mandrill Studio, Parnell, Auckland, again failed to set the local pop charts on fire but whenever Russ le Roq was asked how he and his band were doing he would always be upbeat and positive and hint that they were enjoying success. Graham Silcock's memory of events is rather different, as he told the *New Zealand Listener*: "He used to say he was doing really well and the other guys and I looked at each other – if you say so, great. If we were doing that well, we never made much out of it. We used to see the records in these old bins for fifty cents. My friends used to remind me of that."

A lot of people found Russ le Roq arrogant. But then he had lived in Sydney and he'd seen for himself how competitive life could be and how difficult it was to get ahead. Until someone voluntarily offered to manage him, he reckoned he had no choice but to do everything himself. And he kept up his show of arrogance just to get himself talked about.

The next single, *Shattered Glass*, was produced by Trevor Reekie, a member of a group called Car Crash Set who were heavily into a more electronic sound than Russ le Roq And The Romantics were used to. Reekie took the studio controls at Russell's request in an effort to inject the band with a different, more immediate, fuller and funkier sound. "We tried to jazz this piece of shit up and it didn't work at all," Reekie was quoted as saying. "It didn't work at all, but he was a laugh."

While Russ le Roq may have lacked musicianship and vocal dexterity, there was no mistaking he had a certain presence when he was up on stage with the band. He'd give it his all and, having observed Tom Sharplin at so many gigs, he knew how to put on a show.

Despite the aura of success that he liked to adopt, Russ le Roq And The Romantics were not gong to be the next big thing. In an *Auckland Star* article just before Christmas 1983, Russell – interviewed as Russ le Roq, not as Russell Crowe – indicated that the whole alter-ego venture had cost him $7,000, but that he might perhaps do one more single. "There's always another $2,000 somewhere to send down the drain."

Within two months Russell turned his hand to another enterprise, this time a night club called The Venue, which he opened at 134 Symonds Street. It was unlicensed and he saw it as just a place where kids could go to hear live music. He reckoned pop groups and live music should be part of their lives rather than an event. But within nine months The Venue had gone under.

The problem was that it was in the wrong location and also that without a drinking license its clientele were teenagers with no money to spend. It did, however, allow Russell to keep his finger on the pulse of the local music scene. He invited groups to play and rehearse at The Venue and hosted a "Battle Of The Bands" competition, which resulted in an LP produced by le Roq called *Dressed Up And No Place To Play*.

But by November 1984 the teenagers who frequented The Venue learned from their local hip publication *Rip It Up* that the club was finished. It reported: "...le Roq said lower-than-expected numbers caused initial problems in covering overheads and when The Venue had to close down for two weeks in August because of violence from outsiders, it dealt finances a death blow leaving him facing bankruptcy court – not a pleasant experience."

Street kids moved on by the police from Aotea Square had apparently posed a problem. Looking for somewhere else to get their kicks they headed for The Venue. "It would be easy to become racist running The Venue," le Roq told *Rip It Up*, "which would be odd, seeing as I'm part Maori myself," he added, referring to his one-sixteenth Maori heritage. Included in the report was the following assertion by le Roq: "I still want to be a pop star."

It was around this time that Russell landed a job as an entertainment officer at a Pakatoa Island resort in the Hauraki Gulf, just off Auckland harbour. He enjoyed living on an island but he loathed wearing a uniform and, so he says himself, used to liven up the bingo sessions by calling out the numbers in irreverent style, such as "Number one, up your bum". Fed up of organising bingo tournaments, he quit soon afterward.

But in 1984 he tried for a musical breakthrough once more when he met up with guitarist Dean Cochran, who was to become one of his very closest friends. Cochran remains so, as well as being a key component of Russell's current band Thirty Odd Foot Of Grunts over the years. In 1985 they recorded a single called *What's The Difference*. There was none; once again the record was a flop, although it did get MTV airplay.

Russell and Dean got on so well together that they went out on the pub circuit playing gigs with other musicians, including Mark Rimington, under the new name of Roman Antix. Their set consisted of some of their own songs and cover versions of familiar hits. Rimington's recollections of Russell are that he was very driven and focused at the expense of everything else. "The women fell by the wayside very quickly. If people had a use he would certainly find it. I wouldn't describe him as the most caring person in the world."

On tour, Rimington witnessed Russell's brash arrogance at close quarters. Russell fearlessly confronted management at venues if things weren't done the proper way and he'd swear at them and call them names if necessary to get things put right. He had a way of rubbing people up the wrong way, including the band members. One heated argument with Rimington almost came to blows. "We got on really well," was Rimington's conclusion, "because I understood where he was coming from. I knew he was an arrogant prick and I told him so."

It was only many years later that Russell could look back at his early records and see them for what they were. Now, of course, since his rise to stardom, they are rarities which are highly prized and fetch extraordinary prices from fans. But, bolstered by healthy sales of his Thirty Odd Foot Of Grunts records, he was able to admit quite recently on an American TV chat show, "I actually have two or three of the worst recordings in the history of the New Zealand music industry. They all went rocketing straight to the bottom of the charts. I've got that whole bottom end covered."

III

ROCKY HORROR

We found Russell in a band in Auckland and
hired him. You could say a star was born.
Peter Davis, co-producer of *The Rocky Horror Show*

While Russell's musical aspirations seemed to be taking him precisely nowhere, his life was destined to take a new direction with
the arrival in New Zealand of two theatre producers, Wilton Morley
and Peter Davis, who were searching for local actors to appear in
a stage production of *The Rocky Horror Show.*

The duo had bought the rights to the stage musical in 1980 in the
knowledge that it had already been a big hit five years earlier in
movie form as *The Rocky Horror Picture Show.* Inexperienced as
they both were in theatre production, Morley and Davis gambled
that the musical spoof of 1950's monster movies could once again
prove popular as a stage show, which was how it had originated.
They were proved right.

Starting at the Pilbeam Theatre in Rockhampton, Queensland, in
Australia, Morley and Davis lured locals to their first show with a
plethora of billboards announcing "Rocky Comes Home". It had the
desired effect, arousing the curiosity of the local residents. But
Rockhampton is a staid country municipality and the theatre-goers
imagined, wrongly as they were to find out, that it was a show
about their own town, which has the nickname "Rocky". Many of
them got the shock of their lives when they took their seats to find
the cast prancing around to raucous rock songs in outrageous
make-up, fishnet stockings and suspender belts – and that was just
the men. In every sense it was a rude awakening for the good
townsfolk of Rockhampton, where they liked their men to be men.

The show was, however, a sell-out and, flushed with the success of their first foray as impresarios, Morley and Wilton proceeded to take *The Rocky Horror Show* on tour around Australia and New Zealand.

Morley is the son of distinguished British actor Robert Morley and he was able to rely on his father's network of English actor chums to fill the leading roles in *The Rocky Horror Show* productions "down under". The rest of the cast was usually made up of local jobbing actors employed wherever the production was staged.

In New Zealand in 1986 the duo were, as was their custom, taking a look at budding actors and musicians to assess their *Rocky Horror* cast potential when they literally stumbled upon Russell Crowe. "We found Russell in a band in Auckland and hired him," says Davis. "You could say a star was born. We discovered a few people along the way and helped launch their careers, but Russell is probably the most famous."

It was a defining moment for Russell when he took to the stage in *The Rocky Horror Show* for the first time. He was still insisting on billing himself as Russ le Roq and wouldn't revert to his real name until he later moved over to Australia with the production. Initially, he was a peripheral member of the cast but he found the experience exhilarating on the five month-long tour that year and showed enough potential for Morley and Davis to urge him to forget about a pop music career and to concentrate on acting. They also suggested that he base himself in Australia, where there would be more opportunities and where they could offer him work in their Australian productions of *The Rocky Horror Show*. Between 1986 and 1988, Russell clocked up a total of 416 performances in three tours of *The Rocky Horror Show*.

The show had first surfaced in London in the mid 1970s. It was the product of the fertile imagination of Richard O'Brien, an actor-writer born in Cheltenham but, by odd coincidence, raised in New Zealand. As an actor, O'Brien had paid his dues appearing in musicals such as *Hair* and *Jesus Christ Superstar* before coming up with one of his own, called *They Came From Denton High*, which was a spoof of 1950's monster movies laced with catchy rock songs. But by the time it was brought to the stage in London by British producer Michael White, it had become the much more commercially titled The *Rocky Horror Show*. It quickly became a cult hit, an enjoyable mixture of spoof sci-fi and camp horror punctuated by some lively rock music with song titles such as *Dammit Janet*, *Sweet Transvestite* and *Time Warp*.

Central to the story are Janet and Brad, an all-American couple who become stranded in an old dark house belonging to transvestite scientist Frank N. Furter. Introduced to Frank N. Furter's stud Rocky, Janet and Brad subsequently find their old fashioned morals under threat of corruption from all manner of kinky Transylvanians.

The key to the *Rocky Horror* phenomenon, both in the stage show and the movie that followed in 1975, was audience participation, with fans attending prepared for an evening of fun. As Russell was to find out, members of the audience came dressed in their favourite on-stage costume, many wearing garish make-up, she-bitch stockings and suspender belts. Others came armed with rice ready to throw during the wedding sequence or water pistols to shoot during the rainy scene.

Russell learned a great deal from seasoned professional actors like Daniel Abineri during his stint in the show. Russell often played the dual roles of Eddie, the character played by rock singer Meat Loaf in the movie version, and the aged Dr Scott. Eddie is a character who fails to last long on stage – he comes out, sings a song, gets killed and gets chucked in the fridge. This allowed Russell to race backstage, apply a thin film of greasepaint and come back on stage in a wheelchair as 65-year-old Dr Scott. With a pork pie hat pulled low on his brow, a false moustache and a check rug drawn up over his knees, he was virtually unrecognisable.

Being given as a 19-year-old the chance to play an old man in a wheelchair opened Russell's eyes to the possibilities of character study as an actor and he made his mind up there and then that acting, rather than music, should become his major objective. He soon realised that although *The Rocky Horror Show* was an eccentric musical, he was not going to get noticed – sitting in a wheelchair – while so many others were on stage cavorting in fishnet stockings unless he made a convincing Dr Scott. So he went all out to breathe life into the old man.

Naturally, Russell was desperately keen to impress in his homeland but he quickly experienced the reality of life on stage, where not everything tends to run smoothly all of the time. One hilarious instance in Christchurch is etched in his memory.

"There was a sequence in which Dr Scott would come out in his wheelchair, wheel around on stage and stop short in front of Brad, who is standing there in his underwear," Russell remembers. "He gives such a dead stop that he comes flying out of the chair into Brad's arms.

"On that tour we had a 17-year-old guy playing Brad. Brad's playing the show in his underwear, it's a musical, big theatre, two thousand seats, microphones all along the side of the stage. As Dr Scott, I come out and rocket into Brad's arms with such force that it knocks the breath out of him so hard that Brad farts right into the microphone! Brad stands there red as a beetroot, and the audience are too shocked, embarrassed and polite to say anything.

"I'm in Brad's arms looking at him, and he's going red and he's shaking. I know what's happened, he knows what's happened and so do the two thousand people in the audience. But they're very polite. They're not laughing, they're sitting there tight-lipped pretending they haven't heard what had happened.

"My first line of dialogue is now supposed to be, 'Brad, what the hell are you doing here?' But – I was playing it as an American from the southern states – instead I drawled, 'Brad, what the hell have you been eating, boy?'" Just the memory of it brings tears of laughter to Russell's eyes.

In Australia, Russell eventually progressed to the role of Frank N. Furter, wearing fishnet stockings and high heels, and enjoyed the show's every crazily eccentric moment. But he wasn't just out to have fun. "It's high camp, absolutely," he said of *The Rocky Horror Show*, "but if it's played without reality it's completely meaningless – it's just people grinding away in stockings." Colleagues and fellow cast members were always struck by the fantastic energy and sense of daring he brought to the role and as an actor he seemed to get better and better.

Life proved hard for Russell when he first took the advice of Wilton Morley and Peter Davis to cross the Tasman Sea and relocate to Sydney to pursue an acting career full time. He was away from home and his parents for the first time and soon discovered the harsh economic realities of life fending for himself.

Finding accommodation was his immediate problem and all he could afford for the first five months was a dingy rented room, starkly furnished with just a single bed and a cupboard against which he could prop his guitar. A shared toilet was a walk away down the hall.

The rent was A$50 a week and he frequently found it hard to come by. Often he allowed himself just $3.50 a day to live on and precariously existed on fried rice, cigarettes and the generosity of friends who took pity on him. When times were desperate he took a job washing cars and worked as a waiter for a few weeks at Doyle's, one of Sydney's most famous restaurants in Watson's Bay, although he made it very clear to the management that it was only temporary while he looked for work as an actor.

When he couldn't find stage work he resorted to busking in the streets of Sydney with his great friend Dean Cochran. It was the only way he knew how to make a living in between stage roles and he was too proud to accept the dole. Just because the dole system existed, it didn't mean he was going to use or abuse it, he decided. He vowed that he would never accept a grant because, he told his friends, whatever he did should be founded purely on free enterprise. Instead, he resolved to sing for his supper, mainly in the bold, bustling and brassily downmarket area of King's Cross or in the much smarter pedestrianized area of Martin Place, situated right in the heart of the city.

Martin Place was a good bet as a busking catchment area because it was a major promenade. The Martin Place Cenotaph war memorial always reminded Russell of his grandfather Stan and is the scene of a memorial parade every April 25 – ANZAC Day. Russell also became a semi-regular down at the Quay, the city's transport hub, where he could catch the eyes and ears and hopefully the odd coin or dollar bills, maybe even a cigarette, from the tourists swarming on and off the ferries which ply Sydney's waterways.

Thursdays, Fridays and Saturdays would usually find Russell and Dean at King's Cross, where they became adept at blocking off a corner so that they had what virtually amounted to a captive audience. They would run through their repertoire of songs ranging from American country favourites to three-chord hits of the Fifties to Beatles songs to Russell's own compositions. In jeans and T-shirt, often badly in need of a good wash and with one bummed cigarette tucked behind an ear, another smoking away with the butt jammed between the strings in the neck extremities of his guitar, Russell became a familiar figure strumming, picking and harmonizing with Dean for any passing punters who cared to listen. One day, they half-jokingly told each other, these good people who dropped the odd coin their way would pay good money to see them on a concert stage. At least that notion, remote though it may have seemed, kept their spirits up.

Together they worked out that if they managed to finish their set before the police arrived to move them along then they could usually make just about enough to live on. All too often it was a precarious hand-to-mouth existence in which they came into contact with the winos, prostitutes and down and outs who also lived on the streets.

Times were hard but that didn't mean they couldn't have fun and they certainly knew how to party when they got the chance. One pretty young Norwegian backpacker met Russell and Dean in a crowded King's Cross pub and enjoyed a night she will never forget. Elegant Trude is happily married now with three children and living in London but she was just nineteen years old and on her first trip out of Europe when she met Russell Crowe. "I saw him as soon as I went in the bar," says Trude. "He was with his friend and they came up to talk to me and my friend. I got this feeling about him straight away. He was good-looking, certainly, but it wasn't just that. He had this big personality – which even seemed to fill the crowded bar – and I liked him straight away.

"He was friendly but he was not that bothered. He seemed to know that there were loads of girls he could be with if he felt like it. We had to leave the bar to telephone home to my friend's parents as arranged. They were strict and she had to check in every two days at a certain time. We had to queue at the phone box and we were away almost an hour. I was desperate to get back to talk to this guy but when we returned we were like the guests who were late for the party. Everyone was really shouting and larking around and I couldn't see Russell anywhere.

"We were just about to leave when these three really creepy guys sort of surrounded me and my friend. They were horrible and threatening and started to say what they would like to do with us. We didn't know what to do and one of them sort of grabbed me and tried to kiss me. I reached to try to push him off but just then there was a flash of movement from behind and the guy slid to the floor. I got a glimpse of Russell with his arm out and I realised he had hit the guy. His two friends just disappeared. Russell seemed to be on his own but they weren't about to tangle with him. He said: 'Sorry about that. Are you all right?'

"I burst into tears and Russell put his arm round me and comforted me. I didn't know him but I felt good being cuddled like that so far from home. We went outside and his friend joined us and we sort of spent the night together. I don't ever intend to tell anyone what happened in detail but it was a most fantastic night. We went to this scruffy apartment and Russell and I were in the bedroom and we weren't just talking. He was the most unbelievable lover I have ever had and it was a sort of magical night.

"I remember gazing up at the stars together in the clear night sky. He liked to point out the stars. He had all these plans for the future. He said he knew he would make it as an actor and he even didn't mind it being tough at the start because success would be all the more welcome when it arrived.

"We went out for a few weeks after that but then he was going to one place and I was going to another and we sort of lost touch. Really it was just that one night when it was really special. I don't think we slept at all and we looked at the dawn together and talked about our dreams. I'm not at all surprised he has made it so big in movies. He's a fabulous guy."

One option open to Russell to escape the poverty was to try for a student place at Sydney's National Institute For Dramatic Arts (NIDA), which numbered Mel Gibson and Judy Davis among its graduates. But, having spent much of his life on the sets of TV productions since he was a small boy, he felt he already had enough of a grounding in the acting world and had served his apprenticeship. Before he finally made up his mind, Russell talked to the head of technical support at NIDA, a friend of the Crowe family, and asked him what he thought of his spending three years there. It would be a waste of time, came the answer, because Russell was already doing things he would go to NIDA to learn and he'd been doing them most of his life. There would be nothing to teach him but bad habits.

Instead, Russell actively chased stage work and auditioned whenever he could. Theatre was then his driving ambition and he couldn't imagine anything more wonderful than one day being able to act in an Arthur Miller play at the Sydney Opera House. But in his most honest and private thoughts, he also felt that he would never reach that kind of level. So he strove for any opportunity to get in front of a film camera too and when he was eighteen, he made a short film called *A Very Special Reason* for the Seventh Day Adventist Church, in which he played a farm worker who decided to dedicate his whole life to the Christian group.

Eventually his persistence started to pay off and in 1988 he land-ed a stage part in *Blood Brothers*, written by the Liverpool play-wright Willy Russell. It tells the story of a working class mother who is inveigled into handing over one of her twin sons at birth to her upper class employer, who has never had a child. Russell played the working class twin Mickey, who grows up to be unemployed and loses hope. Russell became so embroiled in the portrayal of his character that the role affected him well after the curtain came down each night. "I'd feel a bit funny after each performance and find it difficult to talk to people." But it was worth it. The critics found Russell's performance strong and convincing and, important-ly, the word got around that he was an actor of some promise.

But that year, 1988, also brought Russell great sadness when his grandfather Stan, the man who had been such an inspiration to him, died of cancer aged seventy-two. Stan had visited him in Australia six months earlier, when Russell was just about eking out a living by busking. He scraped up what money he had to take his grand-father out to a Japanese restaurant he had always wanted to eat at but quickly regretted his choice. The very sight of rice and the smell of soy sauce brought back bad memories of his wartime years.

Stan's death was not unexpected but it still came as a severe jolt to Russell, especially because of the manner in which he heard of it. He was sitting in the kitchen in his Sydney digs when a big rare kookaburra bird settled down on his windowsill and looked him in the eye. Something told him it meant that Stan had died. The bird was such an unusual sighting that he phoned other members of his family who related that they had also been visited by the same rare species and that Stan was dead.

Russell was grief-stricken and phoned his grandmother Joy, but she told him not to fly over to New Zealand straight away. She knew how close he had been to Stan and feared Russell would be totally overcome. It was a desperately sad moment for Russell. He would never forget his mentor, not even at his finest moment thir-teen years on.

Russell's stage appearances started to lead to modest television appearances in the courtroom drama series *Rafferty's Rules* and in the daily drama serial *Neighbours*. Russell was roped into the long-running soap when he was appearing at the theatre in Melbourne, the city where *Neighbours* is shot. "I did four episodes in 1987," he sheepishly admitted years later, before adding brightly, "That's one for the grandkids, isn't it? I've got that on video and I can show them when I get old."

Russell revealed that he took the role to get closer to Kylie Minogue, the pretty young star of the series who went on to find international fame as a sexy singer with a string of hit records. He remembers: "I was reading the script and I'm thinking, 'This is awful'. Then I get to the last scene and I've got to punch Craig McLachlan, and Jason Donovan's trying to break up the fight, while Kylie Minogue is riding on my back trying to strangle me. And I went, 'Yes, I'll do it!'

"I did four episodes of *Neighbours* in 1987 and four episodes of *Neighbours* takes about twenty-five minutes to shoot because they work a pretty tough schedule. I got more money for that four days' work than I got for the whole season at Melbourne Theatre." While other actors around him looked forward to the day when they had regular incomes and a house, Russell, however, saw that a certain level of bohemia gave an edge to an actor.

By now Russell had been spotted in theatre by north Sydney-based agents Bedford and Pearce and they were able to bring purpose and direction to his burgeoning career. The trickle of TV work was enough to project him into his first movie role when the following year he was signed up for a small part in *Blood Oath*, a movie starring the man of the moment of Australian movies, Bryan Brown. Written by Denis Whitburn and Brian A. Williams, *Blood Oath* is a courtroom drama with a difference, based on a true story involving the experience of the latter's father as an Australian military lawyer delegated to prosecute Japanese war criminals on Ambon Island.

Williams had had a lifelong interest in bringing the story to the screen and meticulous research had been carried out for the project, including interviews with, and reminiscences of, real former Ambon prisoners of war.

Bryan Brown would be playing Captain Cooper, the tough, tenacious prosecution lawyer who is horrified by the acts committed by the Japanese during the war and who is determined to right the wrongs and bring the perpetrators to justice. In the real trial in 1946, ninety-one Japanese officers and men who had controlled the POW camp stood accused of atrocities, which included brutal treatment and cold-blooded murder.

Russell was to play Lt Corbett, Captain Cooper's assistant counsel in the trial investigations. Like Russell, Jason Donovan, later to become an international heart-throb in the TV soap *Neighbours* and in the pop charts, would also be making his feature film debut in *Blood Oath* as Private Talbot, a young soldier untouched by war.

Russell was grateful simply to be given a role in *Blood Oath*, even though he later said that all he really did was carry Bryan Brown's pencils and appear one step behind him all the time with his head peering occasionally over Brown's shoulder. But as part of the learning curve Russell could appreciate Brown's commitment to the A$7 million film after he had first shown an interest in *Blood Oath* three years before and given his guaranteed support to the screenwriters after reading the first draft. Russell also had the benefit of working with a cinematographer, Russell Boyd, whose credits included Australian movie successes such as *Crocodile Dundee*, *Picnic At Hanging Rock* and Peter Weir's *The Year Of Living Dangerously*.

Blood Oath was not an easy film to make. The movie required many Japanese extras, who were initially confused, guilty and perplexed about what had actually taken place because it was not in their history books. A scene where they had to dig up a mass grave caused them great distress but when it was explained to them that it was based on historical truth, nobody opted out.

Principal photography began on August 14, 1989, and while he was one step behind Brown and the cameras weren't rolling, Russell took the opportunity repeatedly to quiz the star on various aspects of acting and filming. Brown generously allowed Russell to follow him like a puppy and offered advice as often as it was asked for without complaining once. He could see how keen Russell was to learn from the moment he arrived on the set.

"I felt I could ask Bryan any questions," said Russell, "especially about the essentials in the script. I learned a lot working alongside Bryan. He was very generous with his time and was very patient with my many questions."

Bryan Brown was amused by the lesson Russell learned on his very first day of filming. "As I came walking out of the jungle," Russell recalled, "I decided I'd smoke a cigarette, which is fine. The only problem is that they didn't shoot the scene only once, they shot it twenty-seven times from all number of angles. At the end my throat was killing me. Bryan Brown asked me what I'd learned that day and I said, 'Never smoke a cigarette in a scene'."

Forty per cent of *Blood Oath* was shot in a courtroom constructed at Warner Roadshow studio complex in Queensland and by October 6, 1989, when filming was completed, Russell could rejoice in having made his movie debut. *Blood Oath* did, however, have only a short theatrical release, especially in the United States where in the summer of 1991 it was largely lost in the stampede to see *Terminator 2*.

But for Russell it was at least a first film role and now that he'd had a taste of it, he knew that film, not theatre, was his medium. *Blood Oath*, which also came to be known as *Prisoners Of The Sun*, had given him ten weeks of on-set experience. He knew it would prove invaluable because he had just learned that he had been chosen by George Ogilvie, one of Australia's most illustrious directors, for his new film *The Crossing*. But this time Russell would figure on screen as much more than just a pencil carrier. He would be the star.

IV

THE CROSSING

I knew him so well before it got romantic that
the things I liked about him were things
other than his good looks or sex appeal.
Danielle Spencer

She was just twenty years of age, petite, ultra feminine, with a captivating smile, long blonde hair tumbling about her shoulders and
an innocent air of vulnerability that was deeply attractive. She was
an actress by the name of Danielle Spencer and, lying back in the
hay in a farm shed in a state of semi-undress, she was consumed
with nerves about an imminent love scene with one of her co-stars.
Lying beside her, lean, tanned and stripped to the waist was Russell
Crowe, preparing obediently to roll over, seize her in his arms and
make love to her for the cameras on the direction of film maker
George Ogilvie.

In the sweltering heat of high summer in Australia, and on the set
of *The Crossing*, Russell was filming a pivotal scene with Danielle,
which was to spark the first stirrings of a passionate off-screen love
affair between the couple and which was destined to have a profound effect on both their lives for many years to come.

Neither Russell nor Danielle could possibly have foreseen the far-
reaching consequences of what, for each of them, was their first
adult screen love scene. Danielle would have laughed to scorn any
notion then that, ten years on, she would evoke the envy of women
all over the world simply by appearing at the side of the man who
had just won the Oscar for Best Actor and affectionately holding
his hand.

Ambitious and driven actor that he was then, Russell equally
could not have envisaged that the half-naked girl whose ear he was

about to nibble and whose neck he was about to nuzzle for the cameras would be by his side a whole decade later as he celebrated a moment of triumph coveted by every movie actor. Nor could Russell or Danielle have known that the years to come, in which they would be inextricably bound as real-life lovers, would tug them both through such a varied range of emotions. Ahead were days and nights of passion, tenderness, heartaches and tears, sorrowful partings and joyful reunions, loneliness and despair. Very fittingly, it was a film called *The Crossing* which was to transport Russell and Danielle, both separately and as a couple, into a whole new world.

They had been brought together in *The Crossing* by producer Sue Seeary and esteemed director George Ogilvie as two parts of a love triangle in a story of young romance with a tragic and fatal ending. Another young actor, Robert Mammone, would join them as the third side of the triangle. For them all, it was the chance of their young lives, an opportunity to launch a movie career under the ablest and gentlest of directors, a man who had been an actor himself and who understood their anxieties over their lack of experience in front of a film camera.

Hearteningly for Russell and the others, Ogilvie was a man who genuinely wanted each one of them to succeed. In return, they were simply grateful to be working under the aegis of a director held in such general awe within acting circles.

Born into a Scottish family who had settled in Australia, George Ogilvie had been a boy soprano – encouraged by his music-loving parents – and later went on to become a drama student in London. From there he progressed to fully fledged actor, excelling in comedy roles. Subsequently, he was reluctantly persuaded to try his hand at stage directing and chose Lorca's *Blood Wedding* as his first effort in a bid to convince everyone that directing was never going to be his *forte*. To his surprise, he fell in love with it – and he was anything but a failure.

Returning from Europe in 1965 to become associate director of the newly founded Melbourne Theatre Company, Ogilvie then went on to spend four years as artistic director of the South Australian Theatre Company before turning his hand as a freelance director to opera and ballet as well as Australian theatre.

Ogilvie's services to theatre eventually earned him the OBE, but by the time he came to direct Russell in his first starring movie, *The Crossing*, he was still relatively new to major movie directing. He had shared director's duties with George Miller on *Mad Max Beyond Thunderdome*, third in the trilogy of *Mad Max* movies, which first brought Mel Gibson to the attention of moviegoers world-wide, and the following year he was nominated for the Australian Film Institute's Best Director Award for *Short Changed*.

His small screen credits were, however, impressive, notably episodes of the mini-series *Bodyline*, about the controversial Australia v England cricket series in 1933, which became infamous for England's intimidatory bowling tactics, devised to restrict Australia's star batsman Don Bradman, and which eventually became a political hot potato. In 1988, a further foray by Ogilvie into TV with the mini-series *The Shiralee* had secured the year's highest TV ratings.

Now, with *The Crossing*, Ogilvie was going it alone with no George Miller at his side but relying heavily on *Young Einstein* cinematographer Jeff Darling. Set over a period of twenty-four hours in an Australian country town on ANZAC day (Remembrance Day for the troops of Australia and New Zealand who lost their lives in the war), *The Crossing* involves two young men, Johnny and Sam, and a teenage girl called Meg, whose childhood friendships are eclipsed by the overpowering chemistry of the love they share.

The basic synopsis introduces Meg, as a simple farm girl, and Sam, as publican's son, who have become childhood sweethearts. But Sam wants more from life than settling down in the small town where they have both been brought up. He wants to spread his wings and experience life outside his immediate surroundings. So he heads out of town to sample pastures new and leaves Meg behind. But emotions reach boiling point when Sam unexpectedly returns to the town after a year in the city to seek out Meg. He arrives back on ANZAC day when the whole town has turned out to watch or take part in a remembrance parade down the main street. It should be an auspicious homecoming for Sam but he is shocked to find that Meg has now embarked on an affair with Johnny, who happens to have once been his best friend.

Sam's homecoming irreversibly changes all three lives. He has returned clearly believing he can pick up with Meg where he left off. But when he tells her he has come back for her, Meg runs into Johnny's arms and subsequently berates Sam for having left her when he did. She has not forgotten that Sam obviously felt that leaving for new life adventures was more important to him than the relationship they had formed. His return nonetheless leaves her confused and torn between her two lovers. Her parents have been married for seventeen years and after her father has caught her *in delicto flagrante* in the shed with Johnny, she is under pressure from her parents to marry.

When Meg and Johnny turn up together at the local dance, Sam heads off in his car out of town, believing he has lost her. Then he turns around and goads Johnny into a car race to end at the town's railway crossing. Meg sides with Johnny and jumps into his truck. As they speed away jockeying for the lead, Meg screams through the window for Sam to slow down – but in vain. Sam burns Johnny's vehicle off the road from where he and Meg watch in horror as Sam's car slams violently into a train at the crossing.

By coincidence, George Ogilvie had in fact read screenwriter Ranald Allan's script for *The Crossing* many years before producer Sue Seeary had optioned it for a movie. Ogilvie had been enthusiastic about bringing the story to the screen but at that point another independent film producer was considering making it into a film and Ogilvie did not figure in his plans as director. Ogilvie typically took it all philosophically and simply got on with other projects with great success. Now *The Crossing* was back in his hands and

Sue Seeary couldn't disguise her delight when he accepted the director's post.

It was confidently expected that the cast would be inexperienced since they needed to be young and Seeary felt the director's input would be crucial. "It required a director who could give the story the pace and energy it needed," she said. Ogilvie's very prestigious presence also ensured the film attracted funding from the Australian Film Finance Corporation.

Russell was the first of the three leads to be chosen by Sue Seeary and Ogilvie. Relying on his strong background in theatre, Ogilvie had decided that workshopping with dozens of actors and choosing from those groups would be his best method of casting *The Crossing*. "If you spend fifteen minutes with an actor you can get only a superficial idea of what they can do," he explained. "So a whole day of workshopping relaxes them, and finally you can see what they can do." Since the young actors had no major credits, or even showreels, Sue Seeary agreed that this was the most efficient way to see all the contenders. It also enabled her and Ogilvie to judge how they looked in combination.

Ogilvie had already known of Russell through his stage work and boldly told him he would make a great cinema actor. He recognised that Russell was not only keen and ready to spread his wings in a meaningful movie role but that he had limitations on stage. In movies he would break free. Ogilvie was not surprised that when he asked Russell which of the roles he wanted to play, Russell famously replied: "All of them!" Ogilvie laughed and told him, "We don't have the budget!" Realistically, Ogilvie saw him as Johnny, the simple, down-to-earth country farm boy who starts an affair with Meg when Sam leaves her for the big city life. But there was one problem troubling the director: he didn't want his screen Johnny sporting a broken tooth and he felt compelled to raise the issue with Russell.

Russell had never recognised his less-than-perfect dental appearance as a drawback, but Ogilvie gently persuaded him it was time for repairs. "After I got the role, George and I went out for coffee," Russell recalled. "He said to me, 'What are we going to do about your broken tooth? I've been trying to think of many, many ways as to why this character would have a broken tooth and I just don't see it.'

"George was such an artist, such a gentle guy. And then he said, 'What's the problem?' I told him that I just didn't want anything false going on here and I went through my whole teenage years: how I failed these auditions; never got a TV commercial; that I didn't want to do anything false and how all the jobs I got were with this gap in my teeth. And George just said: 'Well, I think it's good to grow out of that behaviour. Let's have two front teeth when we play Johnny Ryan, shall we?' So I got a new tooth." It was Ogilvie who eventually paid for Russell to have it fixed.

Russell learned he had won the role of Johnny shortly before completing his first ever film role in *Blood Oath*. He had already managed to have a borrowed script copied so he could get an early feeling for the movie and he was looking forward to working with Ogilvie.

With Russell now in place, Ogilvie was mindful that his choice of stars for his film required a blend that went beyond mere acting talent. "I needed not only the right people for the roles, but people who could support each other throughout the shoot," he said. He was confident that Russell's belief in himself would comfortably carry him through.

Robert Mammone was enjoying a holiday in his home city of Adelaide when he was asked to audition for *The Crossing* as Sam, Russell's screen rival in love. Mammone immediately cut short his holiday when he heard that he would be auditioning for Ogilvie, only to discover, to his consternation and at one of Ogilvie's workshops, that at twenty-six he was the oldest actor there. He did well enough, however, to be called back for a screen test opposite Russell, which proved to be the pairing Ogilvie wanted above several other potential Sams. Like Russell, Mammone's experience as an actor was limited but he had some film credits and had appeared in Australian TV series such as *Rafferty's Rules*. It now remained for Seeary and Ogilvie to cast Meg, the delicate rose between the two thorns.

For Danielle Spencer, a young actress very much starting to blossom, *The Crossing* represented as much of a career break as it did for Russell and Mammone. Danielle had trained extensively in drama, singing, classical and jazz ballet and modern dance. Realising that dance had its limitations, she had applied to Australia's National Institute of Dramatic Art but at seventeen was too young to be accepted. Instead, she took a small role in the 1987 Sydney stage musical *Rasputin* and began learning "on the job". From there she'd gone on to appear on TV in *Rafferty's Rules* and other series, such as *Mission: Impossible, Dolphin Cove* and *The Flying Doctors*. Among her Australian movie credits she could also list *Crack In The Curtain* and a lead role in *What The Moon Saw*.

Danielle eventually won her way through Ogilvie's extensive screening process past dozens of other young hopefuls. Her reward was a screen test with Ogilvie, which was filmed one Friday morning. She set off for home for the weekend with the promise that she would be informed the following Friday as to whether or not she'd been successful. It was an agonising week of waiting for Danielle and the following Friday she was a bundle of nerves every time the phone rang. By 5:30 in the evening she had still heard nothing and was beginning to fear the worst. Then an upstairs neighbour, who also happened to be an actor, came down to tell her that her agent had been trying to contact her. Danielle hastily hung up on her call and frantically dialled her agent, who told her that she could now call herself *The Crossing*'s leading lady.

Danielle was a shrewd choice by Ogilvie, bearing in mind how keen he was that his three stars should gel as people during what he knew would be a pressurized seven weeks of filming. Danielle was steeped in show business, right from an early age, and was unlikely to be phased by the rigours ahead.

Danielle's father Don was an entertainer who had the distinction of having chalked up a Top Ten hit in the Australian charts and had gone on to tour with such rock luminaries as The Rolling Stones and Chuck Berry. More recently he had written children's albums and eventually became everybody's friend as the highly popular presenter of the children's TV show *Playschool*.

"Because of dad I felt very balanced about the entertainment industry," Danielle was able to say with confidence. Danielle's mother had also been in show business before she married Don, so Danielle felt entirely comfortable making her own way and taking her own place in a world to which she had become accustomed.

When George Ogilvie introduced Danielle to Russell there was a noticeable instant warmth between the two. But a three-month delay in the start of filming to allow for streamlining of the script and final decisions on locations meant that they quickly went their own ways. As part of his preparations for the role of Johnny, Russell spent time on a western New South Wales farm where he sheared sheep and played Two-up – a form of betting favoured in Australia, where bets are staked on two tossed coins – with the old soldiers in the local Returned Servicemen's League Club. He also kept in touch with Danielle and Robert Mammone and organised get-togethers, various outings and even trips to the gymnasium as a trio so they could start to establish some sort of a rapport before they ever set foot on the set. Russell agreed with Ogilvie that it was important that they should all get on. For all three of them *The Crossing* would be a steep learning curve, not least in the actual process of film-making.

Such regular meetings gave the three of them the chance to discuss their characters in *The Crossing* and for them all to get to know each other better. Russell discovered that, like him, Danielle had a genuine interest in music and he delighted in hearing her recount stories of her dad's days on tour with The Rolling Stones. He could not help but notice that Danielle's fresh-faced blonde looks turned heads wherever she went and he wasn't in the least surprised when she told him that she had a steady boyfriend in Sydney.

Chapter IV

Throughout those three months leading up to the start of filming, Russell thought of little else other than how he was going to approach the role of Johnny. He saw him as a typical product of his small town environment, bound to the land and tied to the town through his mother and his dead father. He decided that Johnny was a young man who wanted to progress within that environment; to marry Meg and have a family with all the stability that represented. His task, he felt, was to make the audience like and care about Johnny and to show his sensitive side. "He's not just an aggressive country bumpkin," said Russell.

From Sydney, Ogilvie and Sue Seeary set off on a series of location hunting expeditions into the New South Wales countryside, sometimes driving as much as eight hours a day. Their routes took them across a wide range of landscapes, following rivers and railway lines which would be crucial to the story. They were also looking for a suitable township of some three thousand to four thousand people and after four days of almost relentless driving they settled on Junee, five hundred kilometres south west of Sydney, for the town scenes. Situated midway between Melbourne and Sydney, Junee had been a railway town for more than one hundred years. Much repair work on interstate freight trains was carried out there.

North west of Junee they found the small grazing and crop district of Condobolin, which has a population of around 3,600. The geographic centre of the state of New South Wales, Condobolin's terrain is flat and open and several areas on the outskirts would prove ideal for some specific scenes, notably the car chases, a train stunt and Meg's farm. "It had a broad, endless horizon, so it gave an expression of vastness and nothingness," Seeary observed.

Once filming began, George Ogilvie's own dedication to the task in hand was total to the point where nothing else except finishing the movie seemed to matter. He exuded an air of calm control, which was reassuring for his three young stars, and he was sensitive to their requirements and anxieties. Having been an actor himself he knew what value his quiet encouragement could bring to the production, with just a word here and there, a suggestion or two usually offered with a reassuring arm round the shoulder. Actors are notoriously insecure and Danielle noticed that Ogilvie always made sure she, Russell and Robert felt good about themselves. He also nurtured the camaraderie between the three of them and discouraged them from viewing the daily rushes in case they became too critical of their own performances. Instead, the trio often spent evenings together in character in order to stay focused, or simply watched videos together.

Ogilvie's challenge as a director was to drive the story forward from three points of view – those of the three principal characters. "They were all equally important," he argued, "so we had to carefully and gently draw the audience through their three lives and families, sustaining the momentum, but still retaining balance."

For Russell, filming *The Crossing* was a complete revelation. As an actor, it thrilled him in a way that he had never felt before as a stage actor. He found he was capable of spending hours preparing for a scene then delivering a performance spontaneously for the camera – a quality which Ogilvie seized on. "It seems to me the essential quality that an actor requires is the ability to be spontaneous," Ogilvie remarked. "It's a very difficult ability in terms of art. When you are on a set and you have to wait twelve hours to be spontaneous about a scene that you've gone over and over and rehearsed, then it's a very difficult thing to do. Very difficult."

His workshops, he pointed out, were largely based on teaching the actors "how to become empty and therefore ready to be filled up". It was the preparation for a role or a scene that was important, he said, because it was impossible to teach an actor to act.

Russell constantly surprised George Ogilvie with the invention and originality he brought to his acting and impressed the director with his whole-hearted preparation. "He's the sort of actor you watch work and you have no idea what he'll do next," said the director. "Johnny has an explosive thing in him and at times it has to be released physically. At the same time he had to be played by someone with a very gentle nature. There is that duality."

A pivotal scene very early on in the movie features Meg and Johnny making love in the hay in a farm shed. It would symbolise a personal crossing of sorts for Meg, a physical consummation of her love for Johnny and consequently the mental acknowledgement to herself and to Johnny that she had transferred her affections. Her previous boyfriend, Sam, was now very much yesterday's man.

For Danielle, aged just twenty, the prospect of filming the up-coming sex scene with Russell understandably filled her with apprehension. It would involve some nudity, which unnerved her. Even though George Ogilvie promised that he would clear the set to make them feel more comfortable, Danielle's semi-nakedness for the scene was something she found difficult to confront. Russell was also nervous because this was a crucial scene in the context of his screen character. It was the moment when Johnny would stake the most powerful of claims to Meg's love.

To add to the couple's general uneasiness, the heat of the Australian summer was getting to everyone in the production team, with temperatures soaring to a sweltering forty-four degrees in Condobolin. Danielle, especially, was keenly feeling the collective pressure that she, Russell and Robert Mammone were under to deliver the kind of performances that would carry the movie. "I felt a very big responsibility, not only because this was my first big part in a film," she later confessed, "but also because a great deal of *The Crossing* rests on the cast."

With Ogilvie calling the shots, Danielle's roll in the hay with Russell was never going to be distasteful. What the director was startled – but delighted – to capture on film, however, was a sexu-al energy from Russell that was, frankly, electrifying. Russell threw himself upon Danielle with irresistible vigour and kissed her with an ardour that left Danielle's lips tingling from the sheer force of his embrace. On the shout of "Cut!" she sat up flushed and breathless. She later confided to a member of the crew that she had never been kissed like that in her life. In fact, she confessed, "I didn't know a man could kiss a girl quite like that."

Given that Danielle and Russell were later to go on to enjoy a five-year love affair, the moments of passion they conjured up on screen in *The Crossing* have since become the subject of much curiosity and conjecture.

Danielle has really spoken only once of her recollections of the sex scene she filmed with Russell in the stifling interior of a farm shed. "I was so young and it was summer and very, very hot," she revealed to *Hello* magazine. "The scene starts off with us kissing but it gets pretty steamy and I end up with my top off before my dad walks in, obviously furious with his daughter."

As to whether the scene in reality produced the first sparks of the affair that was to begin much later on, Danielle said: "I had a boyfriend back in Sydney and when you have a crew around it's very difficult to get involved in the sexual aspect of the scene because it's sort of embarrassing. It was a closed set, but it was still very nerve-wracking – we were both very nervous and self-conscious. Russell is obviously an attractive guy but I wasn't thinking along those lines at that point because it was a big movie for both of us and we were very focused on that."

When Ogilvie came to view the footage, such was the dramatic impact of Danielle's and Russell's liaison on screen that their love scene became the natural opening sequence for *The Crossing*. It was the perfect set-up for the return of Sam, which would lead to such turmoil. To Danielle's relief, the final edit showed no more of her body than a brief glimpse of her naked breasts. But it was enough to convince the audience that Meg had quite clearly given herself bodily to Johnny for the first time – with all that the act implied.

Producer Sue Seeary said: "The passion and intense emotions were really exciting to me. I wanted to explore the first love experience on screen as this is often shrugged off by people as insignificant 'puppy love'. But it's a very beautiful and powerful experience. Some films have taken a sentimental approach to this issue, but what I liked about *The Crossing* is that it exposes the raw emotion involved in young love."

To capture the flavour of the mid-1960s in which *The Crossing* is set, Ogilvie peppered his film with strategic and effective use of popular songs from the period, such as *She's Not There, For Your Love, King Of The Road, Let's Dance* and *Here Comes That Feeling* – famous hits in their day for The Zombies, The Yardbirds, Roger Miller, Chris Montez and Brenda Lee respectively. The titles and lyrics added an extra dimension to the unfolding story.

Ogilvie was thrilled with Russell's performance. Dimple-jawed and looking lean, mean and virile in a singlet and white jeans, there was no doubting that Russell had star quality. He brought a brooding hint of menace to the role of Johnny, made a convincing drunkard for a scene at the town's war memorial, and yet managed to make Johnny likeable enough for cinema audiences to be divided in their emotions as to whether they wanted Johnny or Sam to claim Meg's affections in the end. The outcome is left in doubt until the film's final moments.

Crucially, Ogilvie trusted Russell's instincts and let him take risks. "He let me go wild and go for it because he trusted me," Russell remembers. When appraising Russell's talent and appeal, Ogilvie even went so far as to compare him with James Dean, the Hollywood actor who became a young movie idol with attitude in such films as *Rebel Without A Cause* and *Giant* before dying tragically young at the wheel of his high-speed sports car in an horrific crash.

"This is not specifically in looks, but Russell reminds me of James Dean in the way that he has the charisma Dean had," commented Ogilvie. "He's the sort of actor you watch work and you have no idea what he'll do next. That's rare, that mystery about him."

Having given such a flattering eulogy, Ogilvie light-heartedly warned Russell that it didn't mean he could turn up on the set next day in a cowboy hat. Instead, Russell sauntered on to the set in a brand new Australian Akubra hat, climbed into a car, put his feet up on the dashboard, leaned back and said to Ogilvie in a broad American drawl, "OK, y'all, what are we gonna do now?" Fortunately, everyone saw the joke.

Ogilvie found that with Russell, Danielle and Robert, the main problem was not directing them in how to act or interpret character. They all had the acting ability and the intelligence to flesh out their roles, but what they needed was help in understanding what Ogilvie called "the nature of film-making". A high-speed car race with Robert Mammone on a dusty country road in poor visibility was a case in point.

"There's one shot in there that still gives me goose bumps," Russell recalled long afterward. "I'm driving one car and the scene is being shot from the other car. I have to swerve toward it and I missed it by about half a bee's dick. When they said 'Cut!' I pulled the car over and heaved a sigh of relief."

Ogilvie concluded of his young charges: "The actors had an intense seven weeks. It was fairly high-powered for all of them as the story hurls itself toward the final tragedy. Every moment was vital, critical and intense."

Two months before the film was due to open in Sydney, Matt White of the city's local morning newspaper the *Daily Mirror* sat through a preview of *The Crossing* and, apart from praising the film as "brilliantly directed", singled out Russell for special mention. "He's the one to watch," he wrote prophetically. "He's the actor I predict will become not just a screen heart-throb, but a first class performer."

In White's opinion, all three of the main stars excelled in *The Crossing*, "but Crowe's performance stands out". He continued, "As Johnny, the emotionally vulnerable lover of Meg on the rebound from her affair with Sam, he gives a moving portrayal of a young man who is both simple and complex".

Almost exactly ten years before *Gladiator* turned Russell into the hottest of Hollywood idols, Matt White's appraisal appeared on Tuesday August 14, 1990, under the headline: "Russell Crowe could be the screen's next heart-throb."

The Crossing eventually opened in Australia in October that year to generally favourable reviews and similar forecasts of stardom for

Russell. Both Danielle – who had returned to the arms of her boyfriend in Sydney – and Robert were genuinely pleased for him when his performance earned him a nomination by the Australian Film Industry for Best Lead Actor.

Russell would team up again with Mammone seven years on in another movie, called *Heaven's Burning*. As for Danielle, Russell was beginning to find her figuring frequently in his thoughts, but another year was to pass before she was free for Russell to do something positive about it.

V

LOVE IN LIMBO

*He's a very fine actor and I was impressed with his determination.
He's very prepared, quite intense and knows exactly what to do.
Inwardly, it made me smile because he reminded me of myself as
a young actor. It was almost like watching my own reflection.*
Anthony Hopkins

Russell Crowe could have been forgiven if he'd had his head turned
by the plaudits he received from director George Ogilvie and from
the critics for *The Crossing*. Now suddenly he was being offered
advice from all quarters about what he should do next – and most
of it was conflicting.

Some urged him not to take another film role unless it was the
lead. Others tried to sow the seed in his mind of aiming for
Hollywood. But instead of rushing headlong into a starring role in
another movie, he pinned a film poster of *The Crossing* up on the
wall of his Sydney flat and busied himself with renovating a 130-
year-old upright piano – which, perversely, he couldn't play.

But it wasn't long before a most intriguing and original film script
reached him. Called *Proof,* it was based on the extraordinary prem-
ise of a blind man who searches obsessively for truth by taking
photographs of the world around him and who then asks others to
describe the images he has produced.

It was so very out of the ordinary that once he'd read it, Russell
knew there was no way he wasn't going to be involved, even
though it would be a "small film", a first movie by the director
Jocelyn Moorhouse to be made in Melbourne on a minuscule budget of A$1.1 million.

Bizarre as the film's scenario sounds, Moorhouse's project had in
fact developed from a conversation in a coffee shop about a friend's

blind relative who liked to take photographs and have someone describe them to him. From this simple idea Moorhouse created a provocative film about a man's obsessive search for the truth, and a woman's obsessive need for love. There were just three central characters in the film: Martin, who has been blind from birth, played by Hugo Weaving; Andy, an amiable dishwasher at a local restaurant who Martin befriends and trusts enough to show him his photos, played by Russell; and Celia, Martin's housekeeper, played by Genevieve Picot.

Celia has an obsessive love for Martin but, when he rejects her, she embarks on an affair with Andy as a means of breaking up his friendship with her employer. Well acted and beautifully crafted, *Proof* emerged as an engrossing, clever thriller and won Russell the Australian Film Institute Award for Best Supporting Actor. *Proof* earned itself a showing at the Cannes Film Festival and Russell flew to the south of France for some valuable exposure alongside it. It was his first trip out of Australia and he made the most of it, not forgetting to send a postcard back home to Danielle Spencer. Russell was full of the experiences he'd had when he got home.

It was around this time that Danielle's relationship with her boyfriend broke up and she was suddenly available. Now Russell could look at her in a very new light. He had fought for, and won, Danielle from another man on screen in *The Crossing* and now the real-life love rival had moved on and Russell was free to court her.

But Russell's romance with Danielle was slow-burning and did not really take off until after he had invited her out to dinner in a restaurant in Sydney where they swapped stories and filled each other in about what had been going on in their respective lives. Then they went back to Russell's flat on the east side where they shared their first kiss since that sweltering hot day in the hay during the filming of *The Crossing*.

Danielle wasn't slow to realise that Russell was still driven in his desire to be an actor in films of real quality and he was constantly striving to make headway in that direction. But she also discovered

that when he made or found the time for her, he was loving, atten-
tive, generous and passionate. He'd play his guitar and sing to her
and urge her to join him in gazing in wonder up at the stars. He'd
also organise trips out of Sydney, where they'd enjoy the simple
delights of the countryside and tuck into picnics he'd prepared.

A popular weekend escape for Sydneysiders is the Hunter Valley,
renowned for its wineries and idyllic rural countryside, and Danielle
was thrilled when he took her on the two-hour drive north out
of the city to spend a romantic weekend with her there at a
guest house.

Danielle remembers that although his movies were to take him
away from her frequently over the next five years that their romance
was to last, he would constantly try to show her he was thinking of
her. Flowers or some other token of love would arrive for her, sometimes jokey items like an animal-shaped sponge or a miniature grand
piano because he'd noticed her enthusiasm when they gazed together in the window of a shop selling doll's house furniture.

When Danielle landed a role in the Australian TV soap *Home
And Away*, Russell became a familiar figure, arriving at the Channel
7 studios in North Ryde where he waited patiently to pick her up
at the end of her day's filming.

But over the next five years Danielle because accustomed to kissing him goodbye as he relentlessly pursued his goals. They had no
sooner got together as lovers than Russell went off to Melbourne
for another movie. It was a pattern to be repeated throughout
their affair.

Russell was leaving Sydney to appear opposite no less a luminary
than Anthony Hopkins in a new movie called *Spotswood,* the name
of a quiet suburb in Melbourne where the film was set. The story
centres on a no-nonsense time-and-motion efficiency expert called
Wallace (played by Anthony Hopkins), who is bought in to analyse
financially troubled Balls' moccasin factory, which is located in
Spotswood in 1960's Australia. His job is to turn the workers from
a bunch of oddballs into a well-oiled working machine. But, while

Chapter V

facing marital problems and questioning the ethics of his job, he learns to appreciate the laid-back atmosphere at the family-owned factory, as well as the eccentric workforce of whom only sales executive Kim (Russell Crowe) appears to have any ambition or grasp of how to run a business. Russell enjoyed playing Kim as a thrusting, ambitious, aggressive executive who drives a red sports car and has his pick of girls.

"Although it was a small role, Kim's a wonderful little character," Russell reflected. "He's a parody of ambition – or myself when I was a little younger. He thinks he's super-cool, super-happening, but the bottom line is he's just not. But Kim's one of those people who will probably get on in life, although he's such a nasty person he can't really see what he needs to do in order to get ahead."

After working with Russell, Anthony Hopkins forecast a bright future for him as a film star.

"He's a very fine actor," said *The Silence Of The Lambs* Oscar-winner, "and I was impressed with his determination. He's very prepared, quite intense and knows exactly what to do. Inwardly, it made me smile because he reminded me of myself as a young actor. It was almost like watching my own reflection."

Russell returned the compliment by saying it had been a privilege to work with the Welshman and he had learned much from him, especially the power of detail. "Hopkins could map out a twenty-point journey with a coffee cup," said Russell admiringly. "I've seen him pick up a coffee cup, and every time he picks it up, he's doing something different. But nothing that he's doing with the coffee cup is distracting from his eyes, from the internal process."

During the making of *Spotswood*, Russell already knew that in his next film role he would be playing an anally retentive virginal Welsh Baptist in *Love In Limbo*, a coming-of-age comedy about a sex-obsessed trio of young men collectively trying to lose their virginities. Russell took the opportunity to ask Hopkins to coach him in how to achieve a Welsh accent. Hopkins simply told him: "Do an Indian accent badly and you'll be close."

It was simple but effective advice and Russell was able to top it up with a brief visit to Wales on his way back from a trip to Europe for the 1991 Cannes film festival, where *Proof* was being screened. He recorded the sing-song lilt of the locals and made his way to Cardiff Arms Park to enjoy a beer outside the famous stadium home of Welsh rugby.

Set in Fremantle in 1957, *Love In Limbo*, which he filmed in June 1991, once again showed Russell's chameleon-like ability to get inside a completely different character. With short hair and a distinctive parting, a white shirt with tie and tie-pin, he conjured up a busily officious manner for his role as Arthur Baskin, a bureaucratic clothing factory warehouse supervisor who turns twenty-one during the story but whose personal timidity is revealed in his efforts to become a real man along with his handsome girl-chasing colleague Barry and another teenage lad called Ken. Sex is a mystery for the trio, who all work together. Anxious to lose their virginities, they head off on a road trip to a brothel on Kalgoorlie's infamous red light street in a fumbling collective attempt to transform themselves overnight from boys to men. The shoot turned out to be enjoyable although it once again took him away from Danielle for two months, with location filming in Cottesloe, Kalgoorlie and Perth, Western Australia.

The part of Arthur remains one of his favourites. "It was the first time I got to go haywire on screen," he reflected. But Arthur was not the character driving the story, something which bothered others more than it bothered Russell himself at the time. "People are constantly telling me I should not be playing these little characters and say I'm wasting my face," he said. "But I laugh and say, 'Hey, I'm an actor, this is what I physically look like'."

It was his next film, in which physically he looked nothing like the Russell Crowe we have come to know and love, which would elevate the actor to a new, much higher level and ultimately attract the interest of Hollywood and Sharon Stone.

Chapter V

VI

ROMPER STOMPER

What it did in Australia was to put racism on the break-
fast table and it made everybody examine their own big-
otry, which was a very healthy thing.
Russell Crowe on ***Romper Stomper***

There had been moments early in his acting career when Russell Crowe had been scathing about the way his broken tooth may have held him back as an actor because directors could not look beyond the physical when it came to casting. But now he was to find himself grateful for...the very shape of his head.

While making *Love In Limbo*, Russell got to hear of a film that was in the pipeline called *Romper Stomper*, a movie that was destined to become perhaps the most controversial ever in Australian cinematic history. It was to be the story of a brutal street war between neo-Nazi skinheads and the local Vietnamese community in suburban Melbourne. The principal role, that of a vicious but charismatic skinhead leader called Hando, was up for grabs.

Russell was accustomed to being offered scripts that were usually either just right or left of centre of who he really was. But Hando was that rare and therefore much coveted role of someone who is totally extreme. The major problem for him was that plans were already well advanced for another actor to play Hando.

Russell had read the *Romper Stomper* script fully thirteen months before filming actually began and he was desperate to play Hando as soon as he had read the first few pages. He was deeply disappointed when he learned that the producers were already virtually committed to another actor, but Russell was not going to take no for an answer. He adopted the attitude that until the cameras started rolling for the very first *Romper Stomper* shot without him in the frame, then there would still be a chance for him as Hando. Accordingly, he bullishly rang the *Romper Stomper* director Geoffrey Wright on a regular basis, telling him he'd got the wrong man and that he, Crowe, should be Hando. Three times Wright had to tell him that there was no way he could get Russell into the film in the role. On all three occasions Russell said he was still not prepared to give up on it. Finally, one day Wright rang Russell up and said, "You've got it".

What partially swayed Wright to change his mind can be put down to the simple matter of a razor. The original choice for Hando had shaved his head at the audition to give some idea of what he would look like as a skinhead. But, unfortunately for him, his shaven skull did not make him look nearly menacing enough for the character everyone had in mind. The fellow had a longish face and a head that rose to a point. But Russell's, when razored to a skinhead cut, was a rounder shaped head and, quite simply, his would look far more sinister, evil and threatening than his rival's when topped off with Nazi dress, tattoos and Doc Martens boots. Having suffered the broken-tooth no-go syndrome, Russell had plenty of sympathy for his rival but at the same time he was excited at the prospect of playing Hando. He knew he had clinched a role that was right out of the ordinary.

Wright's mind was finally made up when he looked at footage of Russell in *Proof*, in which he played the gentle dishwasher. He watched the scene in which Russell gets involved in a fight at a drive-in movie and decided Russell was his man. "I didn't know anything about Russell at the time," the director recalled, "but I thought he was the most menacing gentle dishwasher I'd ever seen. There's always something threatening about him on screen. Right after I'd seen *Proof* I called my producers and said, 'We may have our boy'."

Wright had first planned his film in 1986 but couldn't get around to making it until he had raised the necessary money, which amounted to US$1million, about A$1.5 million. By then, the skinheads who had first aroused a morbid fascination in him in 1986 were not the same racists he now saw. Back then they were apolitical hooligans but now they had become Nazis and he re-wrote the film to add that element.

Wright was making his first full-length feature film and, although there was no question it was going to be highly controversial, he wanted his purpose behind it to be absolutely clear, not least to Russell. "I wanted to take a serious theme," he explained, "a deadly serious theme – racial bigotry – and present it with as much kinetic energy and authentic sub-culture detail as I could, contradicting expectations, at least in Australia, that such themes require a turgid or angst-ridden treatment.

"In this way, the film would, hopefully, become more fixed in the memory of the audience. I wanted to do a story that revealed the pathetic, personal vulnerability of young neo-Nazis and remind them that, whatever they think, they are primarily motivated by a profound sense of inadequacy. They may lack love, self-respect or simply a real family, but as soon as they allow themselves to be driven by the childish simple-mindedness of race hatred they are set upon a road to eventual ruin. Hate and violence begets hate and violence."

Quite apart from the bulldog shape of his head, Russell was a fitting choice for Hando. "I've seen racism from both sides of the fence," he was able to say quite truthfully. One of the pubs his father Alex had managed was nicknamed The Flying Jug, because it was famous for its fights. "So I've seen racism from Maori to Samoan, Tongan to Maori, not just white to black. My maternal grandfather's mother was Maori. I have an option to vote on the Maori roll. And yet I've been bashed in New Zealand for being white. But you can't stop and say: 'Excuse me, my grandfather's mother was a Maori'."

Russell needed little motivation to gear himself up for the role. He had been informed he was to play Hando while still working on *Love In Limbo* and there were some amusing moments during breaks in filming when he would be seen sitting reading Adolf Hitler's *Mein Kampf* while still dressed in his crisp Arthur Baskin shirt, tie neatly held by a tie-pin and cardigan.

To fire Russell up in the necessary evil direction, Wright had provided Russell with *Mein Kampf*, and later gave him *The History Of The Third Reich* as well as other reading material on mass killers and fascism. When *Love In Limbo* was completed, Russell also volunteered for regular work-outs with Greg Heasley, a Melbourne trainer, to build up his physique and menace. In the gym Heasley proved to be an exceptionally inspirational instructor-cum-mentor, repeatedly bending Russell's ear with Hando's ideology. "This one's for the *Fuhrer*," he goaded Russell as the actor slugged away viciously at a punch bag. When Russell performed bench presses Greg would close up on Russell as he sweated away and whisper in his ear, "You hate…you hate."

Soon Russell was bidding to transform himself into Hando both day and night with a rare fanaticism. He badgered Wright for more appropriate literature, including psychology textbooks such as *Mass Murder In The 20th Century* and *The History Of The Criminal Mind*. He began putting together and painting a set of German Second World War model soldiers and carrying them around in his pocket. He also spoke to members of a skinhead gang and picked up on certain of their characteristics. In the second half of the film Russell would wear a Footscray Bulldogs T-shirt after noticing that one of the gang he talked to was wearing one.

He knew he had delved deep into Hando's psyche when he found himself one day in his hotel room dressed in Nazi regalia with *Triumph Of The Will* on the TV, Wagner on the CD player and, in the background on auto repeat, a tape he had made up of a baying Millwall v Brighton soccer match crowd in England. When he went to bed he'd leave the crowd noise on all night to infiltrate his brain while he slept.

Russell was also anxious to carry out practical research into the effect a tattooed, shaven-headed Hando breathing menace with his gang of skinheads would have on people. It would help him to try to understand the kind of threat such neo-Nazis might impose visually.

Accordingly, he set off for a bar in full Hando regalia – shaved head, tattoos and Doc Martens boots – and patrons stepped out of the way. Then, with several other members of the cast suitably dressed, he headed for a trendy restaurant patronised by Yuppies in Melbourne. There they gathered as a gang outside the restaurant's large front window and peered in through the glass, staring and snarling at the upmarket diners, and gave exaggerated Nazi salutes. The effect was startling. Chairs were pushed back and the more faint-hearted scuttled for kitchens and a back exit while the front door was hastily locked. Others simply looked petrified and were rooted to the spot.

It was Russell's idea to pay the eatery a visit and he surveyed the patrons' sense of panic with glee as a piece of research professionally accomplished. It had been an important lesson in psychology – the public were fearful just because of the appearance and the posture. Interestingly, the fear factor prevailed even when *Romper Stomper* began filming. Russell noticed that not one of the crew felt inclined to approach him.

Further evidence of the ability of the cast to look threatening was soon to follow the deliberately provoked incident at the restaurant. After a pre-shoot drinks party, three cast members "flexing their character muscles", as Wright described it, were jailed for giving lip to a Melbourne policeman. Russell wasn't arrested. "But Russell's never one to be left out," said Wright. "So he marched down to the police station and said, 'How about me you so and-sos?' And they put him in too." Russell was insulting enough to be processed first.

Astonishingly, Russell was, in fact, detained no less than five times during the production because of his threatening appearance and the props he was carrying, although common sense prevailed and all charges were dropped.

Once the hair had been scraped off his head, Russell required seven hours of make-up each Monday morning to apply all the tattoos that were to complete Hando's look of aggression. Two people were employed to create the tattoo crosses, swastikas and slogans on his back, thighs, arms, chest and shoulders using glass paint. Every morning he'd get up and look at himself in the mirror and cringe at the hideous figure looking back at him. It wasn't make-up that could be wiped off. The coloured glass fibre stayed on for weeks.

Romper Stomper opens with a chilling scene at Footscray station, Melbourne, with Hando and his gang viciously beating up two skateboarding Asians then proceeding to go on a shop-wrecking spree. From then on the movie's violence rarely lets up, with the drawn-out brutal running clashes filmed in semi-documentary style accompanied by frenzied punk music. The gang starts to self-destruct when a new girl joins the gang, which attacks Vietnamese youths on their own "territory" at the Railway Hotel. Other Vietnamese are called up to retaliate against the racist attack and the neo-Nazi group loses about a third of its members in the fighting.

The pace only slackens to allow emphasis on Hando's warped ideology, reading *Mein Kampf* to his girlfriend Gabe, raging over what he sees as the demise of Anglo-Saxons and marshalling his hideous gang in their squalid warehouse hideout for more attacks brought to terrifying life with effective, frenetic camerawork.

Encompassed within the furiously paced action is a dramatic scene of Hando subjecting his girl to rough sex, but she eventually becomes the centre of a love story which director Wright cleverly sets within all the mayhem. Hando's right-hand man Davey, played by Daniel Pollock, is the one who eventually claims her in a bloody beachside climax in which Hando tries to strangle and drown her and is knifed to death by Davey. Meanwhile, the entire gruesome scene is witnessed and captured on film by a bemused coach party of camera-happy Japanese tourists as they disembark from their bus.

The impact of the film, shot in just twenty-eight days and now to be found in cult sections in video stores, is truly astonishing and predictably the response to *Romper Stomper* when it was launched in Australia was extreme. Critical reactions ranged from "technical-ly brilliant" to "a terrible blot on humanity". *Romper Stomper* was also compared with Stanley Kubrick's *A Clockwork Orange*, which features a gang of bowler-hatted thugs. One critic even demanded that the negative of *Romper Stomper* be burned. In his review of *Romper Stomper* in the show business paper *Variety* in May, 1992, film critic David Stratton accused the film of being racist "...because the audience is given no positive characters to root for". He said that misgivings about the movie's effect on impressionable audi-ences seemed justified.

Producer Daniel Scharf, director George Wright and Russell were all quick to refute Stratton's claim. "This is a film about neo-Nazi skinheads – they are racist, violent and sexist, therefore the film is racist, violent and sexist," said Scharf. "It shows all those things. The film doesn't say to you out there: you must be racist, violent or sex-ist; and that's what these people are about. How can you make a film about neo-Nazis and not be racist or violent?"

Russell stressed that the characters who believe in that Nazi ide-ology are either dead or in jail by the end of the film and so it very clearly made its point.

"I think the moral of the film is patently clear," he said, adding, "*Romper Stomper* doesn't glorify any ideology, and it certainly doesn't glorify the results of any racial hatred. What it comes down to at the end of the day in *Romper Stomper* is it's just a very harsh and strange place to find a very simple love triangle. But never in any way was *Romper Stomper* associated or in support of any organisations that hold those beliefs. This film is cutting open the flesh of society to show you the maggots."

Russell praised Wright for having the guts to be the first film-maker to follow through on a film about the neo-Nazis. "If you just chose to ignore them, you only make them more intriguing," he said.

Inevitably, the movie sparked much heated debate, which raged for weeks, about how much violent content could be tolerated at the cinema and Wright was accused of glamorizing fascism. In

Melbourne, where the film is set, local politicians called for it to be boycotted charging that *Romper Stomper* painted a thoroughly unpleasant and distasteful picture of their city. Even Paul Keating, the Australian Prime Minister, condemned the movie as morally bankrupt.

But the public gave their verdict with their feet. In Brisbane, cinemas ran record numbers of screenings to cope with the demand for tickets and the film went on to break box office records. All involved with *Romper Stomper* were gratified at the impact the movie had on the skinheads who thought their ideology was going to be glorified on screen. Wright's movie shows their political stance to be immature and destructive.

Russell admitted he had never felt at ease when in the character of Hando and he was desperate to shake him off when filming was completed and he was able to start growing his hair once more.

"The best day I had playing this character was the last day of filming when I got the make-up off, got in my car and drove away from the set," he said. "I no longer had to think like him or read that crap they read or sit in my room listening to Wagner while watching *Triumph Of The Will*. That was enough punishment for anyone. I was getting really sort of depressed about it. Toward the end I thought: 'Jesus Christ, what am I doing here?'"

Whatever the varying opinions of the movie, the critics all marvelled at Russell's *tour de force* performance and it earned him the Australian Film Institute's Best Actor award. Russell was given his grandfather's wedding ring to wear for good luck on the night of the awards and he was thrilled to win. The movie was to be the catalyst for Russell to branch out into much bigger international films.

Director Geoffrey Wright said of Russell that in *Romper Stomper* he "took it to the max". During the climax, in which Russell tries to strangle co-star Jacqueline McKenzie, "he's actually attacking her," said Wright. "It's hard to restrain Russell. If it's in the script and he hits someone, he kinda hits them. He doesn't bluff."

Once the furore over the film – which was to be reprised in every country in which it was shown – had subsided, Russell was able to add a finishing touch of humour to his Hando creation. At the very end of the final series of a kids' TV comedy show called *Humphrey The Bear*, which is about a bear with three fingers, there was a surprise for the young viewers. The man inside the bear was to be exposed – and up popped Russell as Hando from *Romper Stomper*.

VII

THE SILVER BRUMBY

*I'd love some 25-year-old to come up to me one day and
say, "I saw you in that film when I was a kid".*
Russell Crowe

Since its first publication in 1958, successive generations of Australians
have grown up enthralled by the story of *The Silver Brumby*, an
enchanting tale about a little girl, a magnificent wild horse and its
adventures on the hoof roaming the highest mountains in Australia.

The book was originally written by Elyne Mitchell as an attempt
to interest her own daughter in reading and learning and the story
has since become an Australian children's classic. It is essentially a
simple tale about Thowra, a wild Brumby grand in stature and a
beauty to behold, with a silvery mane and tail and striking cream
coat, who is king of all the Cascade Brumbies. Wise in the ways of
the bush, courageous and daring in the face of danger, the Silver
Brumby is revered by all, including his greatest enemy, Man. For
years men have tried to claim the elusive Brumby as their prize, but
without success. Then a horseman, a high country loner known
simply as The Man, sets out to capture the horse that according to
legend could never be tamed.

With its appealing slice of equine folklore, the book has gone on
to prove a hugely popular read with successive generations of
youngsters, not just in Australia, but right around the world, and it
had been reprinted no less than eighteen times when plans to film
The Silver Brumby were announced in 1991. Over the years, general
enjoyment of the book showed no signs of diminishing and producer Colin South and director John Tatoulis, who had both
emerged through TV in Australia, were convinced they could turn
the book into a fine family film.

South and Tatoulis had formed their own company, Media World, in 1981 to produce Australian drama from an Australian base and they had lovingly steered *The Silver Brumby*, with the help and encouragement of Elyne Mitchell herself, through two years of development and pre-production.

Some seventy-five liberty horses would be the real stars of the film and both South and Tatoulis were eager to cast Russell in the key, but largely silent, role of The Man, a lone stockman who is obsessed with capturing Thowra. The two men knew they had a couple of major obstacles to overcome if they were to persuade Russell to play The Man. Firstly, purely on a dramatic level, the role was less than challenging since it contained barely one hundred words of dialogue. Some of those words, moreover, would be little more than utterances delivered to The Man's faithful dog, almost as asides. It did, however, offer a rare physical challenge since there would be hours of hard galloping required across rugged terrain and much energy expended besides.

The second obstacle facing South and Tatoulis was the fact that they were quite literally saddling Russell with a second successive role on horseback. Russell had just been filming a Canadian movie called *Hammers Over The Anvil*, directed by Anne Turner, in which he played a horseman. Although *The Silver Brumby* would be a markedly contrasting movie from *Hammers Over The Anvil*, it would nevertheless showcase Russell once more astride a horse.

Russell's initial reaction to the idea of taking up the reins on screen again so soon after *Hammers Over The Anvil* was to leave the script lying unread almost two weeks after it had dropped through his letterbox. He had never read *The Silver Brumby* as a child but knew enough about the film project to know that he ran the risk of becoming branded as "that horse-opera actor" if he agreed to be in it.

All logic dictated he should have nothing to do with *The Silver Brumby*. Accepting the role of The Man ran totally against the gut instinct of an ambitious actor whose career plan was to keep ringing the changes. But, not for the first time in his life, Russell surprised everyone by deciding The Man was enough of a gear-change for him to agree to take on the role. He explained: "When I read the script, I felt like I was seven years old and had been transported on this magical journey. I just had to do the film."

One look at the script reaffirmed his view that the horses would be the stars of the film. But he didn't object to that. "The humans in the story are totally peripheral," he acknowledged, "but it was a fantastic story so I wanted to do it." He saw The Man as an opportunity to play an intensely physical film role and he phoned Tatoulis to tell him that he would accept but only on one condition: that he be allowed to perform all the physical action himself. "For me to feel good about the role in twenty years time, I felt I had to do it all," he explained.

When Russell arrived for pre-production, he was immediately introduced to animal trainer Evanne Chesson, who would be providing Russell with his canine co-star, Coolie, the faithful dog who would be at The Man's side throughout the shooting of *The Silver Brumby*. Evanne and Russell had barely shaken hands before they were set on a collision course.

Russell saw The Man's relationship with his dog as much deeper than simply master and pet. The trail of the elusive Silver Brumby would be a lonely one, he pointed out, and The Man would treat his dog as a much cherished companion, friend and confidant. To achieve the required mutual devotion between the two, Russell decided he would need to have Coolie living with him around the clock.

Evanne did not take to this idea at all. She was a woman with vast experience of working with animals in movies and she had very definite views about the welfare of her four-footed charges and their method of working. They were her animals and she would control what they did and when. Russell, however, was equally unyielding about his very different opinions on how best he could cement the relationship he needed to establish with Coolie over the next two months. He stressed that if he and Coolie were to look like a convincingly loyal partnership on screen, then the dog must stay with him at all times so they could really get to know and trust each other. He was more than capable of looking after Coolie, he assured Evanne.

She wanted to believe him but told him it was out of the question. Russell later recounted: "She looked at me and said, 'Listen, I've worked in the Australian film business for thirty years and I've never met an actor yet that I'd allow even to wipe my dog's behind let alone live with him. So just forget it. I'll be bringing the dog to work, you'll get the dog at work, and I'll be taking the dog home. You got me?'"

With a look of triumph Russell added, "Within a week, Coolie was staying with me!"

Russell had swiftly got his way. His natural empathy for animals was soon obvious to Evanne and she relented when she saw that Coolie was perfectly at ease in the company of his new co-star and that they had quickly struck up a rapport. "She tuned into the fact that I was someone who genuinely did love animals, and things were fine," said Russell. "The dog then went everywhere I did for the whole film."

As shooting progressed, Russell became ever more attached to Coolie and was full of admiration for the dog's determined refusal to be left trailing behind, even for the scenes when Russell was riding full tilt. Russell was genuinely delighted when, in the final edited film, Coolie was seen so often holding his own at breakneck speed alongside him.

The budget for *The Silver Brumby* was A$4 million, not inconsiderable by Australian standards at the time. A fifty-strong crew and sixty horses headed, on March 9, 1992, for the Victoria High Plains to start filming at Dinner Plain, between Mount Hotham and Omeo, in the hope of catching the early snowfalls of the season. Russell was looking forward to spending two months out in the open up in the mountains and relished the prospect of immersing himself in the business of communication with the film's cast of animals. Caroline Goodall, who had played Robin Williams' wife in *Hook*, completed the main cast as Elyne Mitchell, with Ami Daemion, a 12-year-old schoolgirl from Byron Bay, as her daughter.

Before he had started work on *Hammers Over The Anvil*, Russell had not been on a horse for twelve years. But he had discovered that the basic rhythm of riding, which he had learned at the Christian youth camps his parents had sent him off on when he was a young boy, had never left him. Nevertheless, for *Hammers Over The Anvil*, he'd found himself with a very different proposition – riding a powerful sixteen-and-a-half hand ex-racehorse in his role as East Driscoll, a handsome, skilful horseman and town hero who falls from grace when he becomes entangled in an affair with the much older, aristocratic wife of a landowner, played by Charlotte Rampling. To fully re-acquaint himself with horses, Russell ate near them and even slept near them. He said he wanted to get so close that he could smell them – although he said it in a more colourful way.

Russell had had no choice but to put in the time to raise his level of horsemanship for *Hammers Over The Anvil*, and now, for *The Silver Brumby*, he was facing several saddlesore days spending up to twelve hours on horseback thundering through rivers, down steep gullies, up craggy inclines and across uneven plains. It was a painful process occasionally. He was thrown three times after his steed was scared by a helicopter hovering overhead for aerial shots. Each time Russell picked himself up and clambered back on.

Russell's horse was intelligent enough to realise that the word "action" would mean a kick in the ribs and that some hard riding was in prospect. But, over-excited on the first two occasions, the horse went straight up on its hind legs, throwing Russell off and landing him on his feet. On the third occasion he was not so lucky and landed hard on his backside. Apart from bumps and bruises, Russell did, however, also earn the respect of Buddy Tyson, a former rodeo star who was also along for the ride in *The Silver Brumby*. At the end of a hard day Tyson complimented Russell on clambering back on immediately after each of his three falls. "You're not an actor, you're a horseman," he told Russell.

By contrast, on other days Russell was required largely to sit outside a log cabin in an Akubra hat and wax coat in a downpour, his one line of dialogue comprising a loud scream at the top of his voice through the teeming rain. "I'm going to get you, silver horse," he yells as Thowra the stallion, the object of The Man's desire, plays tantalisingly hard to get. But he was uncomplaining. Having insisted that he would perform all the action himself, Russell also waived away the idea of a stand-in for a scene where he wades into a stream to rescue a struggling calf, hauling it to safety in his arms.

When *The Silver Brumby* was released, film critics generally agreed that visually the movie was a joy and that, apart from an ending which had echoes of *Thelma & Louise,* justice had been done to Elyne Mitchell's book. Thowra proved to be a stallion like no other, roaming the unforgiving wilderness of the Australian mountains. The semi-autobiographical story unfolds on screen as part-fantasy, part-reality, with Caroline Goodall as Elyne Mitchell writing a tale about the Silver Brumby for her daughter Indi. As each chapter of Thowra's exploits rolls off the typewriter, so the stallion's adventures are played out on screen: Thowra contending with the harsh alpine elements; up on hind legs with hooves flailing fighting off challenges from other Brumbies for his supremacy and leadership of the pack; and cleverly giving The Man the slip. There's even a touching equine courtship.

Inevitably, it is the Brumbies themselves, often filmed from a helicopter, which capture the eye, majestically galloping across streams and plains, hooves pounding up hill and down dale, through snow-flecked forest, mud and mire. "Never work with children or animals," is the tried and trusted advice usually given to actors but the critics generally agreed that Russell came out with some credit up against his equine co-stars.

Within the obvious limitations of the role, Russell managed to get across his view that although men are shown to be aggressive, The

Man is never quite the bad guy, despite his desire to shackle the free-spirited horse. Russell perceived The Man as one of the universal characters of film: a loner on horseback pitting all his ingenuity and resources into the capture of the object of his desire. Russell said he hoped that the intensity of the pursuit brought out a nobility of character in both man and horse. While The Man's pursuit of the horse is undoubtedly single-minded and obsessive, he has a respect for the Brumby and for animals in general after spending so much time in close contact with them on the mountains.

The over-riding factor in The Man's make up, Russell had decided, was his closeness to animals and he defended the sequences in which The Man is seen carrying on canine conversations with Coolie and dismissed the notion that they had made him look foolish. "There had to be a situation," he said, "where you see this guy, who is supposed to be Mr Moody Groover, talking alone with his dog. It made The Man all the more human. People say the stupidest things when they are on their own with an animal."

By the end of the shoot in mid-May, 1992, Russell and Coolie had become almost inseparable, which inevitably made for a difficult final parting. "He was a beautiful dog," Russell reflected. "It was really quite upsetting emotionally to have to leave him at the end of shooting. I know that sounds quite stupid, but that's the way it was."

The Silver Brumby remains a film that Russell is proud to have on his CV. Pressed on its release as to why he had taken on a film so far removed from the usual intensity of his work, Russell countered that movies were after all about entertainment and there was nothing wrong in making a film which brought a smile to the face. It showed unashamedly how life is in that equine world up in the mountains.

"It was a kids' film made for pony club girls aged between eight and twelve," he said "and it was a great part of Oz history to document it on film. It's a magical story and I'd love some 25-year-old to come up to me one day and say, 'I saw you in that film when I was a kid'."

Hammers Over The Anvil was having its world premiere in Vancouver just as *The Silver Brumby* was being released in Australia in September 1993, and Russell was by now preparing to go back into the theatre. He had enjoyed no real break since 1988, but still jumped at the chance to co-star in *The Official Tribute To The Blues Brothers*, to be staged at Sydney's Metro Theatre.

This was a show based on the comedy-song act of the original Blues Brothers, John Belushi and Dan Ackroyd, on which the hit film *The Blues Brothers* was eventually based. Quite apart from the appeal of belting out a dozen numbers in a quality stage production, a longish run in Sydney would also afford him time to spend at home. The stage show would be fun and he turned down four major opportunities in America to take it and to alleviate some of the homesickness, which was starting to become desperately grim. "For my own sanity I just needed to be at home," he explained.

Russell worked out that he had spent a total of just seven weeks in Sydney in 1992, ten weeks the year before and nine the year before that. It had left him yearning for days in which he could just watch the world go by or find time to catch up with friends. The long absences had left him looking forward to a spell of simple day-to-day existence. He had reached, he said, an exacerbated state where he had come to feel there was a cloak that was always over him.

He also ached for quality time with Danielle. "I've got a long-suffering woman waiting for me to get off these stupid plane rides all the time," he told *The Sydney Morning Herald*.

Referring to his hectic work schedule of nine movies in two and a half years, he added, "I wasn't enjoying the things I was doing as much as I should have been. Sure, they were all exciting and fantastic and all that sort of stuff, but when all you want to do is sit at home in your own grubby flat, with your own cockroaches and your own mess and being able to just sort of say, 'You wanna go down the road for a coffee?' and all that sort of stuff, it really started to grate on me."

Fate, however, took a hand. An untimely combination of flu, dental treatment and voice strain led to his leaving the stage show just one night after it had opened in July. Doctors ordered him to take a whole week off to rest his voice but the promoter of *The Official Tribute To The Blues Brothers* preferred to re-cast the role instead.

It was a huge disappointment for Russell, but in the end he conceded it needed an enforced break like this one to make him slow down. Suddenly he had two months to himself and by August he had recovered sufficiently to be going to the gym five days a week, to join up with his band to work out some new songs, to catch up with cricketing cousin Martin Crowe and to remind Danielle that he was more than just a voice on the end of a long-distance telephone.

The two months, however, seemed to be flashing by when work almost inevitably intervened all too quickly for Russell's and Danielle's personal liking. On a professional level Russell was heaving a satisfactory sigh of relief because he had finally secured a role in a movie called *The Sum Of Us* – which he had been doggedly pursuing – opposite veteran Australian actor Jack Thompson. As he headed off to stay for a while on Thompson's farm, Russell knew it was a role that would astound many of his closest associates. Thompson would play his widowed father, while Russell would be his gay son, who is searching for Mr Right.

VIII

AMERICA

I have this disease called integrity – something Americans seem to find very disturbing.
Russell Crowe

He'd been called the new Bryan Brown, the new Mel Gibson, an actor with a ring of James Dean about him and a throwback to a young Anthony Hopkins. And in his prolific first five years as a film actor, Russell Crowe had been called a lot of other names besides, many of them unprintable.

But, while it was all very flattering to be compared with other highly regarded actors both past and present, Russell was enraged at any suggestion that he was "another" anybody. If there was one trait that marked him out, it was that Russell Crowe was very much his own man.

As for the accusations that he was arrogant, cocky and rude, well, he could put up with those. He simply put it down to people mistaking his remarkable drive and unswerving passion for his job as mere "attitude". He wanted to be the best movie actor he could possibly be and he expected the same standards of others who surrounded him both in front of and behind the camera on the movies on which he worked.

Self-belief was something Russell was never short of, to the point where he trusted himself more than he trusted anyone else. He had a track record that proved that the career decisions he had taken since he became a movie actor for the first time in *Blood Oath* were, almost without exception, the correct ones.

He had, for example, received four opinions on the merits of taking a leading role in *Proof,* each of them negative, and yet when he read the *Proof* script he felt it was one of the most beautiful he had read in his life and jumped at it. He had also declined to go to drama school despite the urging of colleagues in the business. Instead, he had leap-frogged his contemporaries into movies and in quick succession he had played an army investigator, a downhome boy caught in a love triangle, an amiable dishwasher, an ambitious sales executive, a sick neo-Nazi skinhead, a virginal Welsh Baptist, a revered but flawed horseman and a lone high-plainsman.

Now Russell had reached a point where he was looking to Hollywood, not because he wanted to be a star in Tinseltown but because that's where the opportunity lay to read the best scripts and he hoped that one of top quality might come his way. It wasn't that he had grown tired of making movies in Australia. Having somehow picked – or been picked for – the cream of the crop of Aussie movies over the previous five years, there inevitably came a point whereby the scripts he was being offered either didn't interest him or were too similar to previous roles. Repetition was something he was desperate to avoid.

Russell explained: "Very quickly in Australia I got all the recognition that there is to get there, in terms of awards and stuff. And so I suddenly had to look overseas and look at expanding where I was going to work. In Australia, once you get that level of recognition you're supposed to sit down for ten years and they'll re-discover you in your forties, you know? But I wasn't satisfied with that because I was only just starting to work."

He also came to realise that even though Australia had wonderful actors and performers, skilled crews and able and talented directors, it was still hard to get the money together to bankroll a film. Only the really impassioned people were making films, he realised, and so he turned his attentions to America and, of course, to Hollywood in particular. It didn't mean he was going to turn his back on Australia completely. Russell was aware he was very much a product of the Australian film industry and that he owed that industry. He would work out how to repay the favour in due course while ensuring the Australian film industry continued to be part of his life.

Hollywood has always been a town which lives by the adage "Don't call us, we'll call you". Since he felt the call was unlikely to come, Russell began to explore other ways in, but he knew he had to be careful. He couldn't see himself transferring to Los Angeles to bum around and knock on doors to try and barge his way into the American film industry. Nor was he going to sit by a California hotel swimming pool hoping for a lucky break. On early visits to Los Angeles he had met a lot of ex-patriates and had noticed their lack of motivation. Waking up every day in Los Angeles could quickly dull a man's passion, he sensed. Stay there too long and there was a danger of forgetting the ambition you arrived with and you'd end up clutching at straws.

The *entree*, he decided, was to find himself an agent in Los Angeles but, most importantly, the right agent for him. Eventually, in 1992, Russell signed up with the prestigious International Creative Management company, which meant that he would share the same agent as Hollywood big hitters such as Nicolas Cage, Melanie Griffith and Denzel Washington, as well as Mel Gibson, the last Antipodean actor to make it really big in Hollywood. But it wasn't their impressive roster of big stars that swayed him toward ICM. Russell said his decision was based on who he was going to have the least friction with. "It's very easy for me to have friction with Americans because I'm very positive about what I want to do."

To clarify Russell's idea of "the least friction", it can safely be said that he was not prepared to be dictated to by an agent who would magnanimously send him a script and insist he take the job simply because it was on offer and it was in Hollywood. Russell's method would be for him to read a script and say "no" if he felt it wasn't right for him. "Nobody knows what is gonna be good for me, only me," he stressed.

That, of course, was all very well. But, as he began his flirtation with Hollywood and set off on exploratory trips to Los Angeles, he very quickly became aware that the American film industry is unswervingly driven by the dollar and that everyone has a dollar value. At the start of his efforts to spread his wings in Hollywood, Russell's dollar value was not exactly attracting the interest of Wall Street nor that of top film studio executives. It was a *Catch 22* situation – the best roles wouldn't come his way until he was a valuable property, but he wouldn't become a valuable property until he'd proved his worth on screen and at the box office.

Hollywood didn't have to wait long to gauge some sort of idea of Russell's attitude toward the world's film-making capital when his agent, George Freeman, the man who would eventually guide him expertly through the Hollywood minefields to movie superstardom, threw a party for him at his Hollywood home. The idea was to introduce Russell to guests who might be influential. "It was a very short party," Russell later recalled. "I split. Hollywood parties are not my vibe. I'm into the more traditional Australian party: beer in the bathtub and you have a good sing."

The next two years would find Russell flying from Australia to Los Angeles no less than sixteen times, often funded from his own pocket, but he found the meetings and discussions a frustrating business. The people he met who made their living from acting in or casting feature films were, he discovered, for the most part positive and passionate about what they did. It was the peripheral personnel and the hangers-on, the people who were not really involved in the business of movie-making, who drove him mad. "That's where you get all the bullshit," he said.

He soon discovered that status and the dollar were everything in Hollywood and although *Romper Stomper* had shown the American film industry just what he could do, Russell was naturally way down the pecking order for the juicy movie roles. He did, however, sign up for a Canadian movie called *For The Moment,* a wartime weepie about three young airmen that was to be made in Manitoba. Canadian director Kim Johnston had seen something special in Russell in *Proof* and chose him to play an Aussie fighter pilot called

Lachlan, who accompanies his colleague Johnny home to meet Johnny's fiancee. There the dashing Lachlan meets and falls for her sister, who is experiencing extremes of loneliness since her husband went off to war.

For The Moment was at least a foot in the door of North American film-making, but the Hollywood frustrations continued. One director Russell read for enthused over him only for the film studio to insist on approving twenty-one names before he was allowed to begin casting.

The endless meetings, the favourable reaction to him without any tangible progress, turned up the pressure on Russell and he began to feel it acutely. He'd make disheartened phone calls back to Danielle in tears as he explained his despair. Finally his frustration got the better of him so that he was ready to blow up and he knew he had to get away from Los Angeles that minute. He needed to think his own thoughts or he'd explode.

On the spur of the moment – and without telling anyone – he hired a car and hit the freeway north out of Los Angeles and headed for Reno, Nevada. Every mile he put between himself and Los Angeles brought increasing relief and he began to feel better, singing along to hits on the car radio.

In Reno he tried to take his anger at the tangled machinations of Hollywood out on the gambling tables and proceeded to lose every dollar he had. Next morning he woke up with a fearful hangover and empty pockets. His head would clear and he didn't care about the money, at least he given himself a desperately needed break.

Back in Los Angeles his immediate circle of friends were wondering where Russell had got to. So too was his agent at ICM. He wanted to get in touch with Russell because he'd had an important phone enquiry about him. It was from Sharon Stone.

IX

THE SUM OF US

People are going to go spare when they hear I'm
playing a homosexual football player, and they
already have. They've been just stunned. But the
way I see it is that it's one hell of a challenge.
Russell Crowe

Sydney, Australia, is the second largest gay capital after San
Francisco, California. Far from hiding that fact, or even being concerned, wary or embarrassed by it, Sydney's Ministry Of Tourism is
comfortable enough with the statistic to proclaim it to tourists in its
official guide to the city. The gay scene, it advises visitors in *Sydney*
Welcomes The World, centres on Darlinghurst in the inner-east and
Newtown and Erskinville in the inner-west areas of the city. "The
colourful *Mardi Gras* festival held in February and March celebrates
sexual diversity and draws huge crowds," the Ministry's guide trum-
pets in a manner that underlines its tolerance.

Such enlightened acceptance of the gay scene was not always to be
found in Australia. In a masculinist culture, there has always been a
certain faction of Australian society for whom homosexuality is a subject that is thoroughly taboo. It was no different in 1994 when a film
called *The Sum Of Us* confronted head-on that faction's inability to
cope with homosexuality with a plot featuring character Jeff Mitchell
as a gay young man searching for Mr Right with the full encouragement and approval of his heterosexual widowed father Harry.

With its gay topic, *The Sum Of Us* was always bound to be a film
that would invite controversy. But it was typical of Russell that he
actively chased the role for months, despite the reservations of many
of his friends and fellow actors. From the moment he first got to hear
of the project and expressed an interest in playing Jeff, there was no

shortage of advice for Russell to stay well away from the film. Clearly, it would be a contentious role and one recurring opinion was that Russell would be committing professional suicide if he took it. Why, people asked, did he want to take on the role of a gay young man when such strenuous efforts were being made in Hollywood to groom him as a bright new young star with virile sex appeal? Surely he was shooting himself in the foot, they argued, and they tried to convince him that *The Sum Of Us* offered him a no-win outcome. If he made a convincing homosexual on screen, there would be many who would assume he really was gay, which might possibly harm his Hollywood prospects. If he made an unconvincing homosexual, his standing as an actor could suffer. Since he clearly wasn't gay, he also risked a backlash from the gay community, who might well consider a heterosexual actor starring in the film as unrepresentative.

But the more his friends counselled him against playing Jeff, the more stubbornly Russell went after the role. At one point he was infuriated and bitterly disappointed to learn he was set to lose the part of Jeff to an American actor. Having a big-name American in the key role would help with the film's funding and distribution in the crucial American market.

Fortunately for Russell, *The Sum Of Us* was unequivocally Australian in essence. The film was based on an award-winning play by Australian-based British ex-pat David Stevens, who had also co-written the screenplay. Stevens, who said much of the dialogue and situations were based on his own life, had an admirable pedigree having co-written the highly successful and much praised Australian movie *Breaker Morant*. He had also adapted Nevil Shute's *A Town Like Alice* as a major television series.

His setting for *The Sum Of Us* is Sydney, and Jeff and Harry Mitchell are very solidly Australian. Jeff is a junior rugby league footballer for the Balmain area, an inner suburb of Sydney, and Harry is captain of a ferry boat plying Sydney's harbour waterways. This Sydney scenario enabled Russell to wage a calculated campaign to secure the role in which he strategically placed himself very firmly within the Australian film industry until the producer was in a position where he couldn't hire anyone else. Russell was overjoyed when he clinched the role. He also couldn't help laughing inwardly at the thought of all the people who had loved him in *Romper Stomper* paying their ten bucks at the cinema to see him in *The Sum Of Us* and freaking out.

For Russell to take on the role of gay rugby-playing Jeff was nevertheless an extraordinarily brave move considering that he was at such a crucial point in his career, especially as efforts were being made to tout him among the Hollywood movie power-brokers as leading-man material. It cannot have helped in securing the role of Sharon Stone's love interest in *The Quick And The Dead* when there was such weighty anti-Crowe opinion building up against him on that particular project anyway.

Russell believed the risk was worth it and regarded it as a testing challenge, not least the moment when, as Jeff, he would be required to kiss his boyfriend Greg passionately. (Greg would be played by another up-and-coming actor, John Polson.) Russell had taken heart from hearing the esteemed French actor Gerard Depardieu declare that the hardest thing he had ever done as an actor was to kiss a man. "I thought: if Gerard can do it, so can I," said Russell.

A prime motivation for co-starring in *The Sum Of Us* was that Russell considered it to be an outstanding script laced with warmth and humour. He saw well beyond the obvious reaction that it was a film about homosexuality. He conceded that of course it was such a film but he viewed it primarily as a story about the relationship between a father and a son, a film about shifting generations within one family. To the doubters, Russell pointed out that his character Jeff didn't have a lisp, didn't wear women's clothes and hadn't got AIDS. Unless one knew Jeff was gay, he appeared a regular guy because Jeff was not part of the gay lifestyle as such. In fact, he is a man who does not wish to live in a world that is entirely male and he intimates as much in the film.

Russell's friends still took some convincing that *The Sum Of Us* was a good career move for him. "So many people were saying to me, 'Oh you'd better be careful', so of course that makes me expose myself totally to the gay community, which I did."

In the face of so much adverse opinion, Russell could at least count on the loyal backing of girlfriend Danielle Spencer. She could see the role fitted perfectly with Russell's ambitions, his driven intention to keep challenging himself to get inside the most diverse of film parts and characters. She not only supported his decision to take the role of Jeff but, as his lover, she had no difficulty in demolishing any doubts anyone might have had about Russell's sexual preferences.

As a film project, *The Sum Of Us* had arrived at an opportune moment for Russell. During the protracted negotiations for a Hollywood break, and while there was no concrete progress, he was also searching for a film in Australia that was right out of the ordinary. He had turned down several other roles in Aussie projects because they had failed to interest him. *The Sum Of Us* was startlingly different. Russell also needed to plunge into a film of real quality to boost his general confidence after the acute disappointment of flying to Rome to start work on yet another movie, called *Red Rain*, only for it to collapse with financial problems soon after it had begun shooting.

Red Rain was an Australian-Italian co-production co-starring Jennifer Beals, a young and pretty actress who had made a name for herself as the liquid-limbed dancing star of the movie *Flashdance*. Russell was playing a bearded professor of archaeology who, after years of digging away in the ground, has to dig deep with himself. Unfortunately, the producers lost their money just two weeks into filming and the moment Russell and Jennifer were hurriedly asked to vacate their respective hotel rooms and were informed that the police were on their way because of unpaid bills, he knew the production had run into big trouble. Soon afterward the film was abandoned. It was a major blow for Russell but, he consoled himself, at least he got to go to Italy.

Having already lost weight for his *Red Rain* role, he began attending daily aerobic workout classes so that he was able to bring a lean and athletic look to Balmain junior league rugby player Jeff Mitchell when filming began on *The Sum Of Us*. Jack Thompson, a highly regarded and popular Aussie actor, with whom Russell had taken his first tentative steps into acting at the age of five in *Spyforce*, was cast as his father Harry.

Russell's new screen "love interest", John Polson, happened to live in Paddington, an area of Sydney known to be frequented by members of the gay community and he and Russell went to gay clubs to observe and study the pick-up scene. "I got right inside the gay community without making it known," Russell revealed, "and I discovered for the most part they're people looking for pretty much exactly the same thing as heterosexuals."

The Sum Of Us was eventually shot in thirty days – from October to November 1993 – with a budget of about A$3.5 million, by which time Russell was relieved and excited to be told at last that he had finally clinched the role of outlaw-turned-preacher Bud Cort opposite Sharon Stone and Gene Hackman in *The Quick And The Dead*. He was flattered to be informed that the production of the Sharon Stone western would even be delayed until after he had completed his scenes in *The Sum Of Us*. After all that he had been through, it was a considerable triumph and a sweet moment.

But up against such a tight schedule, there was little time for celebration on the set of *The Sum Of Us* and Russell knew he needed to stay focused. Still to be filmed and looming large, just as he received the good news about *The Quick And The Dead*, was what would emerge as the most contentious scene in David Stevens' script.

The storyline has Jeff going down to the pub and meeting Greg, a young gardener who has not yet admitted to being homosexual. The two young men are clearly attracted to each other and back at Jeff's house they eventually kiss passionately, with Jeff slipping his hand inside Greg's shirt to fondle his torso.

Inevitably, it was a scene to which both actors had given a great deal of apprehensive thought. "Of course I was nervous when the scenes came up in the filming schedule," Russell admitted. "But my job is to fulfil the requirements of the script."

John Polson was equally tense about Greg and Jeff's intimate love scene. This was uncharted acting territory for both himself and for Russell. Neither wanted to offend the other. Both were desperate to appear utterly professional, John Polson perhaps overly so. "I was waiting around," Russell remembered, "when John came over and said, 'Do you want to practice kissing?' I looked at him and said: 'John, are you sick?' He said, 'Well, I've never kissed a man before'. And I said, 'Well, neither have I. But how do you think it would be if I went up to Sharon Stone before a love scene and said, 'Hey Shaz, how do you feel about practising kissing?' I don't think so."

As Jeff, Russell had to make all the running in this crucial scene. But, instinctive as ever, he threw himself into it after a timely mental reminder that although kissing a man might be the hardest thing he would be called upon to perform in his acting career, he could do it if Gerard Depardieu could. It was with some relief, he later jokingly confided to friends, that the next time he kissed Danielle her lips tasted sweeter than he'd ever known.

Only when *The Sum Of Us* was finally released was Russell able to convey fully to his friends why he had accepted the movie. His reasons shone through for them all to see on the screen. Anyone who expected Jeff to be a limp-wristed effeminate dandy had completely misunderstood what Russell was about. He portrayed Jeff as normal in every way, except that he is gay. Apart from the pair of socks Jeff stuffs in the crotch of his trousers before going down to the pub to search for Mr Right, there is ostensibly nothing in his physical appearance to suggest that Jeff is anything other than a heterosexual male. He is a working class man, he goes down the pub and he plays, and is interested in, rugby. He is a loyal, considerate son who loves his father. He meets someone he likes in the pub – Greg – who is also a working man living in the suburbs.

It's left to his father Harry, in a series of quick monologues uttered directly to camera, to flesh out the details of the whole Mitchell family background – including the revelation that Jeff's grandmother was a lesbian – and to explain the circumstances of how and when Jeff's homosexual tendencies came to light. As a boy he'd seen his gran and a woman called Mary in bed together and then Harry subsequently caught Jeff in a garden shed in a compromising position with another boy. The real sadness for Harry was that Jeff became involved with a young man called Kevin, who was training to be an airline steward, and who then broke his son's heart.

Jack Thompson comes across as a deeply compassionate father who cares enough for Jeff even to buy gay magazines – the better to try to understand his son's feelings. He also encourages him to bring his dates home. Harry has long ago accepted – and now approves of – the fact that Jeff is gay and all he wants is for him to find happiness with Mr Right. Harry does, however, want it very much to be known that he himself is singularly a ladies man. "When I was his age I was a right little rooter!" he proudly tells the audience. Despite this boast, Harry eventually resorts to a dating agency to find happiness. A date with a woman called Joyce promises much but their blossoming relationship is abruptly nipped in the bud when Harry's new love cannot cope with his tolerance of his gay son.

The Sum Of Us produced several highly amusing and dramatic on-screen exchanges between Russell and Thompson. Living at home together, widowed father and gay son bicker over trivial matters, such as not turning the shower off fully and Jeff's habit of pushing his plate away across the kitchen table when he's finished his meal. Away from the set, Russell came to develop an enduring friendship with Thompson, for whom he had always had the utmost respect, believing Thompson's performance in *Sunday Too Far Away* to have signalled the start of realism in Australian film. He found Thompson fun, good company and distinctly un-starry.

Predictably, there were some cries of outrage at the film's open tolerance of homosexuality when it reached cinema screens. Audiences, both gay and straight, appeared divided. There were those who felt *The Sum Of Us* was a commendable step toward mutual understanding between heterosexuals and homosexuals while others considered it had failed in that objective by implying that gay men were acceptable only if they looked and behaved "normally".

Equally predictably, Russell's performance was good enough to warrant debate at the bars of Sydney's gay clubs as to whether he might himself have homosexual tendencies, though the subject was usually broached more in hope than anything else. On one occasion Danielle was enjoying a quiet drink in a Sydney pub and became engaged in a conversation about the merits of *The Sum Of Us* with a couple of men without letting on that she was Russell's girlfriend. She listened intently as the subject inevitably got around to Russell's love life and couldn't believe her ears when one of the men solemnly informed her that he knew the man who was Russell's date whenever he was in town. It turned out he was actually referring to the gay gentleman who had simply been helping Russell with his research into the role.

In interviews to support the promotion of *The Sum Of Us*, Russell said he felt that society's violently aggressive attitude to people with a different sexuality stemmed, as it did with racism, from fear – a fear of that which is different. "If we can put a tenth of what we did for putting racism on the table for conversation with *Romper Stomper*, then I'll be ecstatic," he concluded.

Encouragingly for all concerned with *The Sum Of Us*, the film performed well at the Australian box office, taking A$3 million in its first nine weeks. It went on to prove a surprise minor hit in America as well. "Move Over, Mel Gibson," said *The Village Voice*. Gradually, Russell's name was counting for something in America, the Canadian-made wartime drama *For The Moment* having been screened earlier in the year at film festivals in both America and in

Canada. *For The Moment* had earned a welcome accolade for Russell from *Variety*, the US show business trade magazine, which recognised in Russell a "stardom-in-the-making lead performance". Russell had also collected the Best Actor trophy at the Seattle International Film Festival in June for *Romper Stomper*.

John Polson was so taken with Russell's performance that he went and saw the movie five times and picked up on different nuances in Russell's portrayal of Jeff every time.

As for *that* full mouth-to-mouth kiss he shared with Russell, Polson commented, "It's probably one of the most unsexy experiences you can have". More than anything, he said, it was uncomfortable although he expressed the view that kissing any woman he was not in love with was invariably as uncomfortable. "Like when I had to kiss Nicole Kidman," he added. "But I can say that kissing Nicole was marginally more enjoyable."

Russell barely had time to kiss Danielle Spencer a tearful goodbye before he was boarding a plane for America and a whole new adventure with Sharon Stone. After thirty days as gay Jeff Mitchell, he was on his way to romance the woman regarded as the sexiest screen siren in the world.

X

THE QUICK AND THE DEAD

Russell Crowe is the sexiest actor working in movies today.
Sharon Stone

If Russell Crowe had been able to hand-pick an ally to help him fight his corner as a fledgling international film actor seeking recognition in the intimidating arena of Hollywood power politics, then he could hardly have wished for anyone better than Sharon Stone. There were, it need hardly be said, worse fates to befall a young actor than to have Hollywood's sexiest and most glamorous actress casting admiring glances in his direction, championing his acting ability and calling him up to suggest his lips met hers as her romantic lead in a multi-million dollar movie she was about to produce and star in herself.

At the very point when Russell was trying to break into Hollywood big time, he won the largely unsolicited support of an actress who was not only regarded as one of the world's great screen sex symbols, but who was a woman newly enjoying the ability to flex her now considerable muscle among the movie power-brokers after years of Hollywood mistreatment, which had occasionally bordered on humiliation and ridicule.

Thanks to the phenomenal world-wide success of the sexually charged thriller *Basic Instinct*, Sharon Stone was, by the mid-1990s, one of the most bankable movie stars in the world. And with that status went the ability to call the shots – at last. She was ready to re-invent herself as a movie producer and she wanted Russell Crowe in her movie. Even if she didn't know much about Russell Crowe at that point, Stone knew all about re-inventing herself. She'd done it very successfully once before.

As a teenager spending half her day in a special school for gifted children, it was Sharon's brain that had been remarkable, not her looks. She was skinny, wore thick glasses and hated the way she looked. "I just wanted to fit in," she recalls, "to be like other girls and get a date. Then I realised I could re-invent myself. I wasn't born beautiful but I learned how to make myself a lot more attractive. I bought all the fashion magazines, gained weight, bought tight jeans and high heels, got contact lenses, dyed my hair and went off to college."

The all-new Ms Stone won a local beauty contest, which led to a modelling contract in New York for $500 a day and provided a way into movies. But movie fame and acclaim with *Basic Instinct* had arrived at the age of thirty-three, comparatively late for the actress. Now, realising she had to move on from being regarded as just a sex symbol, she was turning her hand to movie producing for the first time with a project called *The Quick And The Dead*. This was a western in which she would play the leading role of a raunchy gunslinger seeking revenge for the death of her father.

What intrigued many, infuriated not a few and aroused the jealousy of others in male-dominated Hollywood, was that Stone not only wanted the then little-known Russell Crowe to be given a star part in her movie as her romantic lead, but that she was also prepared to fight for what she believed in and dig her stiletto heels in deep until she got her way. She certainly believed in Russell Crowe, and when he got the call indicating she would like to lock her lips with his as her love interest in *The Quick And The Dead*, who was he to say no?

But who was this Russell Crowe? And why was Sharon Stone making such a stand for him? These were the questions frequently asked around the film studios as Stone considered whom she might cast as her co-stars in her $35 million movie. The answer, quite simply, was that once Stone had met Russell Crowe she found him excitingly masculine as a man, and when she reviewed his work as an actor she believed Russell had real ability and the potential to be a major movie star. Of this she was adamant, while the studio continually voiced their doubts.

Chapter X

What is certain is that Russell's Hollywood movie career might never have happened had Sharon Stone not shown such belief in him and used her influence to back him when the odds were so heavily stacked against him.

By the time Russell was knocking on the door of Hollywood and being touted for *The Quick And The Dead*, there was much more substance to Sharon Stone than the sex siren who had so sensationally starred as bisexual killer Catherine Trammell in *Basic Instinct*. That movie, with its daringly explicit sex scenes between Stone and co-star Michael Douglas, had undoubtedly been an extraordinary turning point in her fortunes as a movie actress fully ten years after she had broken into films with a role in Woody Allen's *Stardust Memories*.

One scene in particular in *Basic Instinct*, in which Stone, as Catherine Trammell, seductively blows cigarette smoke at drooling cops then controversially uncrosses her legs while seated in the interrogation room of the San Francisco police department, had given her a world-wide notoriety. One Hollywood showbiz expert cryptically remarked that she had turned the simple act of parting her legs into the greatest cinematic special effect since Charlton Heston parted the Red Sea in *The Ten Commandments*.

Stone had wanted the *Basic Instinct* role desperately badly. After years of B-movies and bimbo parts, she knew, she said, that *Basic Instinct* was an all-or-nothing roll of the dice. "This is the opportunity of a lifetime. I'm either going to play this part and rock things or hang my head in shame at the supermarket."

Several other big name Hollywood actresses had turned down the part of Catherine Trammell, fearful that the sexual content was just too explicit. And, as the credits had rolled at the premiere of *Basic Instinct* in Los Angeles, Stone was still anxiously questioning inwardly whether the movie would be a hit and whether the film's sexual content, in which she had virtually given her all, had indeed gone too far. She didn't have long to find out.

Rising nervously from her seat, she was taken aback to find the crowd erupting into wild applause. At this moment of longed-for triumph, and before she could take a bow, Stone was conscious of an arm being slipped around her waist and an obviously female hand giving her a congratulatory squeeze. It was Faye Dunaway, who whispered excitedly in Sharon's ear: "You can tell them all to kiss your ass now. You're a star." And so it proved.

Basic Instinct was a world-wide blockbusting success and became the must-see movie of the year. For Sharon Stone, the years of toiling away in forgettable movies were over. What she wasn't going to forget, however, was the ridicule she had endured in her first few screen outings, where she was regarded as little more than a pretty, empty-headed appendage. All the more galling for a woman with an IQ of 154. Nor would she ever forget a series of agents who had told her she had no talent, or the casting directors who had rudely poured scorn on her auditions by carrying on telephone conversations while ordering her to go through her paces.

Suddenly, *Basic Instinct* elevated her to a position of undeniable strength and, just as importantly, one of respect. And Sharon Stone was revelling in it. "No more cheap remarks," she said with undisguised relief, "and the condescending attitude of casting agents and directors who think you are just a piece of meat who can be replaced by the next Hollywood blonde waiting in line."

So immense was the transformation in Sharon Stone's standing that in 1993 America's *Premiere* magazine placed her at number fifty-four in their much vaunted "100 Most Important People In Hollywood" list. From that lofty position she could look down below her at the names of several distinguished movie tycoons, and such established female Hollywood luminaries as Barbra Streisand, Goldie Hawn and Jane Fonda. Sharon was now a formidable force in Hollywood and respected all the more for the fact that she had paid her dues. "I took the shitty beatings and the crummy locations to get to this point," she said with feeling.

Stone had built on the success of *Basic Instinct* with another controversial role in *Sliver* which, although not critically acclaimed,

LEFT: Cricket runs in the Crowe family, but at school Russell was overshadowed by cousins Jeff and Martin who both became star batsmen for New Zealand.

RIGHT: As an army cadet, middle of the front row, during his schooldays in Sydney.

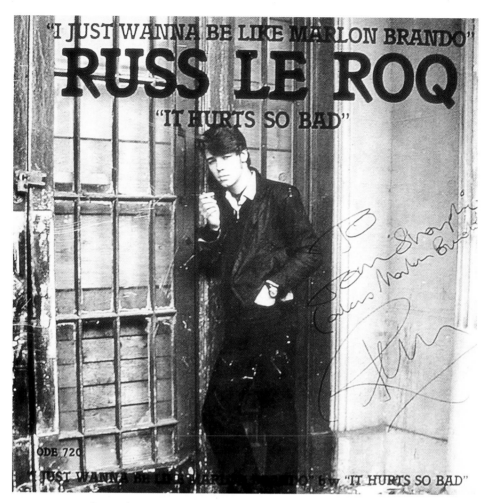

"I JUST WANNA BE LIKE MARLON BRANDO"
RUSS LE ROQ
"IT HURTS SO BAD"

ODE 720

"I JUST WANNA BE LIKE MARLON BRANDO" b/w "IT HURTS SO BAD"

ABOVE: Striking a pose for a record sleeve after reinventing himself at 17 as singer Russ Le Roq. Russell's first record was a flop, but the title "I Just Wanna Be Like Marlon Brando" was prophetic.

LEFT: A first stage role in *The Rocky Horror Show* persuaded Russell to forget his dreams of pop stardom and to concentrate on acting.

RIGHT: Abseiling in Sydney in a guest role in the Australian TV action drama series *Police Rescue*.

LEFT: First star role, aged 25, in *The Crossing*. Russell played a country boy caught in a tragic love triangle with Danielle Spencer and Robert Mammone as co-stars.

BELOW: This intimate scene with Danielle Spencer in *The Crossing* sparked a five-year off-screen love affair.

Three very different screen faces of Russell Crowe: as an amiable dishwasher and friend to a blind man (Hugo Weaving) in *Proof* (LEFT, TOP); shaven-headed, tattooed and menacing as evil neo-Nazi Hando in *Romper Stomper* (LEFT, BOTTOM); and as an unworldly Welsh factory supervisor with two adventurous colleagues (Craig Adams and Aden Young) in *Love In Limbo* (BELOW).

ABOVE: Courting controversy: Russell as a gay rugby-playing plumber who found his Mr Right (John Polson) in *The Sum Of Us*.

RIGHT: But there were very different amorous on-screen adventures for Russell as an idolised horseman in *Hammers Over the Anvil*.

reaffirmed her pull at the box office with takings around the world topping $100 million. When the film was released on video, it also rapidly became America's top rental.

It was with this newly-earned clout as a prime box office attraction that Stone won the backing of the Sony Corporation's Tristar Pictures for *The Quick And The Dead*. (Tristar had been the distributors of *Basic Instinct* so there already existed a successful relationship between the two.)

After a number of years when they had slipped out of fashion, westerns had made a notable comeback to cinema screens. Kevin Costner, with his *Dances With Wolves*, and Clint Eastwood, with *Unforgiven*, had demonstrated emphatically that the genre was far from forgotten, need not necessarily invite box office failure and could garner Oscars.

Stone saw *The Quick And The Dead* as an opportunity to make a western with a twist. The story was essentially an archetypal tale from the Old West about a gunslinger seeking to avenge a father's wrongful and most hideous death. The difference was that this time the chief protagonist would be a sharp-shooting woman tracking down the bad guy to settle the personal score.

The role perfectly reflected Stone's new status. She'd be the one riding into a corrupt town infested with odious lowlife characters with names like Ratsy, Scars, Flatnose, Spotted Horse and Fly, blowing the whole nasty lot away before getting even with Herod, the real villain of the piece and the man responsible for the death of her father. Stone seized the project with relish. She'd be in control of the movie – on screen and off.

Russell had already been alerted to the possibilities the movie might present for him by the time a list of no less than forty directors was sent to Sharon to choose from. Several experienced and prestigious names were suggested but she surprised her backers and her co-producers by sending back a blank sheet of paper with just two words typed upon it: Sam Raimi.

The reason for raised eyebrows at the studios was that Raimi was best known for *The Evil Dead*, a low-budget horror picture notable for its showy outbursts of special effects gore and graphic violence. In some film circles *The Evil Dead* was crudely described as "a splatterflick". But to be fair to Raimi, *The Evil Dead*, which had been filmed in 1980 at locations in Tennessee and Michigan for under $400,000, had also displayed a talent by Raimi for maintaining suspense and a nightmarish mood. This, combined with considerable black humour, eventually led to cult status for the film, which is about five youngsters holed up in a remote cabin, where they unwittingly summon up dormant demons living in a nearby forest.

Raimi's sequel, *Evil Dead 2,* which was released seven years later, was a further excuse for the writer-director to explore shock tactics on screen. Yet another excursion into the same territory, in *Army of Darkness, Evil Dead 3*, completed the trilogy of horror-kitsch. Thereafter, Raimi's reputation was greatly enhanced with a show of wit, pathos and visual flamboyance in *Darkman*, which he also helped write. It starred Liam Neeson in a gripping story of a hideously disfigured scientist seeking revenge on LA mobsters who have dipped his head into a vat of acid and blown up his laboratory.

Whatever misgivings the studio may have had about Sharon Stone's choice of Raimi, the actress herself was adamant that Raimi was the man she wanted at the helm. Raimi had the reputation of not taking anything too seriously and his dark humour would be invaluable if Stone's perception of the gender-bending tale of the Old West was to be realised. "It was never Sam or somebody else," she said. "He was the only one who could make this film. He's a true visionary and I knew he could turn *The Quick And The Dead* into his own kind of film. Sam is his own genre. This isn't a western, it's a Sam Raimi film."

Both Stone and Raimi soon settled upon Gene Hackman as their first choice to play Herod, the evil, villainous mayor who presides with ruthless cruelty over the town of Redemption, where he holds quick-on-the-draw shoot-to-kill contests every year which he always wins, thus eliminating his rivals as town ruler in the process.

Raimi went to visit Hackman, who was working on location for *Geronimo*, to secure his signature. Having taken a role in just one western during his long and distinguished career, Hackman had starred with Clint Eastwood in *Unforgiven*, followed up with *Geronimo* and now he was prepared to star in his third western in three years with *The Quick And The Dead*.

Two other main roles remained to be filled: a sharp-shooting youngster known as the Kid, who might or might not be Herod's illegitimate son, and Cort, one of Herod's former henchman who has revoked violence and become a preacher. Matt Damon was tipped to play The Kid but Sharon subsequently picked out a then little known actor whom she felt showed rare promise by the name of Leonardo DiCaprio to play him. And it was the role of Cort that Sharon Stone eventually earmarked for Russell after Sam Raimi had put up his name.

Raimi had seen Russell in *Romper Stomper* and encouraged Stone to take a look at Russell's performance in the film. Raimi had been impressed by the sheer force of Russell's portrayal of the evil Hando and felt sure that Sharon would form the same opinion.

Stone's conclusion after seeing the movie was that Russell's qualities went beyond acting ability. She described his performance as courageous and riveting. "When I saw *Romper Stomper*, I thought Russell was not only charismatic, attractive and talented," she declared, "but also fearless. And I find fearlessness very attractive. I was convinced I wouldn't scare him."

Not for the first time in Russell Crowe's career, it was the actor's animal magnetism, laid so brutally bare in *Romper Stomper*, which stood out for Sharon Stone. It was something she frequently remarked upon as discussions continued on Russell's suitability for the role. "We must meet him," Stone decided, and it was arranged that Russell would fly over from Australia.

Not for one minute, of course, did Stone expect the shaven-headed monster Hando to walk through the door at their appointed meeting, but she was nonetheless totally taken aback by the contrasting appearance and demeanour of the actor who held out his hand in warm greeting and called everyone "mate".

Stone remembers their first meeting vividly. "He wasn't this cold, isolated tough guy," she recalls. "He was a funny, vulnerable goofball, with this beautiful head of hair and beautiful blue eyes. I thought 'Wow, this guy's going to be a movie star'." She also sensed at once that Russell thought enough of himself not to be intimidated by her if they were to work together.

Stone particularly liked Russell's forthright attitude. He remembers that right when they first met he and Stone had had a conversation in which she revealed that she was considering getting married. The conversation moved on to a discussion about the merits or otherwise of a pre-nuptial agreement, a common form of insurance taken out by the wealthy in America to protect their wealth in the event of the marriage breaking down. Russell says he told her from his naïve perspective, "If you're going to have a pre-nuptial agreement, isn't there something wrong with the person you've selected for your marriage partner for life?" He might have earned a slap round the face for his cheek but instead he earned Stone's respect. She thought he talked a lot of sense and appreciated his honesty.

Russell for his part was struck not just by Stone's natural physical beauty and sex appeal but by her obvious intelligence and perception of what being a glamorous film star is all about. They both agreed they would get along just fine.

Crucially, Russell also made a good impression upon Josh Donen, son of famous film director Stanley Donen, who was one of four names who would ultimately end up on the film credits as co-producers with Stone. "What struck me when I met Russell for the first time," remembers Donen, "was that he had this implication of power and threat." Interestingly, it was the opposite reaction to Stone's.

Even with Stone rooting for him, there were several hoops for Russell to go through before he was cast as outlaw-turned-preacher Cort, not the least of which were three screen tests. While the half-dozen meetings Russell had with the film's decision-makers appeared to go swimmingly, he came to accept that he wouldn't really feel the role was his until he was literally standing in front of the camera waiting for Raimi to shout "Action!". The delays, the indecision and the uncertainty made for trying and anxious times for Russell, although Stone's support was unwavering. She wanted Russell in her movie and she told everyone she was not for turning.

To complicate matters, the name of Liam Neeson also kept cropping up as a possible Cort in some quarters and there were many at Tristar who liked the sound of it. Neeson was at least an established film actor whereas Crowe was little known. Neeson had also worked well with Raimi in *Darkman* and had expressed an interest in *The Quick And The Dead*. The Irish actor had also starred in *Under Suspicion*, written and directed by Simon Moore, who just happened to have written the original script for *The Quick And The Dead*. The jockeying for roles and, particularly in Russell's case, for a decent fee was to be long and protracted.

Russell's cause was hampered still further by the fact that he was already contracted to work on *The Sum Of Us* back in Australia. To hire him would mean holding up filming of *The Quick And The Dead* until he had completed filming. When the idea of Liam Neeson faded from the picture and Russell came further into the frame, Stone once again put her foot down. Bravely she insisted to the studio that filming of her movie would simply have to wait until Russell was available. It was again a courageous stand, particularly since the studio personnel who had not wanted Russell in the first place were now further alarmed at the thought of Stone's new co-star gaining any sort of a homosexual screen image from the gay footballer he was playing in *The Sum Of Us*.

Sharon Stone remained resolute. She was determined to have Russell in her film and ultimately she got her way despite the continued misgivings of the studio. Russell remembers: "Basically the studio said to her, 'We don't know who's going to play the role but it's not going to be that guy, some unknown fella from Australia'. And she just went, 'Oh really?'"

Once *The Sum Of Us* had finally wrapped, after a thirty-day shoot in Sydney during November 1993, Russell flew off to America the following day. The contrast could hardly have been more marked. Ahead of him lay a sixteen-week shoot, mainly in the Arizona desert, and he arrived on the set to find a crew of two hundred and forty and twenty-one principal actors who almost to a man hadn't heard of him. After the camaraderie of working with good friends Jack Thompson and John Polson and an Australian crew on *The Sum Of Us*, it was a testing transition for Russell. "I felt more isolated than I'd ever felt," he remembers. "It was hard going from the closeness of *The Sum Of Us*. There was no slow build-up. It was like jumping straight into the fire.

"This was my first American film and there was a lot of pressure on it. On paper I'm supposed to be the third lead and there were twenty well-known actors there going, 'Who is this guy?'. I think only Sharon and Leonardo DiCaprio had seen any of my work when we started the film."

It was an uncomfortable and strange environment, with Russell having to cope with the whispers of "Why is he here?". As the new boy surveyed the faces around him he could spot veterans of many a western, including Woody Strode and Pat Hingle, who had done it all before.

Russell had flown out from Australia with everyone wishing him well, especially Jack Thompson and his five-year-old son Billy, of whom Russell had become very fond. To speed Russell on his way, Billy gave him a little blue plastic cowboy for good luck and there were moments in the coming three months when Russell would take out Billy's little toy and gaze at it to remind himself that there really was a sane world outside of the frenetic and often mad business of film-making Hollywood style.

Depressingly for Russell, he had ultimately been forced to accept a low fee just for the chance of playing the third lead in *The Quick And The Dead*. The budget for the film may have been $35 million, but to secure the services of Leonardo DiCaprio, Sharon Stone and

Sam Raimi had to agree to top up the young actor's fee from their own pockets to meet his asking price. They both thought it was worth it.

For Stone, it was just one more battle won. *Sliver* had been a steep learning curve for her. She'd had the right in that movie to say no to a wide variety of things. So much so, she said, that she had rolled over in an effort not to be difficult, to be a good girl. "Then everything I rolled over on became the enormous errors in the picture," she said. "So I got to the point in the production of *The Quick And The Dead* of fighting for everything."

The continual battles Stone felt she had to fight before the cameras had started turning eventually took their toll on her. "By the time we were ready to make the movie, I didn't want to make it," she said. "I was worn out." The night before the read-through of the script, Stone was running a temperature of 102 degrees because she didn't want to face going in. But by the time she left the rehearsal she was feeling a great deal better and more optimistic. Once the whole production had moved to its key location fifty miles out into the Arizona desert she was able to say with relief: "We did all the fighting before we got here."

What immediately struck Russell on the first few days of filming was the fear that seemed to cloak everyone involved with the production right from the top down. Russell noticed that there was general apprehension because, he learned, it was almost traditional for a director to fire some of the crew in the first couple of weeks. Raimi himself was under intense pressure because he had been hired by Stone wearing her co-producer's hat and now he had the task of directing her as the star of his film. He was desperate to do his job without falling out with her. "I was worried that she was both the producer and the star," Raimi confessed. "If I didn't hit it off with her and if we got in some horrible fight it would be a nightmare for me because I'd be overpowered by her."

But sure enough, one of the first things Raimi did when Stone hired him was to fire her costume designer, the very same designer who had made her look so desirable and alluring in *Basic Instinct*. "Sharon called me and said, '*I* hired *you*. What are you doing?' I told her I didn't want that lipstick and blow-dried look. We went for a no make-up look."

Raimi reasoned that the whole believability of the story of *The Quick And The Dead* was already in question from the start since there never were female gunfighters and no woman ever cleaned up a town shooting from the hip. "The truth is that these towns, as we knew them, were really just movie creations. So we can't push the dreaminess of it too far," he patiently explained to Stone.

To reinforce the reality, Stone and Raimi eventually raided the costumes from Sergio Leone's spaghetti westerns, which had been stashed away in Italian warehouses. "I cast a lot of the background people based on the sizes of the costumes I had," Raimi cheerfully revealed.

The director had been stunned when Stone had first called him to direct her film. He thought it was some sort of joke. "I couldn't believe it," he said. "I wanted to call her back and ask if she was sure she had got the right guy."

Summoned to meet Stone over breakfast at a smart hotel in Vancouver he admitted he was terrified. "I felt like Dorothy going to meet the Wizard of Oz," he said. Stone's memory of the meeting was that she was charmed by Raimi's lack of *savoir-faire* and his boyish enthusiasm, which made everyone, including herself, act like they were fourteen years of age.

Despite jumping straight from *The Sum Of Us* into *The Quick And The Dead*, Russell arrived having done as much preparation as he could, trying to second-guess Raimi's methods of movie-making before the cameras started rolling. He studied all Raimi's previous films and noted how the director liked to move his camera around.

Russell also learned to perfect a Texan accent and had to familiarize himself with the art of gun-slinging. True to form, he didn't want to be just adequate when it came to spinning guns around in his hand and shooting. He wanted to be perfect and managed eventually to score forty-eight out of fifty at the Tucson competition

Chapter X

ranges with the sheriff's department's SWAT team. It was a more than creditable effort but he was annoyed with himself that the remaining two points had eluded him. It irked him, too, that when it came to being quick on the draw, he was hard pressed to compete with Gene Hackman. "Gene has the quickest draw around here, maybe in the business," confirmed Thel Reed, gun coach on the movie. Russell did, however, learn to spin a handgun with a dexterity that rivalled the best, although he collected blisters and bruises in the process.

Russell was intrigued by Sam Raimi, who arrived on set every day wearing a tie because he had seen old pictures of D.W. Griffith wearing a tie while directing some ancient desert epic. Apart from the tie, Raimi tended to look somewhat rumpled. He also addressed everyone as "sir" or "ma'am" explaining, "I do it as a sign of respect for cast and crew". Russell found Raimi to be "a gentleman", a director who never lost his rag, especially not with his actors, and he and Raimi developed an excellent working relationship. Russell soon discovered Raimi was not one for motivating his star actors with endless conversations and directions. Raimi believed the very fact that they were there in such a big film was motivation enough. But he did expect his star quartet to deliver the goods on the shout of "Action!".

Sharon Stone excepted, Russell's relations with his co-stars were not always cordial. He developed an elder brother-style relationship with Leonardo DiCaprio but confesses he felt like the meat in the sandwich between Gene Hackman and Sharon Stone.

There were tensions and rows with Hackman, not helped by Russell's reported jibes at Hackman's hairstyle. "I think I made a joke about the permed hair," he confessed. But Russell explained away any rows and bad feeling between them by pointing out, "I was playing Gene's adversary. A lot of it had to do with the simple relationship of the characters. I was quite surprised there was very limited contact outside of actual scenes between myself and Gene and Sharon."

On further reflection, he felt that he shouldn't really have been surprised at his hostile reception. "Here's this young Australian guy coming in to play what, on paper, is the third lead in a $35 million film and nobody's heard of him except Sharon. So I wouldn't say it was easy for any of these guys to accept that they should give over any kind of respect or consideration at all." At least Russell could console himself that, after two years of biding his time, he was at last part of a major Hollywood movie.

As the days went by, he felt more integrated within cast and crew and endeared himself to many by handing out souvenirs of his beloved South Sydney "Rabbitohs" rugby team while trying to enthuse them about a sport of which, inevitably, the predominantly American contingent knew nothing. Russell was able to derive some satisfaction and a frequent reminder of home from seeing members of the crew wearing "Rabbitohs" hats and the world's sexiest movie actress sporting a South Sydney rugby jumper.

Raimi's and Stone's eventual adaptation of Simon Moore's original script promised to make for an action-packed story. John Herod (Gene Hackman), the sadistic mayor of Redemption rules ruthlessly and violently over the thugs and miscreants who make up his town, circa 1870. Each year, in order to weed out his rivals and to protect his power, he holds a shooting contest which attracts people from miles around, including his son, The Kid (Leonardo DiCaprio). It is a quickdraw, shoot-to-kill contest, which Herod wins every year. Then into Redemption rides Ellen (Sharon Stone), a mysterious lady gunslinger who signs up for the contest, which has a prize for the winner of $123,000 dollars courtesy of Herod and the Wells Fargo Bank. She is the lone female entry, but it is not the prize money she is after. She is seeking revenge for the death of her father and her real target is Herod.

Another new arrival in Redemption is Bud Cort (Russell Crowe), a former hotshot with a gun and ex-henchman of Herod's. Cort has now renounced violence and found God but his new-found peaceful principles are compromised when he is pressed by Herod into picking up a gun once more or face death anyway. After Ellen saves him from a slow death from hanging by Herod in the town's main saloon, he eventually sides with Ellen to bring Herod down. Meanwhile, Herod's contests continue apace. One by one the gunfighters square off against each other in carefully stage-managed duels, permitted to draw their guns from their holsters at the tick of noon on the town's tower clock. At first the winner of each round is the one left standing, but eventually it's the one left alive. When Herod tries to woo Ellen after inviting her to his home for dinner, she passes up the chance to shoot him. Also in the running for Ellen's amorous favours are The Kid and Cort. In an ending which was to be similarly echoed in *Gladiator* five years later, the balance is unfairly swayed before the final showdown between Cort and Herod when Cort's hands receive a fearful battering from the butt of a pistol wielded with savagery by one of Herod's henchmen. He has to face his final test severely disadvantaged, but Ellen comes to his aid and, mission accomplished, she throws him the sheriff's badge once worn by her father before riding off into the sunset.

Russell's name may have been destined to appear as the first below the title of *The Quick And The Dead*, but as filming progressed it became obvious that his was to be a role he would spend mostly manacled and dialogueless. "I spend ninety-nine per cent of the film chained up, being bashed up and having horse shit thrown at me," was his summary of his contribution.

Chained up for the most part in the street, Cort is allowed off his leash only when it's his turn to square off against one of the other competitors. Mostly he sits and watches the shoot-outs, gets pushed around, punched and kicked, and thrown down in the dirt. When it is his turn to pick up a gun and join in the carnage, the odds are literally loaded against him. He is given just a single bullet for his six chamber gun.

By a wry irony, Cort's predicament seemed to sum up the Hollywood struggle Russell had endured for the previous two years – hands tied, pushed from pillar to post, unable to speak up, an outsider who observes the action going on until invited to join in. Like the single bullet in the chamber, Russell had little chance of making his mark. The parallel was further mirrored in *The Quick And The Dead* by the timely intervention on more than one occasion of Sharon Stone, who rescues Cort from oblivion. On the point of being hanged by a noose looped over a beam in the saloon bar by Herod, Cort is saved by Ellen, who expertly shoots through the rope. Later she rescues him from a savage beating.

Russell had nothing but admiration for the way Sharon Stone went about her work on set in the stifling heat of the Arizona desert, where the town of Mescal doubled as Herod's helltown. Collected at 5:30 every morning ready to be taken to the set, Stone impressed him with her professional approach at a time when she had a lot of other personal matters going on in her life that might have distracted her. Under extreme pressure as star and co-producer, she developed a tight working relationship with Russell and was prepared to listen and discuss movie matters with him.

He couldn't help but admire Stone's whole-hearted approach to filming. She willingly spent several draining, uncomfortable days bespattered with thick mud, her hair dirtied, greasy and dishevelled, and wearing a wet suit under her frontiers-women outfits and plastic bags on her feet so she could pad through the wet after a downpour. Russell liked the way she talked his plain language too and enjoyed a laugh. "Your penis has been shot off," she jokingly yelled at one of the fallen protagonists whose nether regions were being copiously coated in fake blood.

Russell warmed to her further when one morning Stone arrived on the set and asked him what plans he had for Christmas day, which was fast approaching. The festive break would be too short for Russell to travel far from Tucson and he told her there was nothing special in the offing. "Then why don't you come with me to the Salvation Army?" she suggested.

Russell later recalled: "So we spend Christmas morning serving food at the Salvation Army. And from there we went to a home for battered children. We just played with the kids, gave them presents. You look into the eyes of a woman like that, what she could be doing on Christmas Day, and you realise what she is doing on Christmas Day and she is still in that single percentage of actresses who know what glamour is and what being a movie star is all about. Man, I'm a big supporter of hers. I think she's a great person."

Long before the production ever set foot in Arizona, there was one important issue troubling several executives at Tristar about *The Quick And The Dead*. They had a multi-million dollar movie on their hands starring an actress noted for her smouldering sexuality on screen. But where in a movie about gun-slinging would there be room for scenes in which their sex siren Sharon Stone would be naked, they fretted?

With one eye very firmly on the box office and the kind of scenes Stone's huge following would anticipate from their glamorous heroine, they fully expected that somewhere along the western trail she would be involved in some sexual action for the cameras. They had bowed to her wishes in the casting of Russell Crowe, and now they were worried that their hot property wasn't going to smoulder on screen. They had good reason to be worried. "I think we've pretty well established my gender by now," was Stone's caustic reminder to everyone that she was much more than a female to be ogled at.

It was obvious from the film's story that Ellen would not indulge in any intimacy with Herod, the man responsible for her father's death, nor could she become embroiled with his son, The Kid, who is little more than a boy anyway. If there was to be any sexual activity on screen, it would involve Ellen and Russell's character, Cort. As producer, Stone of course had the power of veto, but she eventually agreed to film a love scene with Russell knowing she had the power to have it excluded from the final print.

By the time Russell and Sharon were preparing for a steamy clinch, the pressure on her to flaunt her famous curves was intense. It had been building right from the start. The very first shot would show Ellen riding into town and there were some studio high-ups involved in the movie who actually wanted her to wear a dress. "I thought: Oh yes, the gunslinger's gonna ride into town side-saddle," scoffed Stone at this suggestion. Costume designer Judianna Makovsky agreed it would have been absurd. "The studio discussed her wearing a skirt," she said, "but Sharon and I never liked the idea because we were afraid it would make her look like Annie Oakley in Buffalo Bill's riding show." The answer was to dress Stone in sexy brown tight-fitting leather lace-up pants tapered to show her figure to best effect.

As for any thoughts of Sharon appearing naked, the actress countered, "There are lots of ways to be sexy other than flouncing around in your birthday suit. I don't think my sexiness is just related to whether or not I look good without my clothes on. I'm thirty-three years old. I can't be thought of as a sex symbol much longer. I can see the butt sliding down the legs," she said matter-of-factly.

During the making of *The Quick And The Dead*, Stone's own love life had been going through a turbulent stage. She had broken up with her boyfriend, producer Bill MacDonald, with whom she had taken up on the New York set of *Sliver* in 1992. The parting was described as "amicable" by her press agent, despite a rumour that she had sent her engagement ring back to him from Arizona via express mail. Now she had become romantically involved with Bob Wagner, a second assistant director on *The Quick And The Dead*. And despite Danielle Spencer paying Russell a welcome visit during filming, Russell's own relationship with his girlfriend was inevitably under strain from such a long separation.

Russell had telephoned Danielle frequently, begging her to come over and join him. Not only was he missing her terribly and longing to see her, he genuinely felt Danielle might not do her own acting prospects any harm by putting out some exploratory feelers in American movie circles while she was there. He was overjoyed when Danielle told him that she would be flying out to see him. But the demands of the movie schedule meant that they did not have the most relaxing of times when they were together.

It was in these uncertain personal times that Raimi called Sharon Stone and Russell together to film a sexy scene bathed in fractured light streaming through the slats of a barn in which Stone, as Ellen, was to make all the running since Russell was still manacled and helpless. Basically, Ellen was to back Cort up against a barn door and ravish him. The gusto with which Stone went about her work in this "obligatory" scene was the talk of the set. The woman regarded as the world's sexiest actress appeared almost to devour Russell with passionate kisses. Stone wrestled herself into Russell's arms as if her very life depended upon it. It was an unbridled show of passion for which even Raimi had been unprepared, even though the only nudity she permitted was a glimpse of her breasts when Cort feverishly responds by ripping open her shirt.

Later Sharon confided that the physical encounter she had enjoyed with her co-star had confirmed her original view that Russell was an incredibly sexy man. "It was very, very beautiful and very sexy and very nice," she said of their love scene. "I mean, let's face it. It was with Russell. It didn't hurt my feelings."

Russell clearly enjoyed the experience too. "She's a real expert on those scenes," he told one interviewer. "We rehearsed that scene a number of times and then had to do it over and over again. I urged that we try it again. It wasn't the several-back-flips-off-the-high-plat-form thing that she's been involved in," he added.

What fascinated everyone on the set was that Stone later openly admitted that it was never her intention to have her sex scene with Russell included in the film at all. "It wasn't appropriate for this movie," she said. "We always knew it would never be in. I don't want to be trapped in sex scenes. People have to let me move on."

So why did they go ahead with filming it? That was what many con-nected with the movie were asking themselves. The studio doubters would have been appeased, but only temporarily as Stone had the final say-so. Some close observers believed, however, that there was an incredible physical attraction and sexual chemistry between Stone and Russell that, through circumstance and because of their respective involvement with others, was not destined to lead anywhere and that this was as close as they were going to get. Certainly for now, at least.

In their love scene, Cort's ability to explore Ellen's body is severely hampered by the handcuffs on his wrists. And in a film that was to be stuffed full of allegories, was this Raimi's final jokey allegory, that both Stone and Russell had the hots for each other but at that point in time their hands were tied? There were not a few who thought precisely that.

Raimi took a more simplistic view of the whole thing. Explaining why he and Stone took the decision to cut her sex scene with Russell, he said: "Although it might have seemed nutty to do that, the scene just didn't work. Of course the studio had a different opinion of what I did. They asked me if I was out of my mind. But they changed their minds after a test screening when a woman came up to me and thanked me for not throwing in an obligatory sex scene."

Nonetheless, Raimi still surprised himself that he had cut the one scene where Sharon was doing what she was best known for on screen. "I guess it was pretty amazing that I did that," he said, "considering that everything I do in life normally comes out of a sense of desperation and cowardice." Ultimately, the very absence of the sex scene caused ripples in movie circles. "The director is quick, the nude scene is dead," was one headline when the news broke that Sharon Stone would not be disrobing or engaging in screen sex in her latest movie.

The Quick And The Dead finally reached cinema screens with Russell marking his first appearance in a Hollywood movie with an entrance that was certainly dramatic – awkwardly manhandled and bundled into a saloon bar, helplessly trussed up like a chicken having been hurled through the saloon's swing doors.

The movie opened to varying reviews. Some critics emerged from a screening not knowing whether they had watched a drama or a comedy. Others waxed lyrical over Raimi's fast-moving spoof of the great Sergio Leone/Clint Eastwood spaghetti westerns. "Very quick, many dead," commented one. "The film is both a homage to the spaghetti western and a clever send-up of the genre's best-known clichés," said another.

There was no denying that Raimi had stamped his own indelible mark upon *The Quick And The Dead*, with outrageous clichés, eye-catching visual trickery, a swirling camera, quick cuts, gimmicky close-ups, wild sound effects and a generous blood-splattered body count. Allegories abound, right from the naming of the villain as Herod – in the Bible, Herod presided over a massacre of innocents. A torrential downpour symbolizes a cleansing of the evil which pervades Redemption. In most westerns, the showdown is normally reserved for the climax in the final reel. Raimi introduces a showdown every few minutes.

On a promotional tour to bang the drum for *The Quick And The Dead* he giggled, "The movie is riddled with clichés". He added with tongue firmly in cheek that he was looking forward to making a movie that didn't have either of the words "dark" or "dead" in the title. "I aspire to the lowest common denominator," he said. "It's just that I fail!"

Pistol-packing Sharon's dispensation of her own brand of frontier justice – and the absence of any sexual shenanigans – were predominant topics among the critics. But up against Gene Hackman, sporting mutton chop whiskers and bowler hat, and exuding a cruel sadism which oozes from every snarling pore, Russell had little chance to shine in a drastically reduced role. Cort's continual, mostly silent, mistreatment did not earn Russell many glowing notices but at least it earned him the sympathy vote from moviegoers.

Raimi, however, was effusive in his praise for Russell's Hollywood debut in a role that the director admitted was severely curtailed. "He crafted a great performance, even though he didn't have the lines," he said. "Sometimes he could do it with a gesture, even a subtle raising of the lip. He knew the exact moment to deliver the beat.

"But he is a tough bastard to get along with. The problem with working with Russell is that he always has a good idea. And he has no tact! He tells you! Sometimes he stood the whole scene on its head. It's not easy by a long chalk to work with Russell. But it's exciting and it pays off dramatically.

"Russell is bold and likes to challenge people. He reminds me of what we imagine the American cowboy to have been like." Raimi added sagely, "Russell's not dangerous physically. He's dangerous because he's always thinking."

It's fair to say that *The Quick And The Dead* did not set the box office alight in the way that Tristar had originally hoped. But that was partly put down to the fact that audiences were disappointed to find that sex goddess Sharon Stone remained firmly buttoned into her skin-tight leather pants and rarely took off so much as her hat, let alone a holster. The much-debated sex scene between Sharon and Russell did, however, find its way into the European version of the movie. In the glorious certainty of hindsight, Sharon Stone's determination to have Russell Crowe and Leonardo DiCaprio in her movie showed extraordinary foresight. She felt at the time that she had picked two actors who were going places and was prepared to back her own judgement to the hilt despite the scepticism of many around her. *Titanic, L.A. Confidential, The Insider* and *Gladiator* were ultimately to prove her absolutely correct.

Stone could walk away from *The Quick And The Dead* knowing she had done her best for Russell. She had engineered a vital Hollywood break for him and ultimately she had some sympathy for the limitations of his role. But then she herself knew better than anyone of such frustrations on the way up the ladder of movie stardom. Reflecting on some of her own early films she said, "I was like a big mannequin – a prop in the movies I appeared in. I felt so compressed. It was excruciating. Often I got really sick in the middle of production." She could, however, offer Russell comforting advice based on her own experience of her transition from budding starlet to sex queen to film producer. "There's no replacement for experience," she said. "I'm sorry my butt has dropped four inches but my brain is elevated. There's not one tight-bottomed 25-year-old I've met who knows what I know."

Generously, she left Russell with one final, very public accolade. "Russell Crowe is the sexist actor working in movies today," she stated when promoting the film. "Did she say that?" Russell asked incredulously when he got to hear of it. "That's a real compliment coming from her." He added that the fact that his hot scene with Stone had been cut from the film did not bother him at all.

By the time he flew back to Australia, after filming had been completed in February 1994, Russell was looking forward to going home and recharging his batteries, even though he would initially have to stay in a hotel, having let his own apartment out. *The Quick And The Dead* had been an unforgettable, though not always pleasant, experience for him. Working on a movie of the scope of *The Quick And The Dead* had been a steep learning curve, he concluded. "I brought a lot away from it that I won't forget...including how to fire a single-action Colt."

On the downside, after sixteen weeks of filming a big budget movie in which he was third lead behind two major Hollywood stars, it was irritating for Russell to be returning home heavily in debt.

"I did Schedule F for that movie," he grumbled in one interview, "so I got paid less than anybody who was an extra for the whole film. Finally, the only thing between Sharon getting me in the movie and me doing it was money. She pushed so many studio requisites out of the way in order to have me in the movie, based on the fact that she thought I was good. It was like, well, there's no consideration there. Forget money. It's not about that, I'm coming for the work."

Looking at the wider picture, Russell and his agent still couldn't quite believe that they had pulled off getting him into a big Hollywood film by sticking to their guns – literally in the case of *The Quick And The Dead* – by only taking readings on quality scripts. It had been a long wait, more than two years of negotiations and patiently turning down scripts and having the courage to say no. But they had been prepared to wait, and when *The Quick And The Dead* finally came along they had been prepared to attend the protracted meetings, submit to the three screen tests and put up with the hostile reaction. It had all paid off in terms of opportunity, if not, as yet, in dollars.

Back in Australia, Russell bristled when fellow Aussie actors grandly insisted that they would never have accepted such low pay for the opportunity to make a debut in a Hollywood movie. "They don't realise it took two years out of my life to get that role for which I got no money," he said. "Nothing you want to do is ever easy."

He was equally miffed when others took a very different view and tried to build him up as "the new Mel Gibson" and assumed he was bound to move to Hollywood sooner rather than later. "I don't believe I'm a movie star," he ranted. "I don't believe I'm this sizzling up-and-coming new star, bloody new Mel Gibson crap thing. I don't believe any of that. I'm just who I am and I just get on with what I'm doing."

Russell acknowledges, however, that he will forever be grateful to Sharon Stone for the entrenched stand she took in Hollywood on his behalf. "She was very gracious to me," he said. "It took her a lot of pressure and conversation and effort to convince people to hire this basically unknown actor." They parted on good terms, Stone heading off to Florida to begin work with Sylvester Stallone in a new movie called *The Specialist*.

She told Russell how excited she was at the prospect. "I have to pinch myself," she said. "When I hear 'Stallone and Stone', I jump all over the room in my underwear, shouting, 'Yes! Yes!'." After all the nonsense Stone had suffered at the hands of Hollywood moguls down the years, she felt she was starting to get her just rewards. "I'm not going to choke at the plate just now," she vowed. Russell knew exactly how she felt.

Russell's first Hollywood platter had not tasted quite so sweet. But already there were exploratory talks taking place about a star-ring role opposite Denzel Washington in a sci-fi movie, as well as another movie called *Rough Magic*, with Bridget Fonda. And Russell was certain he wasn't going to choke at the plate either.

XI

VIRTUOSITY

*He has that gravity and masculinity that is
disappearing from leading men. If you were casting an
Australian remake of* Raging Bull *then Crowe is the
only actor you would consider.*

Film producer Al Clark

The Quick And The Dead may have enabled Russell to get a foot in
the door of Hollywood but he was a long way from kicking it
down. Just holding his ground would be an achievement, but
progress still seemed maddeningly difficult and a sci-fi chiller called
Virtuosity was a case in point.

Brett Leonard, who had made his directorial feature film debut with
The Lawnmower Man starring Pierce Brosnan, wanted Russell to star
in *Virtuosity*, a new cyber thriller he was making about a computer-
generated killer who runs amok and the one man who can stop him.
Again, it was *Romper Stomper* which had put the name of Russell
Crowe in Leonard's head. It had made Leonard enough of a fan to
write letters to Russell to urge him to come on board with *Virtuosity*.

The movie had a budget of $14 million, which leaped to $40 million once it became known that A-list actor Denzel Washington
would star in it. But the sudden interest from Hollywood's money
men brought attendant problems for Russell. It took Leonard a long,
tedious and drawn-out seven months to convince Paramount
Pictures to use Russell in the movie. Like Sharon Stone before him,
Leonard held firm and finally got the studio to agree to at least
allowing him to screen test Russell with Denzel.

It turned out to be the strangest of experiences for both actors,
with Russell spitting right in Denzel's face – not the cleverest thing
to do, even if it was unintentional.

Russell remembers it well: "The very first thing we did was a scene where there was a wire cage between us and the first time I did it sort of low-key. The second time, now I was going to pump it up a little bit. I'm going do a little bit of acting. So the director says 'Action' and I jump down off this thing and start screaming at Denzel. The scene was dialogue heavy for me, but with the very first word I say, this piece of spittle comes out of my mouth and winds its way very athletically through the wire fence straight on to Denzel's lips. And I've only just met the guy.

"Now, see, ninety-nine per cent of actors would have been just, like, out of there, you know? But Denzel just stayed in there because he knows it's my screen test and the camera is on me. If he moves and my mind goes into the reality of what's just happened, he knows he's going to blow it for me because he'll mess up my concentration. So he didn't flinch and he says his line. Absolutely cool. He swallows my spit. The director says 'Cut' and Denzel rubs his mouth going 'Yuk'. And then he starts screaming 'You spat in my mouth! You spat in my mouth!' Then he looks at me very seriously and says, 'You know, I love the taste of warm saliva in the morning'." Russell was then relieved to find Denzel breaking out into hoots of laughter.

Despite the totally unscheduled special effect Russell had provided, he passed the screen test with flying colours and also won the backing of Denzel. "I only got the gig because Denzel wanted me," said Russell.

Virtuosity is set in a futuristic computer age where boffins have created SID 6.7, a terrifyingly evil computer-generated man who is no less than the most diabolical villain ever. (The name stands for Sadistic, Intelligent and Dangerous.) SID was created for police training purposes. In virtual reality training, the cops come up against SID in simulated conditions and the idea is that if they can get the better of this superpowered criminal, then they can take on anyone.

But things get scary when SID has too much intelligence pumped into his programming. Suspicious that he's about to be terminated, and equipped with human emotions but no moral sense, he escapes from the land of the Internet and into the real world. Now he's a senseless killer who cannot be stopped by gunfire and there is only one man clever enough and brave enough to bring him down. That man is a police officer called Parker Barnes, who is serving time for avenging the death of his wife, who was killed by a terrorist.

The two key roles had their obvious but very different attractions and Denzel Washington was undecided over which one he favoured. Naturally, he had first choice in the matter and he finally plumped for the cop who would hunt SID down, leaving Russell to play the bad guy – the baddest of them all. "It helped that there's a sense of menace about him," the director said of Russell.

That suited both Russell and Leonard, who had originally sent him the script with the idea of him playing the good guy. But since *Romper Stomper,* Russell felt he'd had enough of good guy roles and he'd told Leonard that although he was very keen on the project it was SID 6.7 he wanted to portray.

Russell was aware that Leonard's movie would be full of computer trickery. The director had conjured up twenty minutes of dazzling computer graphics and clever digital manipulation in *The Lawnmower Man* and cleverly integrated it into a live action story. He would bring that same wizardry to *Virtuosity,* but SID 6.7 would still give Russell plenty of scope.

SID is a composite humanoid drawn from a rogues' gallery of 183 of history's most ruthless and notorious pathological killers. As well as obvious figures, such as Adolf Hitler, the list includes latter-day serial killers Jeffrey Dahmer and Ted Bundy and, decided Russell with cheeky humour, he'd add a touch of his own dentist. Russell compiled data for himself on the killers on his laptop computer so he could gen up on them all.

When they first arrived on Brett Leonard's futuristic set, Russell and Denzel Washington found it bewildering. Often they were asked to play scenes to things that simply were not there. It was only when they saw the final version with Leonard's imaginative effects added that they totally understood how the missing gaps had been filled in.

Leonard gave Russell plenty of freedom in portraying SID 6.7 and he came up with a cherubic rake in flashy suits who displays a wicked sense of humour, dishing out violent and bloody havoc with undisguised glee. SID's view of people once he steps into the real world is that humans appear to be behaving as though they are doing their best to try to die and since death is going to be their ultimate fate he's going to help them achieve it. "Within SID's programme there are no such things as regret, conscience, human remorse or anything like that," Russell explained. "So basically the platform you jump off is just pure enjoyment, where terrorising the piss out of people is absolutely funny."

Russell was having so much fun and making such a good job of SID that two weeks into filming Denzel Washington said that he wished he'd taken the role of SID instead of the cop Parker Barnes.

A bonus for Russell was that Brett Leonard was delighted enough with Russell's performance to sign off *Virtuosity* with *The Photograph Kills*, one of the songs that Russell had recorded with his band Thirty Odd Foot Of Grunts.

After *Virtuosity* hit the screen, scripts began arriving for Russell in a rush. At one point, the actor reported, no fewer than thirty scripts were offered for double the money and half the time. It meant a great deal of information for Russell to digest and much to discuss with each of the various parties involved. "But I break the rules," he said. "If I don't like it I say no. I'm meant to play along and tease people about whether I'll take it or not, but I can't be bothered."

Having at last attracted the interest of the big studios, it was typical of Russell to line up two new movies, *No Way Back* and *Rough Magic*, which were micro-budget projects but which offered him roles that attracted his interest. Most of the thirty offers were just variations of the same story, he noted. And anyway, just doing studio movies was not his aim, he explained to those who tried to persuade him to carry on the momentum in Hollywood that *Virtuosity* was giving him.

No Way Back was a $1.3 million independent movie about a mobster who, shattered by the murder of his son, kidnaps in retaliation the young son of FBI agent Zack Grant, who is played by Russell. It was the first time Russell had played a dad on screen.

Rough Magic was a romantic comedy based on the novel *Miss Shumway Waves A Wand* by James Hadley Chase. It was a story, set in 1950, about ex-Marine Raider Alex Ross, played by Russell. He is working in Mexico as a stringer for the *Los Angeles Times* when he falls in love with Myra Shumway, a magician's assistant, while she is running away from an arranged marriage.

Bridget Fonda would be Russell's *Rough Magic* co-star and when Russell first arrived for a casting session with director Claire Peploe, she wasn't sure he would hit it off with Fonda, who had actor approval for the movie. Russell and director Peploe had been out to dinner and afterward they had gone back to Russell's agent's house where he later produced a gun and demonstrated how quick on the draw he had become since making *The Quick And The Dead*. Peploe was impressed but wasn't at all sure Fonda would have been since she was a sensitive soul with a deep loathing for macho men. Russell decided he would go and meet Fonda where she was working on America's east coast and two weeks later Claire Peploe was somewhat surprised but delighted to hear from Fonda that Russell would make a fine co-star for her in *Rough Magic*. Russell was pleased to be making what he felt was a significant film with a significant actress but the shoot, which took place in Guatemala, Mexico and a warehouse in Los Angeles, turned out to be a problematic.

But after the strange film-making experience of *Virtuosity*, Russell was first looking for a return to a more basic, real and performer-aligned project and it presented itself in the form of *Breaking Up*, the story of a couple's on-off, on again, off again, maybe on again relationship in which he would star with the very beautiful Salma

Hayek. Russell had only a few days to prepare for the role, the movie was shot in just twenty-eight days – again on a minuscule budget by Hollywood standards – and Russell, who showered Salma with gifts during the shoot, emerged from the film with her attesting provocatively that of all the male co-stars she had kissed in her acting career, Russell's kisses tasted the best.

Salma also spoke of Russell being one of the two best actors she'd ever worked with and that she'd learned so much from him. "I learned the hard way, too," she said, "because he's very…he's a little difficult. I'm sure you've heard this before, many times. But we ended up bonding because we both fell in love with the film.

"One day we got to a set in New York and they put two cats on the floor and they tried to separate them and said: 'That's your role.' It was a tough shoot. We were overworking, we were going crazy and you don't want to see Russell Crowe in those circumstances." One day Salma arrived for filming to find no dressing room, just a blanket on the floor. She just looked at Russell quizzically. "Did you throw a fit already?" Salma remembers asking Russell. "He said 'Yes' and I went 'OK then, I won't say anything'. Because I knew he must have killed them!"

It was almost inevitable that Russell's relationship with Danielle Spencer would struggle to flourish under the sheer weight of his film work and the enforced absences of American movie making. Danielle had her own career as an actress and singer in Australia to think of and she was not about to abandon everything and traipse round after Russell on his movie travels.

Both did their best to keep their love alive. Russell proved a considerate lover for Danielle, phoning, writing cards and letters and sending her gifts when he was away. She was a soft and feminine shoulder for him to cry on during his often thwarted efforts to push himself on to a higher level as a film actor in Hollywood. Danielle had never seen anyone work as hard as Russell in her life and while she wished she could see more of him she respected his inner drive. She never doubted that he would achieve his goals and reap his reward. But, when Russell himself had occasional moments of doubt, when he was beating the carpet with his fists in frustration at the machinations of Hollywood, or close to tears with loneliness on some far away film set, Danielle was the quietly reassuring and loving voice of reason and support.

Shortly after Russell had turned thirty, there was no question that his thoughts were turning toward marriage and children. "I'm thirty years old now and I think it's got to that 'must have a baby soon' stage. Shocking, huh? I never thought I'd start speaking like this."

Danielle did. She had frequently witnessed Russell exhibiting an exceptional respect for mothers with babies. He would make a great father, but for Danielle, however, the timing was all wrong. She felt she was too young for marriage and, with her career progressing nicely, her maternal instincts weren't taking precedence.

But, two months later, in September 1994, Russell was still dropping hints. "I have a few work obligations to fulfil. Then I want to focus on the woman I love and see if I can't make something more permanent out of it," he said.

Then, six months on, Russell was solemnly describing his relationship with Danielle as one "that flounders greatly with a particularly strong individual whose career is very important to her". It wasn't very much longer before it was over. There was no bitter ending or dramatic finish to their love affair. Their lives just slid in different directions. They had simply found it impossible to develop any rhythm to their affair because of Russell's work commitments. Whenever they appeared to be establishing some sort of pattern, it was disrupted because it was time for Russell to step on another plane.

"We love each other a lot, but we needed to be practical," Russell said after the break-up. "I had things to achieve and she had things to achieve, so we had to kind of let go. But she's one of the strongest women I know. She's a very impressive talent." Imagine, he said, what it must have been like for Danielle. "I've done fourteen movies and been fourteen totally different people – she didn't know who the hell she was sleeping with."

After six American movies in three years, Russell returned home in October 1996 to make an Australian thriller with an underlying element of comedy called *Heaven's Burning*, which owed not a little to the influences of Quentin Tarantino, *Bonnie And Clyde* and road movies in general.

With slicked back hair and long Elvis-style sideburns, Russell played Colin O'Brien, a man whose crash repair business has gone bust and who then hits the small time as a petty criminal getaway driver who accidentally leaves a bank robbery scene without his partners in crime but with more than just the cash.

Due to a bizarre chain of events, he finds himself speeding away from the bungled bank job across the sunburnt Australian countryside with Midori, a passionate bleach-blonde Japanese honeymooning wife, played by Youki Kudoh, who has faked her own kidnapping. She embraces life on the run with gusto, opting to pursue an uncertain future with Colin instead of returning to her husband. On their way, the fleeing duo meet a number of oddball characters, including a wheelchair-bound crippled accordion player whose repertoire consists of a few bars of Wagner's *The Flight Of The Valkyries*, a drug-addicted palm-reading hairdresser, a blind dress store owner and a blousy barmaid. On the trail of fugitives Colin and Midori, who bizarrely end up at a Bachelors and Spinsters ball held in a beach town – with Russell looking suave in a dinner jacket – are a bunch of mean hoods baying for blood, two droll Sydney detectives and a crazy kamikaze motorbike-riding jilted Japanese husband.

If all that sounded far fetched, then that's exactly what it was. Director Craig Lahiff intriguingly claimed in the *Heaven's Burning* production notes that one of the most compelling aspects was the idea of making a contemporary *Tristan And Isolde*. One film critic had another view: "Just call this one *Reservoir Dingoes*."

At least Russell, as Colin, was always in the thick of the action, displaying machismo either by pulling a gun, putting his foot on the accelerator behind the wheel of a speeding car, surviving his hands being nailed to a hotel room dressing table by thugs, or undressing the runaway bride by using his teeth to pull down the zip of her dress before making love to her.

A staggering forty-eight locations were chosen across Australia, which obviously caused logistical difficulties on an eight-week shoot involving fifty actors. Part of the film was shot in and around Adelaide which, despite providing outstanding vistas, also supplied several dust storms that wreaked havoc with camera equipment and tight schedules.

Russell and the diminutive Youki Kudoh apparently made an uncomfortable screen pairing. "He can be very difficult and certainly arrogant," she was quoted as saying. "When he's in a good mood, he's your next best friend, but on a bad day he's not easy to be around."

But Youki did claim that it was she who decided her love scenes with Russell should be a little more animated. "It was my idea to make them more passionate because Midori starts out so weak and subservient. Russell and I had an OK professional relationship in that sense, but he's a hard guy to get to know and to become close to, especially since our on-screen relationship has to strengthen throughout the film. We spent very little time together off-set."

The film's producer, Al Clark, had nothing but praise for Russell. "There's an elusive amalgam of sensitivity and strength, which most actors don't have at all," he said of him. "With Russell you always felt that when he was doing it he meant it. He has that gravity and masculinity that is disappearing from leading men. If you were casting an Australian remake of *Raging Bull* then Crowe is the only actor you would consider."

Heaven's Burning opened in Australia around the time Russell was promoting *L.A. Confidential* and he talked enthusiastically about his change of fortunes in America. He was now able, from an artistic point of view, to talk to people whose films he grew up watching and they were talking to him as a peer. "I had Francis Ford Coppola cook me pasta in Paris a little while ago," he said. "So things change."

XII

HOME

*I think in a funny sort of way it's like buying myself an
island. Somewhere in the middle of that place I can find
somewhere to be by myself and have a cup of tea.*

Russell Crowe, on his home in
northern New South Wales, Australia

It came as quite a shock to Russell Crowe when he realised that
he'd spent so much time working on film sets outside Australia that
he hadn't actually got around to seeing his parents for fully two
years. He regretted such neglect but the months had flashed by as
Russell pursued his acting goals.

Then, in 1994, Alex and Joyce Crowe unexpectedly ran into
financial difficulties and Russell quickly found a way of helping
them out which would eventually allow him to see a great deal
more of them. He decided to put down some roots by buying a
farm in northern New South Wales, some forty minutes inland from
the coastal town of Coffs Harbour, and he installed his mother and
father to help look after it while he was away.

Russell had lived in the same flat in Sydney for five years and the
move out of the city, some seven hours north by car, made sense
in every way. Sydney by now offered him too many distractions. He
knew too many people and too many people knew him. There
were also too many things going on in Sydney that would make
him fritter his time away. A place out in the country offered a
peaceful refuge to offset the frenetic life of Los Angeles, where he
was spending much of his time.

Countless people in the American movie industry tried to persuade him to move over full time to Los Angeles but Russell said it

would feel like unrolling his swag in the office. He reckoned he could be far more objective about his work if he stayed well away from the movie centre of the world and brought his energy to it from outside.

The home he found near Coffs Harbour was a ramshackle affair when he first bought it. But by then the Hollywood pay cheques were handsome enough for him to send his parents off round the world while he had the place done up. When he was there during renovations he was content to sleep in a trailer surrounded by his favourite CDs and choice bottles of wine. Now his home is an impressive ranch-style spread with a swimming pool and an old stable converted into a gym, but it retains its rustic feel and rural charm.

The setting is idyllic, in the heart of a valley that had once been a rainforest. "It *was* rainforest," stresses Russell, who will now not allow a single tree on his property to be felled, "but much of it got chopped down at the turn of the century for wood. So there's a lot of pasture land there. Originally, they ran dairy cattle but the dairy cattle destroyed the soil so now they run beef cattle.

"The tree logging was pretty extreme. As soon as the white man landed there they were basically saying, 'Righto, let's chop them down'. The thing I'm most proud of doing is replanting forty acres on my farm with rosewood, red cedars and a lot of other trees that were once native to the area.

"What I'm trying to do is to bring it back into being a productive area of land through natural means. I'm bringing in eighty acres of hardwood trees. But preparing and clearing the land takes money and time."

Russell has frequently mentioned that he feels he didn't have a home of his own until he was aged fourteen because of his parents' nomadic working lifestyle as TV and film set caterers and hotel managers. Now he had a beautiful home and, although it was not a working farm when he bought it, he set about surrounding himself not just with his immediate family but with dogs, horses, cows and chickens – the odd platypus and turtle or two also appeared – to provide the perfect welcome on his return from making the movies he was notching up in rapid succession. Just as Maximus is desperate to get back to his farm after his battles in *Gladiator*, Russell, too, needs to "fill up on home", as he puts it, at his own farm after his battles in Tinseltown. The animals helped him to open up his mind again, he said, when the small world of show business threatened to close it down.

Being surrounded by animals and six hundred acres of land is not something Russell merely enjoys; he positively cherishes it. Asked recently to re-live the best moment of his life he said: "I worked as a cow cocky (farmer) on a high country property on the border of New South Wales and Victoria in Australia in late summer, when the mountain still had the remnants of snow and we had to bring down a couple of hundred head of cattle who'd been let loose some two and a half years earlier. They had a really bad attitude and didn't particularly want to see any human beings. But on a daily basis, even though it was hard work, it was such beautiful country that it was a transcendental *arabesque*."

The dawning of a new day at Russell's home often brings with it an early morning mist, which hovers like a shroud low over the lushest of green valleys which dip down in front of the Gibraltar Range. Early risers have compared the mist-blanketed valley scene that greets them first thing as akin to living on the banks of a Scottish loch. Russell's farm is situated a little higher than other points in the valley and first-time visitors often just sit and watch the spectacle of the changing vista from Russell's farm as the sun comes up and moves around the valley, dispelling the mist and turning it into a completely different spot from the loch-like image they had seen at dawn.

Long before that mist starts to dissipate under the heat of the burning sun rising to fry the sky, Russell likes to pick up one of the little backpacks he keeps in all the main buildings on his farm – ready packed with powdered milk, coffee, sugar, a metal cup and

Chapter XII

a billie can – and set off with a dog or two to walk the fields, check on a cow that may soon be giving birth, and sniff the sharp morning air. He is in his element in an oasis of country calm of his own making. A recent boundary adjustment has meant the acquisition of yet more land and now, instead of going for a forty-five-minute walk on his own property, he can stride off for hours over his own cleared pasture and woods seeing not a soul, but plenty of birds and his own animals.

"I just enjoy the fact animals are around me, they calm me down," says Russell, who likes to take an active role in the running of the farm. "It's a simple existence, but if you're going to look after the animals the way they should be, you can do ten, twelve hours of work a day easy.

"But I'm a bit of a farmer's nightmare. Once I befriend an animal I cannot then use it for anything. What can you do? You watch a cow born, you grow up with it, you see the cow discover the world and everything and then at a certain point you say, 'Sorry, mate, you're hamburger'. You can't."

While he's building a commercial herd, every year there will be a couple of new calves. But he finds it painful to cull from the herd, especially a cow he's had for nine or ten seasons.

Russell started out with three dogs: two highly-bred cattle dogs and a Jack Russell who, ironically, turned out to be far better at working the cattle than the other two. But, just as *L.A. Confidential* was opening in America, Russell sadly learned that a snake had claimed the life of his Jack Russell. "It may be a very civilized place but we've got three of the most poisonous snakes in the world," said Russell, "and it got taken by a Taipan, one of the most poisonous."

Visitors to the farm are made aware of the dangers posed by the Taipan family, king brown and red-belly black snakes. The king brown is an exceptionally aggressive reptile, which unusually does not restrict itself to one deadly bite of a victim before running away; it keeps on biting.

The dangers literally keep everyone on their toes, but sometimes the unexpected happens. On a walk with a girlfriend a bull suddenly started charging after them and Russell had to bundle her over the fence quickly and explain that it hardly ever happened. Then, shortly afterward, just a little way up a track, Russell had to pull her out of the way of a venomous and deadly red-bellied black snake.

"I get a lot of energy from being somewhere where there's not much noise nor many people," Russell says of the home he returns to at every opportunity. He has put a lot of money and effort into ensuring that the farm runs smoothly, under the aegis of his mother and father and elder brother Terry, while he is away.

Ironically, the more successful he becomes, the more he needs to be there. And yet his very success dictates that he be elsewhere. He spends less and less time being able to "fill up on home". At the end of the year 2000, after what would be a momentous year for him, he counted up and realised that he had been able to spend just twenty-one days under his own roof.

XIII

L.A. CONFIDENTIAL

There's a fire in him that burns all night long, all day long, all the time. And that may hurt him because people don't understand that kind of flame.

Burt Reynolds

L.A. Confidential was the film that changed it all for Russell Crowe. He hates the word, but it was the hit movie that made him a "star". Until the surprise success of 1997 came along, Russell Crowe was just another highly promising leading man. But as soon as *L.A. Confidential* reached the cinemas and fans saw his electrifying performance as tough Los Angeles policeman Bud White, Russell was not just a star, but a superstar – which is a word he hates even more.

Many of the young cinemagoers who were switched on to Russell Crowe were much too young to remember the original *Confidential*, the Fifties magazine that specialized in outrageous revelations about the indiscretions of the rich and famous. It was the forerunner of the modern tabloid but nowadays there is almost a naïve innocence about some of those early stories it published. The intrepid Los Angeles policemen who seemed to spend their lives bravely raiding "reefer parties" and investigating the brutal murders of impossibly beautiful movie stars became just as glamorous as the film stars they appeared to be mixing with.

When acclaimed crime writer James Ellroy wrote the wonderful *L.A. Confidential* novel he insisted that the extraordinary characters all came from his astonishing imagination. Ellroy says: "In the entire book, I was trying to create the big, bad, ugly, evil, down-and-dirty dark romance of Los Angeles in the 1950s."

Ellroy writes from experience. In 1958, when he was just ten years old, his mother was murdered. The killer has never been caught and brought to justice and this remains a wrong the writer is determined one day to see righted. That obsession helped to launch Ellroy's lifelong fascination with crime and criminals. The seedy side of Los Angeles life is what fascinates Ellroy and the eloquence of his book captivated film writers Curtis Hanson and Brian Helgeland. They were enthralled by this vibrant tale of two cities; of a sunshine and beach Los Angeles where everyone smiled and looked glamorous on the surface coupled with a sleazier criminal Los Angeles underneath, populated entirely by pimps and hookers and other seedy elements. Director Hanson enjoys presenting settings and characters that are not at all what they seem to be, such as the psycho nanny in *The Hand That Rocks The Cradle* or the dark deviant drifters in *Bad Influence* and *The River Wild*.

L.A. Confidential was adapted by director Hanson and writing partner Helgeland from Ellroy's best-selling novel. The double world of good and evil is a theme that runs right the way through the film. It was a massive task to distil the key factors of this enthralling 500-page novel into a two hours-plus movie. Hanson and Helgeland spent more than a year writing their script. Hanson said that for simple reasons of screen time they obviously had to eliminate many sub-plots and much of the enthralling back story. But they also had to rewrite certain things so that they could be as true as possible to the characters.

"What grabbed me when I read the book was the emotional reaction I had to the characters. Relevant to that influence, a theme that has always interested me is the difference between how things appear and how they are.

"So this was a theme that I wanted to deal with, and *L.A. Confidential* was an opportunity to deal with it in a full-blown manner. It's without a doubt my most personal movie. It was the one where I used whatever commercial credibility I had earned by being lucky enough to have a couple of successes to step up and say, 'OK, I'm not a director for hire on this one. This is the picture I want to do.' I found the book and initiated it, and made it happen.

"The thing about the locations…well, first of all, I grew up in Los Angeles, and I always wanted to make a movie about Los Angeles. It starts with that first frame, that old postcard of Los Angeles. When you say "L.A." and you say "period" and then you say "crime", everybody immediately thinks *The Big Sleep*, *Chinatown*, Raymond Chandler, *film noir* and so on. While I love that, I didn't want to do that. I didn't want this movie to be perceived by my collaborators as being about that.

"So I put together a group of fifteen photographs and mounted each one on a piece of posterboard – the first one was that post-card that's the first shot of the movie. And what the cards did, I would sit with each collaborator and, in fact, each of the actors – and I would go through these pictures, and they represented how the movie would look, feel, and the theme of the movie. The first one I did it with was Arnon Milchan, who financed the movie. He hadn't read the script, and when I finished he said: 'Let's make the movie'."

Hanson did not want instantly recognisable, top-ranking film stars in every role. He wanted great actors who might one day become the household names of the future. And most of all he wanted Russell Crowe. The character of big Bud White is one of James Ellroy's greatest creations. He is the biggest, toughest Los Angeles Police Department operative there has ever been.

And when director Hanson showed his first choice, Russell Crowe, in a brief screen clip to Arnon Milchan, it was a key point in the whole production. The director breathed a huge sigh of relief when he played the tape and said, "This is my Bud White". The shrewd millionaire scarcely paused before he nodded approval and said, "OK".

For both streetwise Bud White and for Ed Exley, the ambitious career cop who is quite prepared to testify against fellow officers to further his career, director Hanson was determined to have unknowns. He said: "With Ed and Bud I wanted new faces for people to recognise there and then. I wanted people that the audience could discover as the story went along in the same way I discovered the characters as I read the book. It's very hard to do that with a movie star because you already invest the character with what the movie star brings to the part. Russell is an actor I knew from *Romper Stomper* and I knew that he could play the brutal side of Bud White. What I didn't know was if he could play the whole character. So I flew him over and met with him, worked with him and ultimately put him on tape doing a couple of scenes. And it was just unmistakable that he had the goods to be the perfect Bud White."

Russell Crowe was slightly alarmed when he heard that Bud White was the largest man in the Los Angeles Police Department because he is under six feet tall himself. He says he rang Curtis Hanson and said: "I don't know what you've seen. It must be smoke and mirrors because I ain't that big. But we did a certain amount of physical work with large weights. And there is something that happens to increase your physical presence. If it's on the page it is very easy to fulfil it."

He was keen to do as much work as possible to prepare for a role he knew was crucial. The schedule gave the actors a luxurious eight weeks in Los Angeles to get ready. Russell says: "Having two months to prepare was fantastic because it allowed us to get really steeped in all the characters. We watched a lot of old movies. Curtis introduced me to some fantastic films, like *In A Lonely Place, Private Hell 36* and Stanley Kubrick's second feature *The Killing*, with Sterling Hayden. Apart from that we read a lot of books; there are a lot available on the subject. And as the LAPD are at the centre of the film industry there have been a lot of films on them. We had access to some fascinating documentary footage from the Fifties."

But for glamorous Jack Vincennes, the cop with showbiz links to the TV documentary series *Badge Of Honor*, he chose Kevin Spacey. Hanson explained: "With Kevin, I wanted an actor who had that charisma to play the movie star among cops, but an actor good enough to play what's going on behind that facade – that this guy has lost his soul."

The breathless opening features ace sleaze journalist Danny DeVito, proud publisher of *Hush-Hush* magazine, telling it like he wanted his readers to think it was in Los Angeles around Christmas 1953. "Life is good in Los Angeles," says DeVito. "It's paradise on earth." That was the image the media of the time was selling and in the hit TV show *Badge Of Honor* DeVito continues: "The LA cops walk on water as they keep the city clean of crooks." But then he adds: "You'd think this place was the garden of Eden, but there's trouble in paradise." He goes on to describe how gang boss Mickey Cohen runs dope rackets and prostitution with the aid of henchman Johnny Stompanato, most famous as the boyfriend of Lana Turner. When Cohen is locked up on tax charges gang warfare erupts as villains fight to take over his empire.

Russell Crowe dominates the first action. As big Bud White he sits with his fat drunken partner outside a house where a large man is savagely beating up a small woman. His partner insists their priority is to pick up the rest of the booze for the station party, but White ignores him. He steps out of the car, rips the electrified Santa Claus display from the roof and waits to confront the enraged bully inside. When he emerges Bud White delivers a savage beating and leaves the thug handcuffed and waiting to be arrested.

It is a sensational introduction and it establishes that Bud is his own man, that he can't bear brutality to women and that in hand-to-hand combat he is roughly equivalent to a small tank. From that fabulous moment the film brilliantly exposes the real LAPD and the dilemma facing the force is personified in the three main players. Russell Crowe is the old-fashioned form of justice. He would rather fill in a villain than a form and he doesn't care who gets in his way. Ed Exley, played by Russell's fellow Australian Guy Pearce, is the ambitious, by-the-book cop who would rather be one of the bosses than one of the boys. The smoothly charming Jack Vincennes, who helps to maintain the glossy TV image of the department, is played by Kevin Spacey.

Back at the station it is Christmas Eve, 1953, and Bing Crosby is crooning on the radio as cops pick up cartons of free booze to fuel their holiday parties. They pause in their celebrations to hand out a mass beating to three hapless Mexicans. The officers' brutality makes front page news and our three heroes are hauled in to the initial inquiry. White refuses to testify against any fellow officers and is instantly suspended. Exley enthusiastically sees the chance of promotion if he blows the whistle on his violent colleagues. Vincennes agrees to give limited testimony in return for the protection of his privileged lifestyle. The three different types of police officer are there before us.

The plot is complex and demanding but all the more enthralling for that. In a force which is usually satisfied with any sort of a conviction, White prefers to find the people who actually committed the crimes. His work leads him to the door of elegant millionaire criminal Pierce Patchett, played by David Strathairn. He runs an imaginative high-class call girl operation in which aspiring young actresses are given plastic surgery to make them resemble movie stars. One of them is Lynn Bracken, played by Kim Basinger, who has been "cut" to look like Veronica Lake. She looks more like Kim Basinger to most filmgoers, but Bud White calls for lovely Lynn, who appears drawn to him, saying, "You're the first man in months who hasn't told me I look just like Veronica Lake".

By then Bud White's two rivals have teamed up together and when they spot White and Bracken making passionate love behind some unwisely uncurtained windows they realise he is not as dumb as he seems. The black humour of the movie is brilliantly spliced with the shocking violence and the wonderful Raymond Chandler feel of the whole story. One of the funniest scenes takes place in the famous Formosa Cafe, when Exley and Vincennes arrive to question Johnny Stompanato. When his date starts to abuse the officers verbally, Exley snaps, "A hooker cut to look like Lana Turner is still a hooker". But Vincennes knows better. "She is Lana Turner," he says with enormous amusement.

But the film has all shades of emotion and Russell Crowe's Bud White is certainly at the centre of some of its darkest moments. His scenes with Kim Basinger, where the officer unwinds and opens up, are surely some of the finest acting he has ever done. White reveals why he loathes women beaters with such a dangerous passion when he says bleakly, "When I was twelve years old my old man tied me to a radiator and I watched him beat my mother to death with a tyre iron".

Russell was fascinated by the character of Bud White. He said: "Bud is a very basic meat and potatoes kind of guy. He sees things in a very clear-cut manner. He knows, or believes he knows, the difference between right and wrong. And even though when I first read the script, I saw him as an extremely immoral man, using his badge and his authority for his own ends, after a while – and having read the book – I began to see it from the other way round. I saw him as a very strong moral centre who has a great belief in things that are important to him. And he will fight and die for those and what he believes in. He is a racist. He is self-righteous. He is foul-mouthed. His is a son of a bitch. However, in the course of the movie you get an indication as to why he has taken this attitude in life. He doesn't realise just how much he is looking for life and affection and confirmation of his good points, buried as they may be. He finds a woman strong enough to deal with the posture that he has taken so he finds within himself the ability to open up to her. I think he is a good man, but he is very much a product of his environment and his job."

Russell was so keen to get as close to his character as possible that he telephoned James Ellroy for advice. He asked what branch of service Bud had worked in during the Second World War and was told: "He didn't go to war. He had a battle plan since he was ten years old and his battlefield is the city of Los Angeles, and his enemies are the domestic abusers. That is his war. That is the battle he is fighting. He went out of high school into the LAPD training programme. End of story."

One of the most painful aspects of *L.A. Confidential* was that Hanson and Ellroy always insisted that Bud White was not a beer drinker. Russell said: "Come on, this is 1953. He is a blue-collar bloke. A cop. You're telling me he doesn't sit around with the boys after his shift having a beer? And Ellroy says: 'Absolutely not.' So for five months and seven days I didn't have a drink. That was hard for a young Australian. It's probably the most painful period of my life. James came up with this thing that Bud White only drinks single malt scotch straight and that was part of the script as well. And the one time you actually do see him ask for a drink is when he is doing the first interrogation scene with Lynn Bracken and he doesn't take a single sip from the glass because he only asked for a drink to relax her. That's a relaxation technique. And all the cops that see the film go, 'Hey man, he's trying to get her to relax'. This guy is smarter than you might think he was."

Russell Crowe prefers not to think of *L.A. Confidential* in terms of the impact that it had on his ranking as a star. As the movie was launched he said: "I don't see it as 'having made it' or anything like that. I see it as being great work and a terrific chance for me to do the kind of work I want to do with great people like Kevin Spacey and Curtis Hanson, who is a really great director. I was also extremely happy to be doing this one as I'm a big fan of James Ellroy. But I never tried to 'steal the show' or upstage anyone. I was merely wrapped up in the Bud White character, someone who allowed me to be physical and someone who really leapt off the script page.

"Well, Curtis went around explaining to lots of people that having a couple of Aussies like me and Guy as LA cops was a daring thing to do, but then when we sat down and talked it through, it seemed less so. It was a gamble, but it was also important to have rather lesser known actors as Bud and Ed. If they'd been played by bigger stars, the audience would have assumed these people were going to rule the narrative. And *L.A. Confidential* isn't about just two characters, it's about a group of characters, and how they interact and move the story. The casting is brave, but it's also very smart."

But Crowe is very definite about Guy. "One of the best things about doing this movie was working with him. It was so great to have someone like him there to help me through. I mean, when the days were long and the thing feels like a real job...hard work...it was terrific to have someone there who was both a great actor and a great guy."

When it comes to the luminous co-stars, though, Russell loathes all the endless gossip. "Kevin Spacey is a brilliant actor, Kim Basinger – now there's someone who really fits in with the tone of *L.A. Confidential* – her image is so against what she's really like, just like her character. All that stuff the media say about her, and then she shows up, so unaffected, in jeans and a T-shirt, and gives off this tremendous energy in her acting. She's going to go on to even greater things."

L.A. Confidential's wonderfully nostalgic setting has attracted a great deal of attention from cinemagoers who delight in pointing out minor inaccuracies while presumably missing out on the enjoyment of the movie. For instance, it is alleged by Nitpickers Anonymous that Bud and Lynn are seen watching the film *Roman Holiday*, which did not actually premiere until months later. A car is seen with a seven digit licence plate, but these were not introduced into California until the 1970s. Similarly, Johnny Stompanato did not meet Lana Turner until 1957. Russell Crowe's response to these picky complaints is unprintable – I understood him to mean that he thought it was rather more important for people to enjoy the movie.

But the success of *L.A. Confidential* meant that Russell had yet another character he was anxious to distance himself from. "I am no more like Bud White than any of the other characters I play," said Russell. He would much rather reflect on the movie as a whole. He said: "It is a really nice movie. Guy Pearce does a great job. Kevin Spacey is fabulous. Kim Basinger gives her best performance. I shouldn't say that because it sounds like I am judging her work, but she takes you to a fluttering, emotional core that she has not brought to you for some time. She has been doing *Wayne's World* type celebrity stuff and this is a real acting role. My favourite moments in the movie are hers.

"And it has got Danny DeVito in it. It is a wonderful ensemble cast. We went to Cannes together and the thing I really felt was how much we all liked each other and we had a wonderful time of discussion and discovery on the movie. It is the first truly ensemble piece I have done in America. I don't mean that negatively but so often when you work here, you're in your corner, the other actor is in his corner and somebody rings a bell and you come out and do your business.

"We all kind of ganged up on Curtis Hanson and he was pleased because he saw we were so passionate. The great thing about Curtis Hanson is that if you ask him a question he will answer it. It might take him seven days or fourteen days to give you an answer, but as long as you're working, as he is, he is fine and dandy. When he does give you an answer it is thought out, considered and every single thing you asked is given a satisfactory conclusion. Curtis loves the fact that you pick up the ball. I really enjoyed myself. I'm not saying I didn't annoy the hell out of him, but he was a big enough guy to allow me to annoy him."

Some reports indicated that Russell got so close to Bud he even started dreaming about the character. He said: "You have to do what it takes to blow life into characters. Some things come without any real understanding. I don't bother to question it or myself anymore. If you get into a situation like *L.A. Confidential*, where you can just totally get inside the character, that's a privileged position. Now that I am aware of the process I realise it is the position you always want to aim for."

The ensemble went in triumph to Cannes, where the film was highly praised, and Russell was asked if he realised it would make him a star and a sex symbol. "I don't think of myself in the terms you mention, but I do have a sense of humour about what I do. I think *L.A. Confidential* changed the nature a little bit of what I do in America. I took a few of what I considered to be quality jobs, like *The Quick And The Dead* and *Virtuosity,* and they didn't necessarily find their mark commercially. *L.A. Confidential* was kind of like a watershed. It very definitely changed the way I do things. I have got a lot more responsibility now in terms of when I am on a job. There is a different level of respect."

Russell waited fully fourteen months after *L.A. Confidential* before he took on another movie. During that time he turned down dozens of tough-guy roles before opting to join an ensemble cast in Disney's *Mystery, Alaska*, written by *Ally McBeal* creator David E. Kelley, and for which he had to learn to ice skate.

Starting from scratch, Russell had just two months in which to become proficient enough on the ice to play John Biebe, the sheriff of Mystery, a small ice hockey-obsessed town which suddenly gets an unexpected chance to play a big NHL team, the New York Rangers, in a major televised event. As a former player, Biebe joins forces with town judge Walter Burns, played by Burt Reynolds, to whip the team into shape for the game of their lives.

The cast were amused to find Russell running up a flag of the Southern Cross – which covers both Australia and New Zealand – each day before filming began to get the competitive adrenaline going. He'd in turn exhort the cast to sing their respective national anthems before they hit the ice.

One day Russell called for a halt in filming and had the crew sing *Happy Birthday* to actress Megyn Price. Then his assistant appeared carrying a huge platter of strawberries for her. He also kept their collective spirits up in more ways than one by keeping everyone in party mood at night after a hard day's filming. Burt Reynolds was moved to say: "There's a fire in him that burns all night long, all day long, all the time. And that may hurt him because people don't understand that kind of flame."

Thirty timber workers in Canmore, Alberta, close to the movie location, apparently failed to understand that flame one night when Russell reportedly sparked a massive pub brawl with a few choice words at a bar where he was drinking with members of *Mystery, Alaska*'s crew. The place erupted, tables were overturned, glasses hurled and chairs were thrown after Russell allegedly described ice hockey as "a game for wimps" then stood on a chair and branded Alberta "boring".

By the time the movie was in the editing stages, executives at Disney, who bankrolled the movie and who were to distribute it, suggested that *Mystery, Alaska* should be more of a Russell Crowe vehicle than an ensemble piece. But Russell backed director Jay Roach in rejecting this idea, believing the movie was about a town, not any one individual, and that it would be detrimental if he were pushed to the forefront.

Russell was distinctly underwhelmed by his lack of prowess on skates when he saw the movie for the first time. He said: "It was the one time I sat back after a movie and started laughing and said, 'You just bit off a little bit too much, man. There's just no way you could ever be an ice skater. Forget about it.'"

It did, however, tempt Russell into buying a motorbike. "I thought if I can ice skate I can do just about anything," he said.

XIV

THE INSIDER

*I wondered why they'd hired such a young guy to play a
50-year-old's part. But I soon realised there's a great
actor inside that young man's body.*

Al Pacino

Russell Crowe first started smoking when he was ten years of age.
He remembers well how the habit started. It was in the days when
his father ran a hotel and a young Russell, inquisitive and greedy
for experience of life, would gaze up at the packets of cigarettes
arranged on the shelves and wonder to himself whether one of
those packets contained something more than just cigarettes.

Discreetly he tried one of the smokes from each of the different
packets and found out that any suspicions he might have had were
unfounded. Each one contained no more than tobacco. But by the time
he had finished sampling all the different cigarettes, he soon discovered, like millions of smokers before and since, that he was hooked.

The habit has been with him off and on – but mostly on – ever
since, and he is the first to see the irony since a film about Dr Jeffrey
Wigand, a whistle-blower who exposed shocking tobacco industry
malpractice, gave him one of the great film roles of his career.

That movie was *The Insider*, the real-life story of one man's
exposé of the way an "impact booster" was added to tobacco to
enhance the nicotine hit delivered through cigarettes. *The Insider*
failed to persuade Russell to give up smoking, something he lives
to regret occasionally when he's singing with his band Thirty Odd
Foot Of Grunts and the vocals don't roll off the tongue quite as
smoothly as perhaps he'd like.

Despite earning Russell enormous critical acclaim and his first
Best Actor nomination, *The Insider* failed to make him a big star,

which, in its own perverse way, is a tribute to Russell's extraordinary and brilliant portrayal of a man almost twenty years older than himself. With thinning grey hair, a bulky frame and a plump, worried face behind gold-rimmed spectacles, Russell is physically almost unrecognisable. Movie-goers who have come late to Russell's body of work after being introduced to him in *L.A. Confidential* and then *Gladiator* have expressed astonishment at his dramatic change of appearance when checking back on his role in *The Insider*.

When Russell first received the script of *The Insider* while on the Alberta set of *Mystery, Alaska*, it gave him goose bumps. He could see at once that it was a well-written piece of work and he judged it to be a script right up there among the best two or three he had ever read.

It was based on the story of Dr Jeffrey Wigand, the real-life tobacco company executive who blew the whistle on the industry's orchestrated denial of cigarette addiction and its inherent dangers. The film would detail how Wigand was persuaded to spill the beans by producer Lowell Bergman, producer of America's top-rated CBS news magazine show *60 Minutes*. By doing so, Wigand opened the floodgates to legal moves against the tobacco giants and his evidence left the industry fighting a $246 billion law suit in 1998. But his evidence also made him the target of death threats and a smear campaign, and resulted in the loss of his home and marriage. It was a remarkable, sad, dramatic tale, made even more so because it is a true story.

What Russell found puzzling was why the script had been sent to him. He couldn't fathom which part he was being invited to play. He figured there must have been some mistake if he was being targeted for the role of research scientist Dr Jeffrey Wigand, Bachelor of Chemistry and Endocrinology in the study of hormones who, at the age of fifty-two, was almost eighteen years his senior. Even the most minimal research indicated to Russell that he looked nothing like him either. Wigand is thick-set – chubby even – with grey thinning hair and glasses. Russell couldn't work it out.

He was such an unlikely Wigand that he decided it must be a case of stunt casting – a casting decision that is so way out of character that it attracts attention. But when he checked up, he was assured that the script hadn't been sent to him in error. Director Michael Mann, who created the massively popular TV series *Miami Vice* and whose directing credits includes *Last Of The Mohicans* and *Heat*, genuinely had him in mind.

Now Russell began to study the script more closely. He was thoroughly intrigued and on his one day off from *Mystery, Alaska* he accepted Mann's invitation to have himself flown down to Los Angeles for a meeting. As he boarded the plane Russell felt he was going to the meeting more out of curiosity rather than any real belief that much would come of it. On the flight he even rehearsed what he was going to say to Mann – that he was totally unsuitable for the role and that he could think of a handful of actors in their fifties who would make a good fist of it.

At their meeting Russell got straight to the point and suggested to Mann that he look for an older actor to play Wigand. He was strongly voicing his reasons why he thought he was utterly wrong for the role when Mann stopped him mid-sentence. "I don't care about your age," said Mann with great urgency and conviction. "I want you to play this part because of what's in here," he declared, prodding Russell firmly in the chest with his forefinger.

Suddenly Russell looked at the director in a new light and decided that if Mann could look past Russell's own doubts and the more obvious casting criteria of age, girth and volume and colour of hair, then that was the kind of director he would be happy working for.

Not long after that initial meeting, Russell signed up knowing he would have just a seven-day break between completing filming of *Mystery, Alaska* and starting work on *The Insider*. Time enough, he decided, to fly back from Canada to fill up with some all too rare home life on his farm in Australia. There he tried to empty his head of his *Mystery, Alaska* small-town sheriff character by rising early, strolling through his paddocks and fields talking to the horses and cows, and simply enjoying the tranquil surroundings with his dogs. Then he flew off back to Los Angeles.

Russell had just six weeks before filming on *The Insider* would begin and he threw himself into researching the role with Mann, involving him in all the character discussions and in every meeting about Wigand's clothes and props. Russell read the court transcripts avidly and pored over the infamous television footage of Wigand's testimony to *60 Minutes* reporter Mike Wallace, who was to be played by Christopher Plummer. This was the TV segment which the channel originally declined to screen because corporate powers at the CBS network feared that a multi-billion dollar lawsuit from the tobacco giants might damage the network's share price.

The more he prepared for the role, the more Russell realised what a rare opportunity it offered him to stretch his acting talents to new limits. Not only was he playing a real-life character for the first time in his twenty-one-movie career, but someone who physically looked nothing like him. He had a cracking script and a very capable director in Michael Mann, who had been nursing the project to fruition for several years.

Mann told Russell that physically he could be any size he chose because the idea was not to impersonate Jeffrey Wigand. But Russell disagreed. "Once I began researching the character I realised it was necessary," said Russell. "Just as you can't suddenly play Abraham Lincoln with a moustache, I had to understand how Jeffrey Wigand felt physically before I could deal with what was going on inside him."

To this end, Russell submitted himself to a long period in pre-production, experimenting with costume, make-up and hair tests. "We bleached my hair seven times, the last time for an hour and a half, cut big swatches out of my temples to give me a receding hairline, took out seventy per cent of my hair's volume." But no matter how hard they tried to age his hair, nothing seemed to bring about the desired effect. Each morning it somehow looked young again. By the end of the first week of experimentation the make-up team were still not satisfied and started working on a wig for him instead. It required Russell's head to be shaved right to the skin, *Romper Stomper*-style, to accommodate it.

Russell then set about bulking up his weight. He weighed an athletic 172lbs at the start and his aim was to put on 30lbs in the six-week run-up. Accordingly, he adopted a sedentary lifestyle, eating and drinking whatever he liked, mainly gorging daily on a smorgasbord of cheese-burgers washed down with generous shots of bourbon. He also took virtually no exercise, even choosing to go by car when he could walk to the shops.

In those six weeks his weight actually rose way beyond his target. It ballooned by 48lbs, which gave him a fleshy 220-lb frame, a podgy face and more than a hint of a double chin. Russell felt he needed the extra weight not just to look like Wigand. There was to be a scene where Wigand falls over and rolls down a grassy hill in front of his house just as his world is starting to fall apart and the added bulk would make him look more pathetic as he tumbled. Also, a lot of people had told Russell that Wigand's diet had changed dramatically as events unfolded and that he had been drinking a bit more, which added to his weight. It was more justification for Russell to bulk up.

In addition, Russell even changed his walk, abandoning his own natural gait and substituting a purposeful short-step waddle. He also picked up on the posture of a man crushed by the crumbling of his circumstances, the sag in the shoulders, the slump of chin on chest. Russell used his flair for mimicry and his ear for accents and repeatedly listened to several hours of tape of Wigand speaking to get his voice and American accent off to perfection.

In the run-up to filming, Mann three times asked if Russell was planning on meeting Wigand to help him with his characterization. Russell was dead set against it. He felt he didn't need to come face to face with Wigand and, in any case, he didn't want Wigand telling him how he wanted to be portrayed in the film. Russell wanted to remain objective, focused on his role without unnecessary influence. The third time Russell turned down Mann's suggestion that he should meet Wigand, Mann told him: "That's all right, but he's flying in tomorrow morning and your appointment is at 8:30." Mann had finally won the day. The opportunity, he stressed, was just too good for Russell to miss.

Russell's meeting with Wigand did not occur until just before the cameras were due to start rolling on *The Insider*. He joined Wigand in hitting a few golf balls and then they sat down and talked. Because of his confidentiality agreement with his former employers, Brown & Williamson, Wigand could participate in the film in only the most tenuous manner so there were many areas of his past work he could not discuss. But Russell was still able to ask some hard and searching questions in other areas, which Wigand apparently answered with honesty and intelligence.

The actor found the experience invaluable and was pleased he had decided to come face to face with Wigand after all because it gave him a whole new, much more human, perspective on his role. "What got me was that, with all the intellectualizing and studying I'd been doing, maybe the thing I hadn't quite set within myself was the basic emotional journey of a real man in a series of true events. What I came away with was the idea that this was a man under siege." This vital insight into Wigand was something Russell felt he would not have picked up on had he not met him and it became a crucial element of his portrayal.

Russell refused to divulge exactly what was said between them. "Let's just say that after it was all over, I felt we had to honour this man. He put everything on the line to tell the truth."

Interestingly, when Russell hit a few golf balls with Wigand he quickly came to the conclusion that Wigand was not nearly as good a golfer as Mann intended to show in the film. Russell saw Wigand's unreliable game as a key element in why he did not fit into corporate culture. Against that argument, Mann wanted to use a night scene of Wigand diligently perfecting his golf swing under lights at a driving range to drive home the man's loneliness. But it didn't fit in with Russell's view and he repeatedly told the director as much.

Many of Russell's pivotal scenes would be with Al Pacino, an eight-time Oscar nominee and Best Actor winner for *Scent Of A Woman*, who would be playing Lowell Bergman, the CBS *60 Minutes* producer and investigative reporter to whom Wigand first spills the beans. Initially, Pacino was of the opinion that Russell might be too young for the role but during rehearsals he was impressed to see Russell transformed. "I thought what he did was just brilliant," Pacino remarked. "I wondered why they'd hired such a young guy to play a 50-year-old's part. But I soon realised there's a great actor inside that young man's body."

Fortunately, famed and illustrious Oscar-winner and co-star got on famously. Russell was expecting Pacino to be intense but found him relaxing company off screen and they forged a friendship by watching games of basketball together. When filming moved to Louisville, Kentucky, Russell spotted the factory that made the famous *Louisville Slugger* baseball bats and he bought one for $40 and paid extra to have it customized with Pacino's name. Unbeknown to Russell, Pacino is a baseball fanatic and was extremely touched by Russell's gift. He went round telling everyone it was the best present ever. When the Kentucky shoot wound up and Russell flew back to Los Angeles for further filming, he found seven large cartons stacked up outside the door of his rented house. As he came to open them, they turned out to be the components of a baseball pitching machine, a gift from Pacino.

The Insider turned out to feature some terrific exchanges between Russell and Al Pacino and Russell is at his best conveying Wigand's deteriorating circumstances and his life under harassment, both legal and otherwise, including death threats – no one was ever charged with making them. Over the course of the film, Wigand loses his job, his home, his wife, his family, his financial stability and his trust in others – including Lowell Bergman – because of his willingness to speak out on what he saw as the tobacco industry's pattern of lies and deceptions. From the position of top scientist in the number three tobacco company in the US, he sinks to a position where he is homeless, financially and psychologically assaulted, and resorts to applying humbly for a job teaching Japanese and chemistry in a high school.

As a rule, Russell likes to watch the final edited version of any film he has appeared in. But this time he found it a painful process. "Playing somebody who's alive and kicking is a tightrope job," he conceded. This time he was putting on screen the most turbulent events in the life of a man who was real, a man whom he knew to be very real because he had met him, a man who was regarded as a hero in many circles although he had not set out to be a hero. Russell felt that the social impact of Wigand's actions was the result of his desperate attempts to protect his family. Russell had put himself into the body and frightening circumstances of Dr Jeffrey Wigand and he just hoped he had done what he had set out to do, which was to honour the man. "I think Jeffrey's a hero because he didn't go and pick up a gun," said Russell.

He was buoyed by the reaction of the real Lowell Bergman and Jeffrey Wigand when they were given a screening of the movie. Both were unstinting in their praise for Russell's performance. "He was incredible," said Bergman. "He delivered the real everyman quality of a man caught in a moral conundrum. Brilliant." Wigand said: "My hat's off to Russell. He's got it down. He even looks like me."

The release of *The Insider* brought with it some glowing notices for Russell. Janet Maslin in *The New York Times* described Russell as a "subtle powerhouse in his wrenching evocation of Dr Wigand". Kenneth Turan in *The Los Angeles Times* called him a virtuoso Australian actor "…who joins an old-fashioned masculine presence with an unnerving ability to completely disappear inside a role".

Eventually, the favourable reaction to *The Insider* pushed Russell's asking price per movie up to £3 million. It made him better known but, perversely, not a huge star. His stock as an actor had risen immeasurably, however, among his peers and within the movie business generally. He had delivered a truly riveting, admirable performance. *The Insider* also earned Russell Golden Globe and Oscar nominations for Best Actor, although he was to lose out to Denzel Washington for *The Hurricane* in the former and then to Kevin Spacey for *American Beauty* for the ultimate movie accolade, the Oscar.

At the Golden Globes Russell caused a stir by turning up for the ceremony clutching the hand of actress, director and single mum Jodie Foster, boasting the next day that he had the best date in the room. Russell and Jodie had been friends for some time and he had sent her a tiny South Sydney rugby league jumper for her son, Charles, when he had been born eighteen months previously.

The downside for Russell of making *The Insider* "on Planet Mann", as he called it, was spending five months bald and bloated, which put a damper on his socializing. It didn't make him the most attractive of men around town and he wasn't used to that. It had taken him six weeks to balloon up to 48lbs above his normal weight for *The Insider* and he fully expected it would take just six weeks to get it all off again. To his displeasure and frustration, he found it wasn't that easy and it eventually took him five months to slim down to his normal athletic shape, during which time he was shocked to find that cholesterol tests he underwent bordered on the dangerously unhealthy.

Despite *The Insider*'s central message of the dangers of smoking, Russell continued to puff away. "The fact that I could go through a project like that and haven't quit is an indication of the power of this addictive drug," he commented. "After *The Insider* I know the exact chemical compounds in a commercial cigarette. But I've been smoking since I was ten. I know it's terrible but I'm a great fan of irony!"

In Australia Russell's Hollywood success naturally was not going unnoticed. At the Australian Film Institute awards in November 1999, he was among an audience comprising most of the cream of the Australian film industry. He should have been feted, his achievements extolled, but he was smarting from a newspaper article on *The Insider*, which read: "Australian culture is hardly promoted by Crowe's American accent."

It was an untimely barb as Russell had just won the right from director Taylor Hackford to keep his natural accent in his next movie, *Proof Of Life*, after the role of a hostage negotiator had originally been written as an Englishman.

But when Bryan Brown went up to collect his Best Supporting Actor award for *Two Hands* he used his acceptance speech to criticise the launch of Sydney's Fox Studios as "a celebration of American film culture". He went on to list Australian actors "who have not only contributed to Australian cinema but also to the Australian identity". Notable by its absence was the name of Nicole Kidman, who was present that night. Russell took the omission of his own name as something of a slight.

Later he got the chance to retaliate when presenting an award. "Bryan, on behalf of Nicole Kidman and myself, we forgive you," he declared. "You're ignoring the fact that, based on hard work, sweat and commitment, there is a bridge that exists between the Australian film industry and the world."

He indicated that there was nothing personal in what he was saying and added: "Twenty years from now people will look back on this period and say this was when the creative force in cinema performance came from this side of the world."

The Best Actor Oscar nomination which followed on February 15, 2000, for *The Insider* went some way to bearing out what Russell had said. He was intensely proud of the recognition he had received from his peers. "It's an extraordinary honour," he said. "The Academy, to me, is a really important thing. It is your peers – people who do the same job – voting for it, so getting a nomination is enough."

He added in typical Crowe fashion: "I'm an Academy-nominated actor for the rest of my career, no matter what shit I do from here on in."

XV

GLADIATOR

*You should take this Ridley Scott project more seriously. It
is my belief that Ridley Scott is in the top two per cent of
shooters who ever existed in the history of cinema.*
Director Michael Mann to Russell Crowe
on the set of *The Insider*

In the beginning it was the doubters who convinced Russell Crowe
to throw his heart and soul into becoming *Gladiator*. The very idea
of a great big expensive film epic of the Roman Empire had wise
men and women in Hollywood shaking their heads. It seemed to
belong to another era, which few of the movers and shakers of the
movie business of today could even remember first hand. Certainly
Ben-Hur, starring Charlton Heston, won eleven Oscars for its char-
iot-racing excitement. But that was made back in 1959. *Spartacus*
came a year later and was so brilliantly directed by Stanley Kubrick
that it remains the most enduring image of Kirk Douglas. The giant
scale and sweeping spectacle of those great historical hits helped to
ward off the relentless threat of television to the cinema box office.
Then in 1963 came *Cleopatra* with Richard Burton and Elizabeth
Taylor at the peak of their powers. But, after twelve months in the
making, and the famous couple saving their strongest performances for their private battles, the most expensive film ever made was
a total disaster as the public stayed away in their droves. Huge
Roman Empire epics were surely consigned to history for good.

But Russell Crowe is his own man and he knows his own mind.
When he first heard rumours of the possibility of a massive movie
that made a big budget return to the might of Rome, he refused to
write off the possibility of a return to old glories. "Russell loves to

buck the trend of conventional thinking," said a close friend. "The fact that the whole concept of reviving swashbuckling sword-fighting in an ancient empire was regarded as ridiculous made it all the more appealing to Russell. Several people told him he was crazy to even think of playing in *Gladiator*, but the more they said it was ridiculous the more he wanted to play it."

Admittedly, when his agent George Freeman first phoned him with the idea that he might star in a gladiator movie his initial reaction was to laugh out loud and snort, "As if I am ever going to be in a gladiator film!" But when Russell started to give the idea some thought he reflected that a generation earlier an actor had not really arrived unless he had been in a gladiator movie, a couple of westerns and appeared as a swashbuckling pirate. He was actually working very hard on *The Insider* for Michael Mann when the director heard that he was playing it cool with the offers from Ridley Scott. Mann walked into Crowe's trailer and told the actor: "You should take this Ridley Scott project more seriously. It is my belief that Ridley Scott is in the top two per cent of shooters who ever existed in the history of cinema."

The idea of *Gladiator* was close to the heart of powerful movie mogul Walter Parkes, who runs super successful DreamWorks pictures, which he jointly owns with Steven Spielberg. Parkes, one of the men behind the success of *American Beauty*, *Saving Private Ryan* and *The Mask Of Zorro*, felt passionately that right at the start of a brand new century was the time to go back in time nearly two thousand years and tell a great story from history. But his own experience told Parkes that this was a massively expensive risk to take. "My heart was in my mouth until I started seeing some of the results," he said.

The film would require a $100 million budget and no-one would really know whether it was money well spent until it was much too late to change their minds. Writer David Franzoni had initiated the project when he approached Parkes with the basic idea for *Gladiator* some two years earlier. There were many twists and turns to the story from that inspirational start but the concept of a hero who could drag the audience through a compelling story set in that turbulent early civilization was born. Parkes wanted a director who could share his vision and his growing enthusiasm and he chose Ridley Scott.

The mogul chose an intriguing way to convey his image of the essence of the picture. Before Parkes showed Scott even a glimpse of the early draft of the script he showed the veteran director a picture by nineteenth-century artist Jean-Leon Gerome. It featured a scene at the Colosseum of a gladiator in the centre of the great amphitheatre looking up at his emperor and waiting for the verdict. The ruler's thumb is outstretched sideways and with his forbidding expression it looks as if he is about to pronounce a death sentence on the fighter as the painting is called *Pollice Verso*, which loosely translated means "thumbs down". It is a powerful, haunting image and it produced an instant and emphatic thumbs up from Scott.

Scott is over sixty years old and can well recall the great Roman epics that had thrilled him as a young man. He had seen *Quo Vadis* and *Spartacus* and *Ben-Hur* as an enthralled member of the audience at his local Odeon and he knew that with the right story and the right star *Gladiator* could be a winner.

But he was aware that there was a great danger of straying into send-up territory if the film ever looked likely to be anything other than one hundred per cent true to itself. More recent films, such as *A Funny Thing Happened On The Way To The Forum* and *Life Of Brian* had very successfully poked fun at the camp image of toga-clad actors who were just a little too mannered. The memory of Kenneth Williams screaming hilariously, "Infamy! Infamy! They've all got it in for me," was exactly what Scott knew he had to avoid at all costs.

The director was very focused from the start on his conviction that a strong and not too complex central story and an extra-special star were needed to make *Gladiator* a success. But the man who began his work as a director on the BBC's classic TV cop show *Z-Cars* was not frightened of the challenge. In his heart he knew that the glory of the Roman Empire provided a magnificent setting for a drama and he believed he had the ideas and the star to deliver.

The film is set toward the end of the second century AD, a time when scholars appear to agree that the Roman Empire was past the peak of its power and was already set on its decline and fall. It was also a period when gladiatorial games enjoyed their greatest popularity. The games were in fact a distraction which disguised the deterioration of the Empire.

It takes a special kind of film-maker to organise the vastly complex schedule that would produce a believable and compelling film. Both Parkes and Scott knew that the action sequences had to be exciting and innovative and the narrative had to be intriguing and irresistible. Money was to be available but with money comes vast responsibility.

Scott was genuinely thrilled by the challenge of recreating enormous set-piece events like the great Roman assault on the last trouble-making tribes on the banks of the Danube. Scott was determined to be as faithful to history as possible and he insisted from the start that this was definitely not to be a "togas and wreathes" Hollywood-style Rome. But he was charged with enthusiasm by the concept of telling his story in the arenas of conflict in which the gladiators lived and fought and frequently died. The games in the Colosseum or the Circus Maximus were tremendously important, impressive affairs. Emperors used them to keep the people happy and involved and sometimes they ordered no less than one hundred and fifty consecutive days of fighting. The paradox of such a learned and sophisticated society organising such displays of savage brutality has perplexed scholars of the Roman Empire for centuries.

Gladiators became great heroes of the time. They were the pop stars or the top football players of their day. The finest fighters were even sponsored or supported by the emperor or by powerful senators and the games also often included bizarre animal fights. The bloodthirsty audiences would be thrilled by the introduction of captured crocodiles or rhinoceroses to the arena. The emperors used the games to show off their power and control. Ordinary aristocrats could put on only strictly limited shows while the emperor's games were always the grandest, largest scale games.

Sometimes the arena was decked out like a forest for hunters to show off their talents. At other times animals were made to fight each other. But the highlight was always the noon shows where unfortunate unarmed criminals or prisoners of war were savagely hacked to death, or mauled and eaten by lions or other animals.

The top billing went to the best gladiators. They were usually slaves captured in foreign lands and forced to fight for their lives in the arena. They fought in dramatic individual duels or in reconstructions of famous real-life historical battles, such as – in the film – the Battle of Carthage, an encounter between foot soldiers and heavily armed war chariots. *Gladiator* was never going to be a film for the squeamish.

Director Ridley Scott and the rest of the production team were delighted to land Russell Crowe for the all-important title role. The producers were determined to choose a man who could convey the strength and ferocity of the ultimate warrior along with the qualities of leadership and authority to stand up to the most powerful man on earth. Scott was impressed by Crowe's screen charisma and physical prowess. It was always going to be a winning combination.

Russell Crowe was just emerging from unknown quantity to rising star when he landed the role and his director was absolutely delighted with his choice. "He's ferocious, a great actor and he looks as if he will kick down walls to get what he wants," says Scott. "Can you think of an American actor of around the same age who could do it more convincingly?"

Selecting Russell Crowe, who was being deservedly lauded for his Oscar-nominated performance in *The Insider* while still some way from being a major star, was a calculated move according to producer Douglas Wick. "You really want to believe that Maximus is a real person and not a movie star in a toga," says Wick, who was impressed by Crowe's sheer screen presence.

"Russell has real authority, an inner engine that makes him pop off the screen. When you think of the movie stars that last, they all have some kind of furnace inside, an inner dynamic. Russell brought that to the character. His standards are extraordinary. If Russell doesn't feel that a part of the character's journey is credible or well thought out he will say so. And if no-one listens he will get on a table and shout until someone does. There is no quarter-inch of any performance that Russell is involved in that he won't fight to the death for." Just like Maximus.

Russell Crowe was undaunted by reports that Tom Cruise had paused and then passed on the towering title role. He was much more interested in the extraordinary character of Maximus Decimus Meridius, a Roman general of amazing prowess. He was a remarkable man who possessed the inspirational integrity and astonishing fighting skills to take on a whole empire. The script was pretty much a moving target in the early days but the essential concept hardly wavered. As the producer and director pored over new drafts Russell could see beyond the detail to a great big hero of a guy who he knew he loved before he even had his first tunic fitting.

Russell especially loved the fact that the role was so different from anything he had undertaken before. He loved the grand scale of the project. And he loved the idea of recreating the corruption at the heart of the Roman Empire. Russell was in awe of the achievements of the whole remarkable period in history and how the sophisticated advances the society made were under-scored by such gruesome and unrelenting brutality.

But he had an awful lot of work to do before he even picked up a script in anger. Months before filming began Russell retreated to his beloved ranch in Australia and set about losing the forty-five extra pounds he had piled on to play the flabby scientist in *The Insider*. He worked long, hard hours in the great outdoors with his cattle and he stepped up a rigorous physical training regime that included some training in sword play ready for the countless fight scenes of *Gladiator*.

It was hard but he enjoyed getting into shape. And he was enormously relieved that he had put in all the hours once he started filming. The exertions were long and unrelenting as his body took a beating just about every day. Russell Crowe and Ridley Scott quickly developed enormous respect for each other's work, which was surely reflected in the end product. Russell believed it was a wonderful opportunity to work with one of the great visual artists of our time while Scott was impressed by the actor's remarkable ability to internalize a role.

In the end, and in a long Hollywood tradition, the movie makers took a genuine historical setting and grafted their own powerful human story on to it. The film opens with Maximus preparing his well-trained and highly organised troops for a final battle on the last rebellious rabble of Germania. It is 180AD and Emperor Marcus Aurelius is reaching the bitter end of a twelve-year struggle to conquer the lands of what is now Germany. His war-weary star general is hoping against hope that the barbarians will settle without a fight, but when his messenger arrives back on his horse – minus his head – it becomes clear that a deal is out of the question. "People should know when they are conquered," says Maximus' faithful lieutenant Quintus, only to receive the laconic reply: "Would you, Quintus? Would I?"

Quintus is played by Tomas Arana, who also worked well with Russell in *L.A. Confidential*. Of *Gladiator*, Tomas says: "I was pleased to find the same old Russell, full of energy, fun, and as passionate and hard working as ever. He really challenges you as an actor and is great to work with. We are fellow Aries – his birthday is April 7 and mine is April 3 – and we have many things in common." The two actors discussed their characters' friendship and decided to leave the details vague and abstract. They had clearly been through a great deal of hardship together. "We did agree that Quintus and Maximus had been through many battle campaigns together, were close and loyal friends, but that Maximus was a bit wilder, with Quintus being more conservative, which is why he is the general and I would be his vice-general."

Maximus goes into ruthlessly professional action as he carefully briefs and prepares his troops and then finally exhorts them to, "unleash hell". Thousands of flaming arrows fill the sky as the Germans discover to their fatal cost that brute force and ignorance cannot defeat a well-drilled fighting machine. Although the barbarians are no match for the might of the Roman army, there is still some savage hand-to-hand fighting.

It's a stunning opening that instantly establishes Russell Crowe/Maximus as a man to be reckoned with. And it's all the more remarkable when you consider that this huge scale slaughter and blood-curdling mayhem took place not on the forested banks of the Rhine or the Danube but in leafy Surrey, in a wood not far from Farnham. Originally, the movie-makers intended to head for an army base just outside Bratislava, not far from where the actual conflict took place. But with winter fast approaching Scott switched to film in a pine forest closer to London, which posed far fewer logistical problems for the producers.

Fortunately, the English Forestry Commission wanted lots of trees cleared so the movie-makers were happy to oblige. Ridley Scott's philosophy is never to let a period film look like a period film. He attempts to take his audience back to that moment in time and he has surely never managed to achieve that more successfully. As Maximus carves his way through some unbelievably brutal confrontations, the physical power of the character is established along with the immense presence of his personality.

For Russell, the opening battle scene was one of the most frightening pieces of filming. The ground was slippery and very uneven and the horse he was riding got a little too close to some of the burning trees and then started slipping backward down a hill. The poor creature collided with trees and one branch cut Russell's cheek quite badly, producing one of the movie's more realistic looking injuries.

The whole event was an amazing exercise in logistics. All the ancient weapons had to be built from scratch and that meant making huge catapults that fire earthen pots full of boiling oil high into

ABOVE: Shooting stars. Russell in *The Quick and the Dead* with gunslingers Leonardo DiCaprio, Gene Hackman and Sharon Stone – who fought for him to make his Hollywood debut.

ABOVE: A bulked-up Russell
was physically barely recognisable
in *The Insider*. He piled on the pounds to
play corporate whistle-blower Jeffrey Wigand
opposite Al Pacino (TOP). The role earned
Russell an Oscar nomination for Best Actor.

Thumbs up for Russell from *Gladiator* director Ridley Scott
(BELOW); tigerish in combat in the Colosseum (BOTTOM);
and standing tall as victorious Maximus (RIGHT).

Two dates to remember: with Jodie Foster (ABOVE), and with Danielle Spencer (RIGHT).

BELOW: Co-star Meg Ryan has the look of love for her co-star in *Proof Of Life*. And so it proved, both on screen and off.

BELOW: Russell's proudest moment: receiving the Best Actor Oscar with his grandfather's MBE medal pinned to his chest.

Two contrasting public faces: all smiles at a formal film function (LEFT), and serious singer in concert with his band Thirty Odd Foot Of Grunts (BELOW).

the air as well as the giant mechanized crossbows that shoot flaming bolts toward the enemy. In the actual battle some five thousand highly trained legionnaires stood firm against a force of wild barbarians of more than twice that number and triumphed pretty easily. In the film several thousand extras and stuntmen staged the brutal battle with the same result.

Russell Crowe was quickly convinced that the film was firmly attended by good vibes from some supernatural power or other when Maximus had to sniff the winter air and confidently predict "snow". About ten minutes before one of the key battle scenes was to be filmed, snow began falling on the woods. Russell laughed: "So suddenly Max is not only a great general but also the only reliable weatherman in history. I mean, that kind of magic just doesn't happen, but it happened all along on this film."

That first battle was very intense. Russell said: "It took place in about two feet of mud because of the snow, so for me trying to get around to seventeen different opponents with horses galloping past and catapults going off and dogs jumping through the frame was a little tricky. Because of the mud people were slipping and sliding and not hitting their marks. When the battle was over the bodies were on the ground and the steam's rising from the bodies and I'm walking down through the bodies and just naturally all the other Roman soldiers came to join Maximus. It as like 'Wow. This is a glorious moment.' Then through the middle of it this one German extra, who had missed his marks, started running trying to run past and I grabbed him. I wasn't going to let him past me at that moment. I pulled him in front of me and he looks up at me and says in this plaintive little voice, 'I'm not supposed to die yet!'"

Maximus is frequently referred to in the film as "The Spaniard", so Russell came up with a suggestion. He recalls: "I said at the beginning, 'Look, I want to play this with an accent. A kind of Antonio Banderas, but with better diction.' But they just didn't go with the idea. So the accent I do in the movie is what I call 'Royal Shakespeare Company – two pints after lunch'."

Russell kept his sense of humour throughout some uncomfortable filming. He firmly recommended the film when he said: "The violence is very fantasy based. I mean, it's not often one sees chariots down the main streets of American towns these days. There is no sex, obviously, because Maximus probably had it lopped off at an earlier battle, which is why he spends so much time away from his wife and child," he joked. "And there is no swearing, obviously, because they couldn't work out how to say those words in that time period."

As the battle subsides an eerie calm descends on the wood. The feast to celebrate the success gets under way but Maximus is reluctant to take part. He is haunted by thoughts of his wife and son back home on his peaceful farm. He yearns to be back there, away from the horrors of war. The last thing Maximus wants to be is enmeshed in the political problems of Rome, but he becomes quickly caught up in the bitter turmoil of the day and can't help becoming involved. "For want of a better expression, he is a good man," says Russell Crowe.

Maximus is congratulated by his ageing emperor, Marcus Aurelius, played by Richard Harris. Marcus Aurelius is a genuine historical figure, who ruled from 161AD to 180AD, and his statesmanlike qualities in the film are thought to be accurately portrayed. Although he was a philosophical, peace-loving ruler, much of his time in power was spent at war, fighting on some far-flung boundary or other to maintain the integrity of the massive Empire.

When Marcus Aurelius congratulates Maximus it is a key encounter in the film and it is totally spell-binding. Even by his own account the veteran Irish actor is not an easy man to get on with. He says he does not often mix with people in the film business and admits they are probably glad of that. He is not normally comfortable with other actors but he established an instant bond with Russell Crowe. "I love the guy," says Harris frankly. "He doesn't carry that Hollywood star crap with him. There is no 'I am Russell Crowe'. He doesn't say, 'Did you not see *L.A. Confidential?* Wasn't I brilliant in it?'"

The respect is definitely mutual. Russell said: "One night we sat in the trailer and he did twelve Guinnesses right off. And he gets to number twelve and he finishes it and looks at me and he says, 'I think it's time for a Scotch'. He's seventy-three, mate. If you could bat that well at seventy-three you'd be doing all right."

Richard Harris certainly believes that Russell Crowe is now a major star and a potential serious hellraiser. He said: "Russell is carved from the same mould as Peter O'Toole, Albert Finney and myself. He is a throwback to the 1960s. He's a great guy and a wonderful actor. *Gladiator* wouldn't have been nearly as successful without Russell in it."

Harris was tempted out of his self-imposed retirement by the prospect of working with the new leading man and with director Ridley Scott. He said: "It's great for an actor to work with a guy like Ridley Scott, who is so in command of his profession and his craft and who knows precisely what he wants. That is a gift for an actor because half your problems are gone. And if you have someone off-camera like Ridley, you have to trust him."

Marcus Aurelius clearly looks upon Maximus as his son, but just as the emperor and thousands of cheering soldiers are hailing another battleground triumph, his real son arrives. This is the charmless, sinister Commodus, played with considerable menace by Joaquin Phoenix, who is indecently anxious to succeed his father to power. The dialogue is brilliant in its simplicity. "Have I missed the battle," asks the pampered Commodus, only to receive the ultimate fighting man's put-down from his aged father: "You have missed the war." Maximus bows his head in embarrassment as Commodus, whose head is full of his own delusions of grandeur, is instructed to honour the brave commander.

The wise old emperor seems aware that he is presiding over the beginning of the end of the Roman Empire. He shudders at the prospect of corrupt Commodus taking over and decides that his vain and untrustworthy son is not fit to rule when he dies. Marcus calls for Maximus, a Spaniard who has never even been to Rome, to tell him that he will succeed instead. "I want you to become Protector of Rome when I die," he tells the stunned soldier. Maximus does not want the daunting job, which proves to Marcus Aurelius that he must have it. "Commodus is not a moral man," he says. "He must not rule. You are the son I should have had." Maximus is given a day to consider the enormity of his new responsibility. Marcus wants him to maintain order, get rid of corruption and one day cede power to the people.

Maximus is hardly helped as he struggles to come to terms with the new task by the presence of Commodus' beautiful sister Lucilla. It is clear Maximus and Lucilla, who is played by stunning Danish actress Connie Neilsen, have been very close when they were much younger. The earlier relationship appears to have been a passionate romance that somehow went wrong. Intriguingly, it is never spelled out but it is clear that there is still strong feeling between them. Lucilla is a strong-willed and resourceful woman but she has a young son to bring up and she knows that she is dependent on her deeply-flawed brother Commodus for protection. The well-read actress, who studied the period in detail during filming, insists that, in a sense, Lucilla is the conscience of this film. "She is someone who, if she had been born a male, would have been emperor," says Neilsen. "Trust me, if this had been just a movie about a bunch of guys with swords I would not have been interested. But there is great character intimacy, considering the scale."

Tragedy strikes when Marcus Aurelius breaks the bad news to cunning Commodus that he is to be disinherited and effectively disgraced. Commodus is incensed and refuses to accept the decision. The monstrous son responds by killing his father, throttling the life out of the old man before he has chance to announce his decision.

This captivating dramatic device propels Maximus and Commodus into a compelling and bitter rivalry that has the famous general fighting for his life against his own men. Commodus announces his father's sad death and gives Maximus the opportunity to accept his leadership. When the incorruptible general stalks past his outstretched hand, Commodus knows he must destroy the potential enemy, not least because he is clearly aware that he has killed his own father. But Maximus jumps the assassination party and heads off across Europe to protect his wife and son. The audience is treated to a brief glimpse of Maximus' beautiful wife and angelic son waiting patiently for him in their idyllic farmhouse. But before Maximus can reach them, they are brutally butchered by Commodus' troops.

In Roman history the real Marcus Aurelius did die on the banks of the Danube and his feckless son, Commodus, did succeed to power. Marcus Aurelius was a distinguished Stoic philosopher who recorded his views on life in his *Meditations*. Russell Crowe took the time to read the writings of his mentor as he was preparing for the role. "If he is your teacher then you are going to be full of his teachings," said Russell, adding that several lines from the movie, such as "the time for honouring yourself will soon be at an end", were taken from *Meditations*. The script evolved a great deal from the early draft and the frequently quoted "strength and honour" was another of the star's contributions.

Russell Crowe took the role because of the general concept of the film, rather than the detailed script, which underwent some changes. He said the original script was too modern and too cynical. Russell knew the movie would require a massive leap of faith from all concerned and so he wanted it to be an honest and wholehearted leap.

The actual Commodus appears to have been even more loathsome that the screen version. He is reputed to have lived a life of excess and debauchery with a harem of some three hundred mistresses and three hundred young boys. He was very wary of genuine warfare but revelled in the wholesale slaughter of the gladiatorial games. Records claim he would descend to the floor of the amphitheatre to kill wounded wild animals and he would cheerfully deliver the *coup de grace* to injured gladiators who were too weak to fight back.

Phoenix is totally convincing in the role. He might not be a towering malevolent presence but he is more interestingly evil than that. His obvious insecurities combine to make him a ruthless and deadly opponent for Maximus and a constant dark force in the film. Phoenix himself said he thought that the best way to describe him was as a spoiled child. He is nineteen years old yet he is the most powerful man on the planet and he is clearly not up to the job. It's a tantalizing prospect and Phoenix gives the character a twitchy nervousness that prevents anyone who comes into contact with him from relaxing. In one wonderful scene he plays with a razor-sharp sword while discussing politics with some far from relaxed senators.

Russell Crowe noticed that the young actor was nervous. He said: "Joaquin is a lovely guy, but nervous. He lacks a little self-confidence. Ridley would say, 'You're now the emperor and you have to walk out into the middle of the Colosseum'. And Joaquin would say, 'But I'm a lad from Florida. What do you want me to do. Wave?'"

Russell took the time to ask the advice of the experienced Harris, who suggested inviting the young man for a few beers to find out if they liked him.

Russell says: "Richard orchestrated that moment and after that we got on like a house on fire. I really get on with Richard, he's got such a lion heart. When I meet someone who has experienced so many things and is still a balanced individual – a man who knows that the sky is blue and that water is wet, who hasn't let it get to him or change him – it gives me inspiration. It shows me that you can do this job for your livelihood. And though the insanities may come and go, it's all in waves and at the end of the day you can still just be yourself."

Maximus is not strictly a historical figure, but he was partly inspired by the stories of more than one lowly born soldier who gained promotion through valour in battle and rose to great power in Roman society. In the film Maximus returns home tragically too late to save his wife and son and is captured by cynical slave trader Proximo, played by a smouldering Oliver Reed in what was tragically to become his final screen appearance.

Chapter XV

Reed is splendid as the former gladiator who has himself managed to fight his way to freedom. It was a tradition of the games for the gladiators to keep one fifth of their winnings so that as long as they managed to stay alive they could buy their way out of slavery. Proximo spots the tremendous talent of Maximus early on and he advises him that simply winning is not always enough. Because the whim of the emperor can extinguish a life even in victory, Proximo warns Maximus that he must "win the crowd".

Reed seemed rejuvenated by landing such a large and important role and told friends right from the start that he knew it would be a major success. He was wary of becoming too close to Russell Crowe even though they both shared a reputation for enjoying a drink or two. Reed was uncharacteristically anxious about his own performances and realised this was a great chance, perhaps his last chance, to show all of the people who had long since written off his career that he could still hack it at the top level. Reed respected Ridley Scott immensely and forced himself into a very private fitness regime so his could deliver his very best performance.

In the film, Maximus is befriended by another captive, Juba, played by Djimon Hounsou, who helps to heal his wounds on the long trip to Proximo's gladiator training headquarters in Morocco. The grim reality of literally fighting for one's life is starkly conveyed in the film as Maximus is forced to use all of his considerable talents as a soldier to stay alive. Maximus gradually fights his way up to become Proximo's star gladiator and is sent to fight in Rome's famous Colosseum.

The producers built Proximo's gladiator training headquarters in Ouarzazate, Morocco. The arena was painstakingly constructed using more than thirty thousand mud bricks assembled in the traditional local way and in the end it was indistinguishable from the many genuinely ancient buildings in the area. Ouarzazate is an ancient citadel town set against the beautiful backdrop of the Atlas mountains and situated near to Morocco's oldest surviving casbah.

The scenes set in Rome were filmed on the island of Malta, where remarkably realistic versions of the Forum and the Colosseum were constructed. The film-makers found the abandoned army barracks of Fort Ricasoli, an old English base dating from 1803 that had been constructed in the Roman style. The elements had aged the building and it looked like Ancient Rome. And best of all it possessed a giant parade ground that could be converted into the Colosseum.

The location was an enormous help to the production. By adapting existing buildings instead of being forced to build from scratch, the producers reckon they saved millions of dollars. But it still took some three hundred building workers five months to turn nineteenth-century Malta into ancient Rome. The film-makers used up all the plaster and plywood on the island and had to start shipping in more. But production was frequently held up by the worst winter in Malta for some thirty years.

Production designer Arthur Max said: "We were in the middle of the Mediterranean in this awful winter and we actually had to have all the materials and equipment brought to the island. Working on an island has its challenges but despite the remoteness of the location and the adverse conditions we triumphed."

Ridley Scott said: "Arthur and I got the original signed plans of the city from the architect. Then we made an enormous scale model of the actual site, and started to play chess with the models to see how our additions would fit within the structure we had. We never could have built all of it. It was just too big."

Arthür Max originally studied to become an architect and enjoyed the task of building Rome not in a day but over several months. "How many people get the chance to build the Colosseum in its original form?"

The Colosseum is the centre piece of the whole film and its impact on screen is electrifying. But that was not achieved without a massive effort from the team. Underneath the stalls was built the massive hidden maze of tunnels and cells and holding pens for animals. In the breath-taking scenes at the end of the film there are more than two thousand cheering extras, but the crowd is enhanced to number well over thirty thousand thanks to computer-generated fans in the sections of the stadium created by technical wizardry.

Rome was far and away the most highly populated city in the world at the time, with more than one million inhabitants. The flocking of impoverished peasants to the city to find their fortunes is by no means a new phenomenon and Ridley Scott wanted to make his Rome every bit as busy and bustling as the real thing must have been.

The costumes were another area where the big budget really shows. The variety of outfits was extraordinary. From the fighting barbarians of Germany to the stylish leaders of Roman society, all had to be suitably clothed. But most elegant of all was Connie Neilsen as beautiful Lucilla, who had genuine gold thread embroidered by hand into almost every garment she wore. The actress even found a 2,000-year-old signet ring in an antique shop that made her feel much more connected to the part. Commodus has amazing white armour for his final confrontation with Maximus, which reflected the character's obsession with being as powerful as his predecessors, whose statues seemed to haunt his unhappy life. Joaquin Phoenix was transported back in time by the authentic looking outfits and insisted that as soon as he put them on he felt as if he were in a different world.

Russell Crowe's role was so physically demanding that his armour had to be light enough for him to move around, so all the pieces were made in foam and covered in leather. And every single thing he wore, from breastplate to tunic, had to be duplicated a dozen times for wear and tear and for his stunt doubles. The costume department even had to have different stages of each piece as the scenes progressed – from clean to dirty to torn to bloody. In all, the hard-working costume department created more than ten thousand different outfits for the cast, the stuntmen and the thousands of extras.

But it wasn't all hard work. Cast and crew of *Gladiator* took their cue from their leading man and played hard as well. There were frequent keenly contested backgammon contests, which were usually won by the super intelligent Joaquin Phoenix. Russell Crowe organised parties on the flimsiest excuse and there were cricket and football matches against local sides as well.

Russell's uncle, Dave Crowe, father of his cousins Martin and Jeff, who are both New Zealand Test cricketers, visited the set. Tomas Arana enjoyed learning this English game in such exotic surroundings. "Russell organised parties, a soccer match and a cricket match. The cricket was really amusing as Russell and David Hemmings joined Russell's uncle, brother and father in playing a local Malta team. I had never been to a cricket match before but I learned to say, 'Well done. Good show. Good wicket.' On balance I think I prefer baseball but cricket has an old world elegance to it, which is fun."

In May 1999 there was the distraction of Manchester United facing Bayern Munich in the final of the European Cup. Russell was betting heavily on Manchester United to win and even when the English side were 1-0 down with only a few minutes to go he was still shouting the odds and taking bets. When United scored their last gasp goals to win in the most dramatic fashion the place went mad and Russell was dancing on the table showering everyone with beer.

The filming was exhausting and Russell really looked forward to the days when Maximus was required simply to sit in his cell looking grim and manly. "I'm really being run ragged," he said of the gruelling schedule. But after filming each night he would wind down in a small local bar called the Tex Mex, drinking Aussie VB beer specially flown in from London.

In Rome the inevitable confrontation with the evil Commodus takes place as Maximus is drawn into the political intriguing of Derek Jacobi – as Gracchus – and David Schofield and John Shrapnel – as Falco and Gaius. David Hemmings added a rare lighter note to the film with his wonderful portrayal of the flamboyant wig-wearing arena impresario Cassius.

Jacobi knows more about wearing togas than most people and he was brilliantly convincing as the scheming senator who was determined to end the corrupt reign of Commodus. There was a light-hearted bond between the senior British actors, which Derek Jacobi noted seemed to worry their American counterparts. He said that English actors giggle all the time and seem to be taking things very lightly when in fact they take their work just as seriously as the Americans. Jacobi has great regard for the work of Ridley Scott and was delighted to land such a prominent part, and he is such an intelligent actor that he was a great influence on the cast.

Jacobi is, of course, still fondly remembered for his title role in the acclaimed BBC television series *I, Claudius*, and he genuinely loves the culture of Ancient Rome. But more than that he instantly grasped the importance of having the story dominate the setting rather than the other way around. "Great films are about people and relationships," he said. "I think it is important always to remember that, however exotic or lavish the setting, it is vital that the characters and the story lead the way."

Suggestions that Scott had hired a group of big drinkers for his key players were rightly brushed off. "I stopped worrying about such things years ago," he said. "I have had too many disappointments to get myself stressed out. I needed guys who could act. They were as good as gold on the drinking, apart from Ollie, who had his moments, particularly after six o'clock. Whatever went down the night before, they could all deliver the next morning."

The fight scenes were truly spectacular and the apparent realism was not easily achieved. Russell Crowe was injured several times but always kept going. "I don't think there is one part of me that has not experienced some sort of physical rupture," he said with a grin. "I have broken a bone in my foot, fractured a hip bone and had both bicep tendons pop out of their sockets," he counted carefully. But he refused to accept the advice from Oliver Reed, who suffered from an old knee injury and told Russell, "If you ever get injured on a movie, you just make sure they shut down the production". *Gladiator* was different, however, and Russell said: "I just had a little shot of Jack Daniels, kind of stuck the tendon back in place and it's been fine ever since. It was a great experience, even if there were a couple of days when I thought, 'What am I doing here?'"

Russell was even up for any extra-curricular activity to enliven the inevitable dull, off-duty moments. And he was distinctly underwhelmed to be instructed not to play football. It came at a time when Maximus was taking on tigers in the Colosseum, a point he was quick to highlight in a memo that he fired back to the producers. He found it a shade ironic that he was facing up to big cats in the arena and he could not spend an hour and a half of his off-duty moments playing "a girlie game" like soccer.

But there was no sign of irony in front of the cameras. Maximus is the very soul of the film and the way he reluctantly trains to become the very best gladiator and is consequently able to mount a challenge to the evil rule of Commodus is the driving force of the uplifting movie. The most successful general in the Roman Empire is forced to start again from scratch in the ruthless theatre of conflict that was the games. The whole of the gladiatorial system, which is so beloved by cowardly Commodus, is hated by Maximus, who has achieved his greatest triumphs in genuine battles. But the arena becomes the vibrant centrepiece of this astonishing movie as the two men move inexorably toward the final confrontation. Maximus always pauses before battle and stoops to rub his hands in the dirt, as if finally earthing himself. "It was a signal that he was going to fight," says Russell Crowe. "It was like, 'Max is back folks, and he is going to kick some ass'." It was a fabulously full-blooded portrayal and Russell's charisma and concentration was remarkable throughout.

An extra who asked not to be named said: "You won't hear a word against Russell Crowe from any of us. I've worked with big stars who looked upon the extras as so many cattle. They would cheerfully leave you out in all weathers while they examined their ego in their trailers. But Russell was always very considerate. If there was a break he wanted everyone to share it and he would talk to the humblest runner in exactly the same way that he spoke to Ridley Scott. By the end I reckon anyone would have done anything for Russell and Ridley. We all knew *Gladiator* was going to be a special film. People always laugh when you say it was the happiest film you've worked on but this really was. By the end I was really sorry to come home from Malta. The *Gladiator* team had become like a real family to me."

Russell was very grateful for the training in hand-to-hand fighting he received from Ralf Moeller, a former bodybuilding champion who also appears as a gladiator in the film. Russell says: 'He taught all of us how to wrestle following the tough rules of the gladiator schools of the period. It was not the first time I have appeared in a film that is physically challenging but I have never had a role like this. I decided I would like to play a bus driver next in a quiet film!"

The fight scenes in the Colosseum as the movie approaches its climax are brilliantly conceived and executed. Every move was carefully choreographed and rehearsed but there were still times when things went wrong. Djimon Hounsou's tangle with a fighter who was wearing a horned bull-head mask left him with a deep cut in his shoulder and an even deeper feeling of relief that the injury was not more serious.

Perhaps the most spectacular scenes are in the Battle of Carthage re-enactment, when Maximus and his men are attacked by racing chariots packed with warriors armed to the teeth. The moment when one of the female archers is sliced clean in two by the sharp blade sticking out from the razor axle sent a wince right round the cinema at most screenings. In fact, the chariots were one of the most difficult things to film as they really do speed along and space for them to turn was strictly limited in the arena. The same top stuntmen helped throughout the production. They would start out being German or Roman troops and then be re-dressed as North African and then, so long as they had not become too recognisable on screen, appear again as Roman troops.

The producers used real animals in order to recreate the games as accurately as possible. Records show that wild creatures were employed extensively to spice up the excitement. More than three thousand animals were once killed in the arena in just three days of the games. The film used tigers, leopards, giraffes, lions, zebras and an elephant. But the tigers became the stars of the show.

Big cats really were used as fighters in Roman games and in *Gladiator* they became one of Maximus' last great tests as he fought his way toward his final battle with Commodus. As our hero strides out for his final rigged fight against the champion – Tigris of Gaul – he is surprised by the arrival, from trapdoors in the floor, of tigers. The cats were on chains but they were still very close to the actors for the spectacular fight sequences. One handler had a lucky escape when a tiger doubled back on her chain and unbalanced him, but he was able to scramble out of reach of the animal without injury.

Russell Crowe was impressed by the idea of working with tigers. He enjoyed a dangerous excitement of being so close to such powerful beasts that he knew could rip him to shreds in an instant. Russell said: "It was a really visceral kind of experience. It was full on. They could have used a stand-in. The tiger sequence is very complicated and I did not do everything in the sequence, no way. But I got to do a couple of things where I hit the deck and the ground under me opened and the tiger comes at me. And that's me and the cat. When you roll out of the way of the tiger and eighteen hundred people go 'Oooooh' immediately it is kind of cool."

Russell Crowe and Ridley Scott built up a firm friendship during the movie. They are both highly independent, strong-willed men but they have considerable respect for each other's talents. They found a surprising common interest in architecture. In Morocco, Russell became fascinated by the intricacies of the local interior design and, as Ridley was building a house with Moroccan details, Russell would go off and photograph tiles to show him.

Russell said: "I honestly felt we had a great collaboration. We all knew that we didn't have the complete narrative when we began but through a long process and a lot of sleepless night we found our story." But Russell was left in awe of Ridley Scott's powerful intellect. As Russell put it: "Working with Ridley was like doing quantum physics with Picasso."

Oliver Reed died in Malta in May 1999, about three weeks before the end of filming. He was sixty-one and his life had always been lived to the full. Richard Harris was particularly shocked when he heard the news and saddened because he felt this film would have revived his career. The producers were able to complete Proximo's part with the aid of his body double and some technical trickery and the film remains, as Russell Crowe put it, a memorial to him.

His death also meant that a slight change had to be made to the ending. Scott says: "I had seen Ollie as a man for all seasons and his character was going to escape. But we had to examine the jig-saw puzzle of the plot and use a body double, with computer graphics, to see that he also died on screen. The only reason Ollie would be pissed off is that he did not finish the movie. But he popped off, flat on his back in a pub, and would regard that as not a bad way to go."

Russell Crowe said: "Oliver was very disciplined while we were in Morocco, which was great. It's a very hard place to shoot and I think this movie is a wonderful memorial to his contribution to cinema. I think it is his best performance in years." Russell believes the tragedy greatly affected the production. "If we'd had to re-shoot with another actor it would have been horrible for us all."

The final showdown in the arena is a tremendously exciting climax to the film. Commodus cruelly taunts Maximus with details of the deaths of his wife and son. He sneers: "They tell me your son squealed like a girl when they nailed him to the cross and your wife screamed like a whore when they ravaged her again and again." But Maximus rises above the vicious abuse and announces himself as "father to a murdered son...husband to a murdered wife...", before adding "...and I will have my vengeance".

Commodus secretly stabs Maximus before their last head-to-head sword fight so that the hero is already mortally wounded before he goes into the arena. But he manages to slay the evil emperor just before sadly expiring himself with the beautiful Lucilla rushing to tell the dying hero that he is on his way to rejoin his beloved wife and son. The monstrous and corrupt Commodus has been defeated and it is now up to the senators to run the Empire. As Lucilla says: "Is Rome worth one good man's life? We believed it once. Make us believe it again."

The film that seemed for all the world like a flop was instead a roaring success. The word in Hollywood had been full of predictions of total doom as even the hype about the film seemed a shade dated: "The general who became a slave...the slave who became a gladiator...the gladiator who defied an empire."

Director Ridley Scott is certainly a master of his craft, but it had been a long time since his last hit. The man who directed *Bladerunner*, *Alien* and *Thelma & Louise* is certainly a major cinematic talent, but his more recent movies had included the rather more forgettable *Conquest Of Paradise* and *GI Jane*. And the distinguished acting names of Derek Jacobi, Richard Harris and David Hemmings did sound as if they might have their best days behind them. When Oliver Reed died after a massive drinking session, forcing last-minute adjustments to the climax of the movie, it was hardly positive publicity for the film.

The movie world was ready to give a thumbs down to *Gladiator* but when it saw the finished product the verdict was precisely the opposite. "Hit, hit, hit," said everyone who saw the early previews. The all-action story of treachery in high historic places sounded exactly the right note. The great sweeping story had a narrative power that was like an ocean wave and the star was just as irresistible. Russell Crowe had turned in some fine performances before he stepped into Maximus' tunic, and he will surely find great roles in the future, but for most cinema fans his mean, moody and magnificent portrayal of the hero of Rome will always be the defining Russell Crowe performance.

Even previewers who came to pour scorn went away cheering the stirring story. Instant verdicts were plastered all over the

Internet, calling *Gladiator* "Awesome", "Fantastic" and "Sensational". Harry Knowles, who operates *Ain't It Cool*, the best-known film review website, rushed to type out his praise. "This is the Ridley Scott that we fanboys and girls drool over," he enthused. "*Gladiator* is a great cool film."

Russell Crowe was delighted to see the impact the film made. On Hallowe'en, after the film had come out, he was in New York and was knocked out by the number of people walking round in gladiator costumes. "I drove round New York's Greenwich Village during the parade. There were so many gladiators. One guy had an ice cream bucket and pieces of plastic cut out of the top for a helmet."

Among the plaudits that came Russell's way with *Gladiator* was his being named "Superstar of 2000" by the London *Daily Mail*. "Crowe made female hearts flutter in *Gladiator,* where he combined strength with sensitivity," said the newspaper. "Even when the script was ponderous and po-faced, Crowe saved it with quiet heroism and gravitas. He was just as impressive as the corporate whistleblower in *The Insider*, taking you into the living nightmare of a very private man with an insalubrious past – gambling his future and not sure exactly why. Crowe made you experience just how heavily the system is weighted against those who stand up to be counted."

Additionally, and on a more light-hearted note, Maximus was voted the sexiest cinema character ever in a poll for *Empire* movie magazine in 2001. Maximus cut a swathe through to the top of the list of the sixty-nine sexiest characters of all time, beating the likes of Harrison Ford in the *Indiana Jones* trilogy – who came fourth. Also below Russell's Maximus were Paul Newman and Robert Redford's Butch and Sundance, from *Butch Cassidy And The Sundance Kid*, secret agent James Bond, and Brad Pitt's lover-boy character in *Thelma & Louise*. Also well below Maximus was Clark Gable's Rhett Butler in *Gone With The Wind*, Steve McQueen's cop in *Bullitt* and Marlon Brando's Stanley Kowalski in *A Streetcar Named Desire*.

XVI

OSCAR

And the Oscar goes to...Russell Crowe.
Actress Hilary Swank, March 25, 2001, at the Shrine Auditorium,
Los Angeles, California

On February 13, 2001, Russell Crowe was trying, with not much success, to sit still and relax in his first-class aeroplane seat on a long-haul flight from Australia to Italy. He was on his way to Rome to begin a round of personal appearances at European premieres for *Proof Of Life* and, strapped into his seat, he was unusually fidgety and not a little nervous since the Oscar nominations were due to be announced in Hollywood that morning.

Frustratingly for Russell, he was thirty-five thousand feet up in the air and unable to establish any sort of telephone link from the aeroplane to anyone on the ground who might be able to relay the news from Hollywood that he was so keenly awaiting.

His plane was high above the clouds somewhere between Indonesia and the Arab Emirates when America's Motion Picture Academy duly released details of their Oscar nominations, including no less than twelve for *Gladiator*. In seconds the names of the Oscar runners and riders were flashed around the world, but Russell Crowe was to remain ignorant of his Best Actor nomination for several hours to come.

Ever since *Gladiator*'s release, Russell had been told countless times that he was a good bet for an Oscar. And this was long before the formality of a nomination. At times it became an understandably touchy subject with him, not least when one TV interviewer thoughtlessly tried to press a small plastic imitation Oscar statuette into his hand for good luck. Russell was horrified and refused to take it, saying it was much more likely to bring him bad luck.

Whatever his outward feelings, so lavish had been the praise heaped upon his performance that he had every right, however, to feel inwardly confident that members of the Academy would consider him at least worthy of a nomination for *Gladiator*, even if he didn't ultimately win. But on that particular Tuesday, at that precise moment, he was powerless to find out if he had been nominated.

A chance to glean the required information appeared to present itself when the plane touched down in Oman to refuel, but again he was exasperated to find that no mobile phones would function. Allowed out just for a breather on to the top of the disembarkation steps that had been wheeled up to the plane, Russell spotted a soldier standing guard and holding a machine gun. "Mate, have you heard anything about the Oscars?" he enquired of the soldier, who looked suitably startled and nonplussed by the question. Russell repeated the question more slowly this time. "The Oscars, mate, you know, the Academy Awards, you know the movies, have you seen the news?" It then became obvious to Russell that he was not making himself understood and when the soldier became vociferously animated and gripped his weapon more tightly, Russell beat a hasty retreat back to his seat on the plane still none the wiser about his Oscar chances.

He had to wait until the plane had landed in Rome many hours later before he learned that he had indeed been nominated for Best Actor along with Tom Hanks for *Cast Away,* fellow Aussie Geoffrey Rush for *Quills*, Ed Harris for *Pollock* and Javier Bardem for *Before Night Falls*. Russell was also delighted, not just for himself but for Ridley Scott, that *Gladiator* had been nominated in so many categories.

Although he subsequently lost out in the Best Actor category to Tom Hanks in The Golden Globe awards – usually a pointer to the likely Oscar winners – and to *Billy Elliot*'s young star Jamie Bell in the British Academy of Film and Television Arts awards in London, there was a growing feeling that come Oscar night it would be Russell who would triumph. But he was the first to acknowledge he faced stiff competition, notably from Tom Hanks, who had garnered some excellent reviews in *Cast Away* as Chuck Noland, a man stranded for years on a desert island fighting off hunger, thirst and the insanity of loneliness.

Geoffrey Rush, who had won a Best Actor Oscar for *Shine*, would also be a formidable Oscar rival for the depth of feeling he brought to his portrayal of the Marquis de Sade in *Quills*.

There was also a strong case for the Academy honouring Ed Harris in *Pollock* for his portrayal of Jackson Pollock, the abstract impressionist who reinvented modern art by splattering vast canvases with rhythmic webs of slashes and loops. Not only had Harris humanely stepped into the skin of Pollock, he had taken ten years to put together the movie about the life of the brawling, boozing, insecure painter who conquered American art only to die in a drunken car crash soon after hitting his peak. *Pollock* was Harris's directorial debut and he'd also put in a committed acting performance.

Less fancied for the Best Actor award was Javier Bardem. He had unmemorably played the villain in the 1999 Bond film *The World Is Not Enough* but now he had excelled in the biopic *Before Night Falls*, playing persecuted gay Cuban writer Reinaldo Arenas. But the movie itself had not created the global impact of those of his rivals.

Emanuel Levy, a historian of the awards, was quoted as saying: "I think this year it may be Russell Crowe. His film *Gladiator* has the most nominations of any – eleven – and that can set up some momentum. He is becoming a real force in the industry. He was nominated last year for *The Insider*, a good movie that was a commercial failure, and the Academy voters may think it is time to reward him for that as well."

A different school of thought had it that because *Gladiator* was a movie pitched to the 14-to-30-year-old audience, it lessened its chances of success because there were many Academy members in their fifties and sixties and they might find it all too noisy and frantic to vote for it.

Beating the drum by those involved with the respective nominations is all part of the pre-Oscar frenzy in Hollywood. The trade

Chapter XVI

papers and magazines are dotted with full page adverts shouting various credentials. With *Gladiator* the hot tip for Best Film, the publicists for the four films up against it were busy putting around the whisper that *Gladiator* was not a movie of any import, just an expensive sword-and-toga opera.

David Franzoni, who co-wrote and co-produced *Gladiator*, was incensed at the slur and despite food poisoning and a bad cold embarked on a round of multiple interviews to bolster the film against the whispers. *"Gladiator* isn't *Ben-Hur,"* he retaliated. "It's *All Quiet On The Western Front* and the people in the stands in the amphitheatre, they're you and me. Besides, if we were doing a purely commercial movie, why would we have the hero die at the end? What do you shoot for a sequel?"

Franzoni thought Russell deserved to win and championed him in his interviews as a return to the older model of movie star. "Steve McQueen, Charles Bronson – people like that. We haven't had stars like that here for some time. He may be it." His mind went back to the day he had just delivered the first draft of the *Gladiator* script to Steven Spielberg at DreamWorks. "A bunch of us were sitting around in Steven's offices just jamming like jazz musicians, throwing names around. There were really only two crucial questions – who was going to direct and who was going to play the gladiator Maximus. Well, we thought Mel Gibson, but we knew he wasn't going to do it and Russell was in our minds because we had all just seen *L.A. Confidential.* And as soon as he signed on, there really wasn't any further question about it. He was the guy."

In the build-up to Oscar night, Russell himself dutifully attended various functions to help improve *Gladiator*'s chances and, of course, his own. Fortunately for him, the members of the Academy had already cast their votes by the time Russell was making unwanted headlines at a pre-Oscar bash after his wandering eye had alighted on Courtney Love.

Courtney, the widow of Nirvana rock star Kurt Cobain, whose life had ended in a shotgun suicide, enjoys a reputation as the wild woman of rock and she and Russell were already well acquainted. After the Golden Globe awards earlier in the year, Russell was reported to have hooked up with Courtney at a party and friends said that the pair had later retired to his suite at the Bel-Air hotel and Courtney didn't leave until morning.

Now she was in typically high spirits, laughing, joking and dancing with Russell into the small hours at a star-studded party. But when Cobain's distinctive vocals rasped from the sound system on an old Nirvana hit, Courtney became quite emotional and loudly informed Russell: "You're not the star. I'm the star." Courtney came close to tears and Russell tried to console her. "But you don't understand," she protested, "he was the greatest rock star ever."

Soon afterward, at 3am, Russell chose to leave the party and emerged into the night with Courtney – very much the worse for wear – trailing behind him and slurring to anyone who would listen, "Do you want my autograph?" Then, spinning round, she enquired aggressively, "Where's Russell?" and was briefly appeased with several kisses from Russell before he promptly jumped into a waiting limousine and into the arms of Danielle Spencer, whom he had invited over to Los Angeles to be his date at the Oscars.

Courtney was far from pleased to see Russell cosying up to Danielle. Poking her head through the car window she brusquely enquired of a startled Danielle: "Are you the girlfriend? The one from Australia?" She never did get a reply as the car immediately began to pull away, leaving Courtney banging with her hands on the windows of the limo in frustration and letting fly with a volley of four-lettered expletives. Her verbal parting shot was to scream at Russell, "Why are you so f— paranoid?" Next day the mini-fracas between gladiator Maximus and the wild woman of rock was filling column inches in newspapers around the world.

The night before the Oscars found Russell at yet another American film industry party, where he felt a tap on the shoulder and turned around to find himself staring into the face of Robert De Niro. The two men had never met and, mysteriously, De Niro said not a word. He just briefly looked at Russell, nodded his head up and down in a friendly and approving manner and then abruptly walked away. Russell, too, was left speechless but de Niro's nod of approval spoke volumes. It seemed to indicate he thought Russell worthy of an Oscar and it was a good omen. On a lighter note, when Russell bumped into Tom Hanks, the two Best Actor Oscar front-runners agreed a pact that whoever lost out on the big award the following night should clean the other's lavatory for a week.

An unmistakable air of optimism pervaded the Russell Crowe contingent in Los Angeles as March 25 dawned. As well as Danielle, Russell had invited his parents and his Australian agent, Shirley Pearce, over to California to enjoy the occasion. After the previous year's disappointment, they shared the general consensus in Tinseltown that this would be Russell's night. Hollywood history shows that they like to favour their own, but if Tom Hanks were to win – and he was indeed Russell's most serious rival – he would set a precedent by becoming the very first three-times Best Actor Oscar winner.

As the favourite ever since the nominations had been announced, Russell had found his own individual way of dealing with well-wishers. It varied from initial delight and *bonhomie* to eventual exasperation with those who flippantly assured him, "You're bound to win the Oscar," as if it was all a foregone conclusion. "Gee whiz, thanks," he'd responded irritably to one back-slapper who told him he deserved the Oscar. "Can you give it to me now?"

Hollywood's biggest and most glamorous social event of the year is not just about awards. It's a night when the status of celebrity relationships comes under the spotlight and onlookers, reporters and TV crews become avid people-watchers to see who shows up with whom. Body language and no-shows are as eagerly awaited as the Oscar ceremony itself. Since Danielle Spencer was in town and would be on Russell's arm, there was much speculation as to whether Meg Ryan and Courtney Love would attend and with whom.

Much to the disappointment of the media, Meg chose to stay away and watch the event on television. But she did, however, deliver a good luck charm to Russell. It was a silver cross with an inscription taken from Banjo Paterson's *Clancy Of The Overflow*: "And he sees the vision splendid of the sunlit plains extended and at night the wondrous glory of the everlasting stars." Russell slipped the cross into the pocket of his Armani dinner jacket for luck, along with a little plastic duck he had been given by Jodie Foster's son Charles.

The star-studded seventy-third Academy Awards turned out to be one of the most glamorous of all, thanks to the one-off designer dresses and dazzling diamond jewellery worn by some of the most famous actresses in the world. As ever, there were excited crowds and dozens of TV crews, showbiz reporters and fashion experts gathered around the great gilt Oscar statues erected in front of the Shrine Auditorium to catch a glimpse of the cream of the film world's most beautiful women as they paraded up the red carpet in an expensive, glitzy and ostentatious show of fashion. It was Versace who led the way with more than fourteen top female guests wearing the famous Italian label, including Catherine Zeta Jones and *Charlie's Angels* actress Lucy Liu. Not to be outdone, Danielle Spencer looked both stylish and feminine in a black halter-neck dress as she settled into her seat next to Russell.

Before his great moment arrived, Russell had to endure several dubious jibes about his love life from comedian Steve Martin, who was hosting the ceremony. Russell appeared distinctly unamused when Martin joked about the unglamorous transformation that Best Actress nominee Ellen Burstyn had undergone for her role in *Requiem For A Dream*. He told the audience: "She added on 30lb and twenty years for her role and Russell Crowe still hit on her." The audience laughed at the jibe but Russell stoically sat stony-faced and showed no emotion other than to raise one eyebrow.

It fell to Hilary Swank, the previous year's Best Actress Oscar winner for *Boys Don't Cry*, to present the Best Actor award. Many inquisitive eyes were on Hilary, anyway, after a story had spread that she had parted company with her stylist. But she looked dazzling in a shimmering gold-beaded, pleated Versace gown with plunging neckline as she stepped forward with the Best Actor envelope.

Russell gripped Danielle's hand tightly at the final moment of reckoning and held his breath. Then came the words he had so desperately wanted to hear: "And the Oscar goes to...Russell Crowe."

Before Russell could rise from his seat, Joaquin Phoenix in the row behind flung himself around Russell's shoulders in an ecstatic congratulatory hug. Then, after turning to Danielle to give her a kiss on the lips, Russell made his way to thunderous applause up on to the stage. For the first time, the assembled celebrities and millions of TV viewers around the world could see proudly pinned to Russell's jacket the red ribbon and the cross of the MBE his grandfather Stan Wemyss had won before Russell was born. Back in New Zealand, his grandmother Joy was in tears in front of her television. "I've never been a believer in ghosts," she was later quoted as saying, "but when I saw the medal on Russell's chest I knew Stan was with me here. I felt his presence so strongly in the room with me."

Russell's acceptance speech was widely regarded as the most articulate and gracious of the night and earned him enormous respect, especially after the squeals of laughter and histrionics of Best Actress winner Julia Roberts – for *Erin Brockovich* – who shrieked: "I want to thank everyone I've ever met in my life."

Russell thanked his mum and dad "who I just don't thank enough, I suppose," and listed members of "an incredible cast". He also praised "a very brave crew collected from twenty-two countries around the world".

With great dignity Russell dedicated his award to those who dare to dream of greater things from life. "When you're growing up in the suburbs of Sydney, or Auckland or Newcastle, like Ridley or Jamie Bell, or the suburbs of anywhere, you know a dream like this seems vaguely ludicrous and completely unobtainable, but this moment is directly connected to those childhood imaginings. And for anybody who is on the downside of advantage and relying purely on courage, it is possible," he said.

Russell made a point of thanking his British-born *Gladiator* mentor, saying: "But really, folks, you know, I owe this to one bloke – and that bloke is Ridley Scott." He also thanked his Australian agent Shirley Pearce and her business partner, Martin Bedford, whom he numbered among the "personal cavalry" who had helped him along the way. He also told the Oscar audience that he owed a debt of gratitude to his grandfather Stan Wemyss and his late uncle, David William Crowe. They were two men "who continue to inspire me". He later explained to the world's press that Stan had won the MBE he was wearing for his work as a Second World War cinematographer.

David Crowe's widow, Russell's aunt Audrey, was deeply touched that he had bothered to make mention of his uncle. Back home in New Zealand she said on local radio: "It was a very special moment and I thank him for it. Dave himself used to act in the odd play, so he had a nice feeling for what Russell was trying to do. They didn't mind standing up and being counted and standing up in front, so they did have a good rapport. Dave loved music as well, which is another Russell love. I'm thrilled for Russell. I think he deserved it too. He was always a lovely kid, perky, but always determined to do something with his life. He has and I'm thrilled for him."

Later still, as he faced the world's press clutching his statuette, Russell admitted that by mistake he had left out one stanza in his acceptance speech. He had intended to add: "For my opportunities at Destiny's forge, God bless America, God save the Queen, God defend New Zealand and thank Christ for Australia."

As well as Russell's Best Actor award, *Gladiator* won Best Picture, Best Visual Effects, Best Costume Design and Best Sound awards. Russell was thrilled for Ridley Scott, although he was mystified for his director and commiserated with him when Scott surprisingly lost out as Best Director to Steven Soderbergh for *Traffic*. To many observers, it was an unfathomable decision since *Gladiator* was voted Best Film. The clutch of Oscars for *Gladiator* were richly deserved in Russell's opinion. "I believe *Gladiator* is a great movie and deserves to be acknowledged," he said.

It's unlikely that Russell Crowe will ever be more powerful in the eyes of Hollywood than he was that night. He had lost out to Kevin Spacey the year before but now he had triumphed.

For Danielle Spencer it was a bitter-sweet moment seeing Russell accorded the ultimate praise from his peers and collecting the tangible prize of the gold statuette. Her mind went back to 1990 when she had joined Russell on a first film venture for both of them in *The Crossing*. She had recognised straight away that he possessed drive, ambition and no little talent, but neither of them could possibly have dreamed that some ten years later they would be sitting side by side in Hollywood sharing the crowning moment in any film actor's life.

Danielle was thrilled for Russell, but it was his very tenacity and unshakeable determination to work for this pinnacle that had contributed to the end of their love affair and changed them for ever from passionate lovers to great friends. It was nonetheless a much appreciated gesture of loyalty by Russell to ask the girl who had endured some of his darkest moments to be by his side to share in his greatest achievement. In the general euphoria that surrounded Russell over his win, Danielle was not forgotten.

The ceremony over, it was time for the post mortems and, for once, there was no controversy. Everyone agreed, especially Charlton Heston, that Russell Crowe and Julia Roberts were worthy winners. Back in 1959, Heston had won the Best Actor Oscar in the movie epic *Ben-Hur*, thrilling cinema audiences with a chariot race against his sworn enemy in an arena in ancient Rome after surviving the life of a galley slave. It was fitting that it should be he who spoke for the large majority of his fellow actors when he remarked, "Russell richly deserved it". He added grandly: "As he came running down, I said to him: 'As one gladiator to another, I applaud you!'"

The Governor's Ball is the Motion Picture Academy's official post-Oscar party and it was there, right next door to the Shrine Auditorium, that for Russell the enormity of his achievement began to sink in. Members of the Academy are obliged to attend the

Governor's Ball and every single one of them appeared to want to come up and congratulate him and shake his hand. All Russell wanted to do at that precise moment was eat something. He was famished, having been too nervous throughout the day to eat much at all.

Fortunately for Russell, with a $1 million price tag, the Governor's Ball prides itself on being the most lavish of the post-Oscar parties and dozens of *hors d'oeuvres* were available, including $16,000 of caviar, followed by a sit-down meal for the 1,650 guests of veal Oscar – a medallion of veal and half a roasted Maine lobster – prepared by two hundred chefs and served by four hundred waiters. Sticking to the culinary tradition of the ball over the past seven years, chef to the stars Wolfgang Puck also prepared Oscars for all the guests – a chocolate replica sprinkled in twenty-four carat gold dust. This year, however, Russell also had the real thing.

Then it was on to Elton John's party, where Russell's mother Joy and father Alex were thrilled to pose for a photograph with Elton. "After that my dad kept going round saying: 'I've just had my photo taken with Elton John!'," Russell remembers with amusement.

Joy was touched that Russell had worn his grandfather's MBE. "He's very much like Stan in looks and personality," she commented. "Lots of guts and hard working. If they want something they go for it. Both of them were men's men, but the ladies still adored them, including me. Good looking, terrific sense of humour."

The celebrations continued far into the night with a final port of call for the victor at his own hotel, the Bel Air, where Shirley Pearce had returned *post haste* after the ceremony to oversee preparations for a private party in Russell's suite. Guests included Joaquin Phoenix, Michael Douglas with Catherine Zeta Jones, and Ridley Scott.

Across town at Mortons restaurant, where *Vanity Fair* was holding its usual prestigious party, Courtney Love was among the one hundred and fifty privileged people invited to dine on steak, crab cakes and mushroom risotto washed down by wines from *Godfather* director Francis Ford Coppola's private vineyards.

Having hit the headlines for her erratic behaviour with Russell a few nights before, Courtney was ready to make a few more. Provocatively attired in a dress which struggled to contain her brazenly displayed breasts, she was sashaying into Mortons when she was stopped by one onlooker and asked: "What goes on at these parties?" Courtney stopped and smirked. "We all get drunk and screw each other," was her reply. Then, stepping through the door, her first words were: "Is Russell here?"

He wasn't. Although he was enjoying several celebration drinks back at his own suite, Russell was pacing himself. Already he was mentally preparing himself for what he had to do in two day's time when he would be on the east coast of America ready to start work on a new film called *A Beautiful Mind*. Russell would be playing John Forbes Nash Junior, the schizophrenic mathematics genius who was awarded the Nobel Prize for economics in 1994 for a complex game theory he had developed forty years earlier at the age of twenty-one. It could, he confided to Oscar guests who enquired what he was up to next, turn out to be his most difficult role yet.

The morning after the Oscars, Russell was naturally besieged with interview requests from every section of the media but he had neither the time nor the inclination to do them, although he did manage a telephone radio interview with an Australian station, which enterprisingly had somehow managed to get through to his room. "Hold on," Russell told the radio presenter right at the start of the broadcast. "I've got someone else here who wants to talk to you." There followed the sound of repeated tapping on the phone for a few seconds. "That," said Russell proudly, "is a young man called Oscar."

XVII

PROOF OF LIFE

*Meg always liked macho men. I think Russell is
exciting and giving her something that was
clearly lacking in her marriage.*
Susan Jordan, mother of Meg Ryan

Ecuador is a South American country of startling natural beauty.
Named after the Equator, which crosses it, it's about two-thirds the
size of Texas or slightly bigger than Britain. It has within its spectacular boundaries the world's highest active volcano – Cotopaxi –
humid coastal plains which stretch down to the Pacific Ocean, and
the magnificent Andes mountains, which run from north to south
and dominate the country.

A Spanish colony from 1532, the country rebelled in the nine-
teenth century and the Spaniards were driven out. But ever since
independence, Ecuador has been ideologically divided between the
liberals and the conservatives. The compromise has frequently
meant military rule or dictatorship – or anarchy. Recent turbulent
political events include a president who lasted just ten days, only to
be followed by a 12-year-old successor.

Ecuador can be a baffling place, not least because of the climate
– glorious sunshine one minute, a torrential downpour the next,
then a mist so dense it is hard to see more than three feet in front
of your face. The area is also prone to earthquakes. To those unfa-
miliar with the weather, the terrain and the country's infrastructure,
Ecuador can be either enchanting, intimidating or infuriating. There
are half a million telephones in the country and most of them seem
to be in government offices. Those without telephones use horses
– statistics show that there are more horses in Ecuador *per capita*

than anywhere else except Mongolia. For those who take to their cars, life can be perilous. There are ten thousand miles of roads in Ecuador, but most of them are narrow, often pot-holed and liable to be blocked by sudden landslides. Alarmingly for visitors, Ecuador also has the world's second highest death rate from influenza.

Baron Alexander von Humboldt, a German who visited Ecuador in 1802, summed up its people by saying: "They are the strangest people in the world. They live in poverty on mountains of gold; sleep tranquilly at the foot of volcanoes; and cheer themselves with sad music." In other words, they are unpredictable. And in that respect, little had changed in two hundred years when Taylor Hackford arrived to make a movie called *Proof Of Life* about a kidnapped hostage.

From the highly-organised safety of a high-tech office in Hollywood, the possibilities of making an $85 million dollar movie in Ecuador over four months with two of the world's most bankable stars looked an exciting, feasible and surmountable challenge that might occasionally be uncomfortable. If there were one or two alarms bells sounding, they weren't ringing very loudly during pre-production.

Taylor Hackford, the Californian director who had scored a huge box office hit with Richard Gere in *An Officer And A Gentleman* and who had directed *Against All Odds*, would be at the helm of *Proof Of Life* and he would be able to draw on his experiences as a Peace Corps volunteer in South America. Hackford was a filmmaker in the grand style and he looked forward with confidence to shooting in the mountains outside the town of Quito, situated right in the heart of Ecuador.

But there was one word which everyone concerned with the movie *Proof Of Life* seemed to be using to describe Ecuador: unpredictable. The country was "unpredictable". So were the weather, the climate and the logistics of transport; they were all "unpredictable".

There was, however, something else totally unpredictable about the *Proof Of Life* production as it headed off for its Ecuador locations. No one foresaw that the film's stars, Meg Ryan and Russell Crowe, would fall passionately in love off-screen as well as on. Nor did they see that Ecuador would form the backdrop for the start of their affair, which would send shockwaves around the world and signal the end of Meg's nine-year marriage to actor Dennis Quaid, a union which was until then thought to be among the most solid in Hollywood.

But that particular turmoil was several months away and, after the heady success of *Gladiator*, Russell was at first glad just to get back to work again on a movie project that offered vastly different opportunities from those of playing Maximus. *Proof Of Life* was conceived as a tense, romantic hostage thriller about an American engineer called Peter Bowman. While building a dam for an American company, Bowman is kidnapped by a revolutionary group of cocaine-farming guerrillas. His wife Alice is relieved when Terry Thorne, an ex-SAS soldier now specializing in corporate kidnap and ransom cases, arrives to take up the trail. But Thorne leaves the day after when it becomes apparent that the company Bowman worked for had not kept up their insurance payments. Thorne, however, eventually bows to his conscience and decides to take on the case anyway, with the help of Dino, another equally tough negotiator. But during their tense negotiations with the kidnappers for Bowman's release, complications arise as Alice and Thorne find themselves drawn ever closer together, falling in love as they work to secure her husband's safety. In an echo of the famous Humphrey Bogart/Ingrid Bergman airport scene in *Casablanca,* Alice finally goes off with the husband her lover has rescued.

At one point Harrison Ford was the actor talked about for the role opposite Meg Ryan of hostage negotiator Terry Thorne. But eventually the name of Russell Crowe cropped up and it clearly went down well with Meg, who was favoured to play the worried wife Alice. The information which reached Russell's ears was that Meg would sign on to *Proof Of Life* providing Russell would agree to star in the movie with her.

If true, as was likely, that was extremely flattering for Russell. But whatever the strength of it, Russell was still sufficiently impressed by Meg's dramatic track record away from the sugar-sweet romantic movies she was famed for to sign up to *Proof Of Life*. He had seen her in *Courage Under Fire* and *When A Man Loves A Woman* and knew she had it in her to be more than America's queen of screen romantic comedy.

The story for the movie was inspired by *Adventures In The Ransom Trade*, written by William Prochnau for *Vanity Fair*. The movie's eventual title, *Proof Of Life*, refers to the first demand negotiators make of kidnappers: proof that the hostage is still alive.

Russell's role of ex-SAS man Terry Thorne was originally written as an Englishman, but he persuaded Hackford to change the character to an Australian. Russell saw no reason why Thorne should not be an Aussie. It was, after all, a fictional story and Hackford agreed to the switch after discovering that among the ranks of the SAS in Britain – the elite among soldiers – were not just Australians but New Zealanders and Zimbabweans as well. Russell went through a couple of scenes for Hackford in his Aussie accent and the director soon saw that it wouldn't affect the story at all. Russell was thankful to be able to use his own voice in a movie for a change, and those critics in Australia who chose to think he'd sold out to Hollywood years ago could take note.

Immersing himself in his preparations, Russell was astonished to find that kidnap and ransom – known in the trade by its abbreviation to K and R – was a multi-billion dollar business based on stealing people's freedom in exchange for money. "We're talking about thirty thousand abductions a year," he said. "Some five thousand alone in Columbia every twelve months. There's about sixteen different companies that insure people for K and R and it affects Americans working for multi-national companies in different parts of the world, mainly in Eastern Europe and Latin America."

Russell learned all about multi-national corporations' expansion into the Third World, specifically South America, where *Proof Of*

Life would be set in a fictional town called Tecala. In the heart of London's east end he met up with half a dozen men still serving in the SAS to pick their brains and help him flesh out his character.

One discussion centred on which knife an SAS man would use to slit a throat. Russell recalled: "There was one bloke about five feet five inches tall and everybody else in the room was scared of him. He pulled me aside and said, 'Mate, Leatherman. That's all you need. It fits in your pocket and if you want to take somebody out and not give yourself away, no gurgles, nothing. You need to put a serrated blade in front of the spinal column and take every part of his neck out immediately.'" So Leatherman it was in the movie. Russell thanked him for the tip and hoped he'd never have to put what he'd learned into real practice.

Filming began first in England and then in Poland, where Russell chose to perform one particularly dangerous stunt himself, hanging on the skids of a helicopter as it rose into the air surrounded by explosions. Russell first took advice from good friend Tom Cruise, who had hung from a rock in *Mission: Impossible II*, before volunteering to feature in the "one hundred percenter" scene himself. "I call it a one hundred percenter," he explained, "because it means it keeps people involved in the movie. If you force a director to shoot a situation falsely it affects the movie." For his pains and his courage Russell received the plaudits from the crew and about twenty cuts to his face from the explosions. Thankfully, none of them were too serious.

Just before filming was due to move on to Ecuador, there was a *coup d'état* in Quito which temporarily threw the plans for nearby locations into confusion. Fortunately for Hackford, the *coup* was short-lived but it opened everyone's eyes to the political instability of the region and it reinforced the view that the hiring of a K and R company to protect Russell and Meg, the film's two big stars, was a wise precaution. In this respect the production company did not duck their responsibilities. Russell and Meg had in their immediate company a former Royal Marine as well as an ex-marine from the

US and ex-SAS men. As Russell said: "If something bad did happen we had a lot of people that had the right skills." It was also vitally important to Russell to have one man around on the set who truly represented his character in the film and to whom he could turn for practical advice if needed.

But, after safety considerations, there were other hazards looming. As luck would have it, the area suffered the worst rainy season in decades, causing mudslides which threatened to wipe out the sets. Every day posed new difficulties. "With the road slides, you'd go round a corner you'd been round a dozen times but now suddenly there was a road blockage," Russell later recalled.

The drive to the set took ninety minutes from Quito through the jungle and rainforest, a journey in which cast and crew more often than not took their lives in their hands. They discovered that sections of the road that had been there one day had vanished the following day. Parts of the road had simply disappeared in landslides, which were daily occurrences. Other days the hill slides made the roads chaotically impassable.

Russell soon reckoned that he would be better off staying in his trailer rather than having to face the hazardous ninety-minute journey to and from the hotel each day. He begged food and provisions from the caterers and set up a barbecue for himself in an oil drum. Apart from having to cope with the damp, he found the whole stop-out experience infinitely preferable to three hours of daily bone-shaking bumping over the potholes. "Some of the potholes are big enough to swallow a cow," he pointed out, and in several instances it was an accurate assessment.

The local Ecuadorians were astonished at his stubborn stance. They told him he was mad camping out like that in the rainforest and he'd have to take his chances with the wild cats and other dangerous animals and reptiles he might encounter. Russell thought they were the ones who needed their heads examining after seeing the cavalier way the locals performed behind the wheels of their vehicles. The roads were narrow enough anyway and although drivers used half the road, he noted that they tended to use the middle half.

High altitude also proved a major problem for everyone. Filming at eleven thousand feet up, around twenty members of the crew succumbed to high-altitude sickness and had to be sent home. Another half dozen picked up various fungal and internal ailments, which unfortunately were non-specific so the medical team attached to the production couldn't identify exactly what the problem was.

Life was far from easy but Taylor Hackford pressed on, gamely tackling the difficulties of travelling with a team of two hundred people trying to make a major Hollywood movie in a country that was not used to supplying the infra-structure that such a movie-making venture requires.

Hackford's relentless pursuit of authenticity was testament to his documentary film background. He'd had his successes with feature films but he had also produced and helped edit the 1996 Oscar-winning *When We Were Kings*, which chronicled the extraordinary "rumble in the jungle" world heavyweight boxing championship fight in Zaire between Mohammed Ali and George Foreman.

At one point during the filming of *Proof Of Life*, Hackford realised he was perhaps striving too hard and issued an apology to the cast. "That was a turning point," said David Morse, who was playing the role of hostage Bowman. "That was the sign of a guy who was really a leader – to humble himself in front of that many people. I was glad to see it."

Russell, for his part, says he could understand that in some aspects the hardship of shooting was beneficial for the film but the risk was that a lot of people were put in danger. "This is a very unpredictable place, politically unstable," he said, using that same adjective that had been bandied about from the start whenever Ecuador was mentioned. It did cross his mind that Hackford could have found the same sort of altitude and similar kinds of locations in the much safer environment of northern Queensland in Australia.

"Lovely country, everybody speaks English and the beer is better," he said.

What with the logistical nightmares of landslips, volcanoes, zero-visibility "cloud forests", oceans of mud and altitude poisoning, it was inevitable that morale was sometimes low. "Eventually," said Morse, "all of us started feeling like real hostages." Then tragedy overtook the production when a stand-in for Morse was killed when a truck in which he was being transported plunged over the side of a mountain road. "I don't think any film is worth losing your life for," said Hackford. "It's something I'll always carry with me."

For Russell there was very personal sadness when he received the news that his uncle, David Crowe, for whom he had such affection, had died after a long illness at the age of sixty-six. His death had not been unexpected and Russell could take comfort from the fact that he had managed to fly to New Zealand to see him one last time shortly before he died.

There was a gap in his film schedule on *Proof Of Life,* which would allow him the chance to go to Australia to promote *Gladiator.* He seized the opportunity with the proviso that he could fly on to New Zealand to visit his uncle David, whom he knew was then desperately ill and had not long to live.

It was to be a moving last meeting between the two men who had developed such a strong bond between themselves. Having enjoyed so many pleasurable moments on his visit to the set of *Gladiator* in Malta – where he'd been an extra – David was longing to see how the movie had turned out and looked forward to watching his nephew's performance.

Thoughtfully, Russell arranged for a private screening of the movie at his uncle's house and the pair of them sat down to watch it together. "They also spent an hour talking," said David's widow, Audrey. "It was lovely and meant so much to the pair of them to have that final intimate time alone." Russell flew back to the set of *Proof Of Life* with a heavy heart, knowing that he would never see his uncle again. David died five days later. "Russell was absolutely devastated by his death," said Audrey. "He was inconsolable."

Back in Ecuador, Meg Ryan provided a sympathetic shoulder to cry on. Not only were she and Russell putting together performances for the camera, Russell and the 38-year-old actress often found themselves clinging together through all of the uncertainties thrown up by the filming and, once again, the sheer unpredictability of Quito.

"Ecuador is a place where you just cannot predict what's going to go on," Russell stressed once more. "One day we were shooting in San Francisco Square. We've got a couple of thousand extras and we're about two takes into it and from a brilliantly sunny day, all of a sudden we're in the middle of a massive hailstorm. So everybody scatters and I grabbed Meg and we ran into the first doorway, which happened to be a men's public toilet. And we were the last people in so there's already thirty in there, mainly Ecuadorians going 'Hi!'.

"A couple of seconds after the rain hits, the sewage system blocks up and a big thing just bursts out through the wall. So we're just standing at the edge of the door looking back at all these people knee-deep in sewage. So we go back into the hailstorm again and through the next doorway, which was a fifteenth-century cathedral full of beautiful ancient carvings on the wall and everything was beautiful. Quiet. And we got asked if we'd like to go out the back door.

"So we went out into this square where a group of schoolgirls were standing in a corner in their little Catholic uniforms. So we go over and see what they're looking at and there's a guitar player and a blind accordion player and they're playing a song and all the children start singing. And we got caught up in that, you know. And the bloke said to me: 'Would you like to play a song?' So I thought, 'Oh, what the heck'. So I grabbed the guitar and played *Folsom Prison Blues* – the Johnny Cash song.

"And now it's turned into a scene from a Beatles movie. Now I've got thirty Catholic schoolgirls who won't leave me alone. And Meg thinks this is hilarious. I'm trying to get back to work and pushing the girls away. So we finally got back out into the square and the two thousand extras were put back in place. Then my eyes started watering and I'm wondering what's going on. Then everybody starts to rub their eyes. It was a riot on another block and the police had used tear gas. All this has happened and this is, like, only 11:30 in the morning!"

There were other less frenetic moments he could share with Meg, like a long walk in Quito to the top of the hill. "On the top of this hill in the old town," Russell recalled, "there's a statue called the Virgin Of Quito. It's a seventy-metre-high aluminium sheet statue of the Virgin standing on top of a dragon. My friends, who I took on the walk there, said: 'That's the most effort we've ever seen put into getting up a virgin!'.

"One night we took a different way home from work and passed a sign that basically translates as 'The Artists Cafe'. It looked happy. So we stop and have a beer on the balcony overlooking this huge gorge. And these blokes walked in with bongos and guitars and they turned out to be Manu Chao, this Catalan band I'd been listening to in England and they basically did a whole concert. They spoke French, everyone else spoke Spanish, and I could barely speak English. It was a great night. The fact that the building kept moving from side to side was a little problematic for me. I'd wonder: 'Is that the last shift before it tumbles off the side of the mountain?'"

Curiously, for an actress with such a wealth of movie experience, Meg Ryan had been uncharacteristically jumpy about the prospect of working opposite Russell in *Proof Of Life*, even though she had dropped the broad hint that she would only star in the film if he did too. The odd explanation she offered for her nervous apprehension was that she felt "out of her league". But why, she was asked? "Because," she said, "let's face it: Russell is amazing. He's unrecognisable from one role to the next."

Perhaps the real reason Meg had butterflies in her stomach was that she sensed she might well fall in love with him. She had seen

Russell in *Gladiator* and, like much of the female audience who saw the movie, Meg found him charismatic, macho and sexy. His screen presence reminded her of Richard Burton in the epic *Cleopatra*, as she was later to tell Russell herself when they became more intimately acquainted.

Surprisingly, shortly before she was to join up with Russell for *Proof Of Life*, Meg had expressed a preference for movies with dramatic substance, such as *When A Man Loves A Woman*, in which she played an alcoholic, rather than the cuddly comedies for which she was so renowned. Dramatic sets are normally much more light-hearted than comedic ones, she said, explaining that there had been a lot of partying off-set on *When A Man Loves A Woman*.

Asked how she would like to be seen in the future as she prepared to fly off to Ecuador, Meg's chillingly prophetic reply was: "Hmm, 'Meg Ryan, woman in distress'. I like that."

By the time filming in Ecuador was over, Meg had clearly fallen head over heels for Russell. In June, they were seen out shopping together in London's Piccadilly. Next they were spotted leaving London's fashionable Met Bar in the early hours one Sunday morning. The following day they were seen dining together at the Mirabelle restaurant, arriving within minutes of one another and leaving separately. The very next day they both attended a secret gig by David Bowie at the BBC, where Meg was conspicuous for resting her head in Russell's lap as he affectionately stroked her hair. It was a show of intimacy which provoked newspaper stories speculating that Meg and Russell were much more than co-stars and the headlines in turn prompted Meg to issue a statement through the publicist she shared with her actor husband Dennis Quaid that their marriage was over. She had been married to Quaid for nine years and described the split as "mutual and amicable".

The announcement that Meg and Quaid were separated came as a huge shock in show business circles and to Meg's legion of admiring fans. Americans, particularly, had enjoyed an enduring love affair with the cutesy blonde with the huge hazel-green eyes, the lop-sided smile and the just-fallen-out-of-bed hairstyle. They had embraced wholeheartedly Meg's beguiling movie image of the adorable sweetheart in sugary romantic comedies such as *Sleepless In Seattle*, *French Kiss*, *You've Got Mail* and *When Harry Met Sally*, where her simulated orgasm during a meal with Billy Crystal at a diner produced probably her most memorable screen moment without damaging her fetchingly winsome image.

Meg's private life had apparently been beyond reproach, too, and she and Quaid had seemingly found their own utopia far away from the temptations of Los Angeles; a one hundred-acre ranch in the northern state of Montana, surrounded by beautiful countryside and animals. They had a home in Los Angeles, too, of course, for when one or other was working.

But now that she was pictured running around London with Russell, the finger of blame for the tarnishing of this reputation inevitably pointed very firmly in Russell's direction. Meg was subsequently to state that her marriage was over well before she and Russell got together. But when the news first broke he was painted as the villain of the piece.

Marilyn Kagan, a Beverly Hills psychotherapist analysing Meg's affair very publicly, concluded: "In order for her to keep her zest, her sexuality, her power alive, there may be a need for her to feel adored and wanted and attained by someone else whose star is really rising – which is Russell Crowe, who's sexy, who's a bad boy, who's powerful, which may give her a reflection of 'I've still got it', which she has."

What compounded the general view of Russell as the bad guy in this apparent love triangle was that Meg's fans simply could not believe that the woman with the sweet-as-apple-pie image could actually do the unthinkable and split up from her husband. For years they had read of Meg's deliriously happy marriage to Quaid, how she had lovingly helped him through booze and drug problems at the start of their relationship and how they were both devoted to their son, Jack.

The story of Meg's marriage to Quaid appeared almost as sugar-coated as the plots in her romantic movies. It was a fairytale in itself. Meg and Dennis had lived within a block of each other in New York when they were both struggling actors. He remembered seeing her walking up the avenue to a health food store and the way she swung her arms in a long green sweater she was wearing that was much too big for her. He had wanted to ask her out but was too shy. Five years later they met on the set of the 1987 comic adventure movie *Innerspace*, in which Quaid played a miniaturized test pilot injected into a body. Meg was his love interest and for both of them it had been love at first sight. "We had an instant connection when we met. We could have been buddies back in Ancient Egypt," Meg gushed in one interview.

Their courtship did indeed have a rare ring of romance about it. There was a day trip to the Grand Canyon where they just sat together gazing in awe at its natural wonders. There was the incredible twenty-fifth birthday greeting from Quaid to Meg on the set of the film *The Presidio*, which she was making with Sean Connery. "Suddenly a high school band appeared with a huge banner reading 'Happy Birthday Meg' and playing songs Dennis had picked," she once dreamily recounted. "You can't resist something like that. I just fell instantly in love with him."

But Quaid's career took a nosedive while Meg's soared and the actor developed a drink and drugs problem. Meg helped to rescue her man from his demons and saved their relationship. By this time they were engaged and she threatened to return the ring unless he cleaned himself up. The ultimatum worked but Meg confessed she still had to "think, think and think about getting married" because she was still haunted by memories of her own parents' bitter divorce. She was also mindful that Quaid's earlier marriage to an actress had failed.

But, true to the sanitized image that was to radiate so glowingly on screen, Meg, the former high school home-coming queen went and got married to Quaid on St Valentine's Day, in 1991. She and

Quaid were staying at the Bel Air hotel in Los Angeles when they called the receptionist and said: "We want to get married." He arranged for a reverend attending a Rotary Club lunch at the hotel to go to their room and proclaim them man and wife.

Meg's life for all the world appeared perfectly idyllic, and in reality it was impossibly so. By her mid-thirties she was attributing her success, her wealthy lifestyle and her happy marriage to New Age meditation and the mantra that creative visualization encourages brain power to turn one's fantasies into fact. Yoga and meditation, she revealed, helped her focus. "Unhappily, one thing it won't do is get rid of my cute image – and believe me, I've chanted for that one a lot," she said. With a giggle, she also commented on her sugar-sweet reputation. "I have in fact been known to cause diabetes. Throughout my career I have remained consistently and nauseatingly adorable."

That was precisely why Meg's affair with Russell appeared so shocking to the public. They had swallowed every sweet moment. Mostly they just didn't want to believe it was now all over for Meg and Quaid. Some refused to do so until television footage emerged of Russell and Meg sitting at a window table in a coffee shop where a laughing and clearly carefree Meg repeatedly pulled his bearded head toward her across the table so she could give him a series of passionate and loving kisses.

The one person who didn't seem surprised was Meg's mother, who believed the pairing of her daughter with Russell in *Proof Of Life* was bound to light some sort of explosive touch paper between the two.

Susan Jordan, who abandoned Meg and three other children when she was in her teens to pursue an acting career, was quoted as saying that when it was announced they were making a movie together, it was obvious Meg would either hate Russell or end up having a passionate affair with him.

"Everyone else was so surprised when Meg's affair became public," said her mother, "but I suppose I wasn't. It was clear her marriage was going nowhere." She added: "She's running all over London with Russell and she's having her picture taken with him and David Bowie. To me this is not a woman who is ashamed of what she is doing."

After the Bowie concert, Quaid filed almost immediately for divorce. There was an attempt at some sort of reconciliation but then Meg later hit back with a divorce petition of her own, citing "irreconcilable differences". Interestingly, Meg had left her marriage at the age of thirty-eight, exactly the same age as her mother had been when she left hers.

The press had a field day over "when Gladiator met Sally". Everyone, it seemed, wanted to have their say on the Meg and Russell love affair once the storm broke, even Meg's father, who apparently told a magazine that he was warning Meg not to marry Russell.

Carol Lieberman MD, a media psychiatrist, spoke for many when she said: "Meg was blinded by her desire to feel some kind of passion and romance that for long was somewhat dead in her marriage." Meg's mum agreed. "Meg always liked macho men," Susan Jordan concurred. "I think Russell is exciting and giving her something that was clearly lacking in her marriage."

Somewhat incredibly, Taylor Hackford claimed that he knew nothing of Russell's affair with Meg until he read about it in the tabloids after filming of *Proof Of Life* was nearing completion. But he was not best pleased about it. Hackford fretted that the couple's off-screen shenanigans stole the thunder from the on-screen pairing.

His fears intensified when Russell and Meg turned publicity shy and balked at giving interviews to support the film's American release, fearing that they would simply be quizzed about their love for each other. Both were mindful that it was a difficult time for all concerned, not least Meg and Quaid's eight-year-old son Jack. But opting out of doing some print interviews did not go down well with Hackford. "I am deeply hurt that they couldn't and that *Proof Of Life* will probably be known best as the film that sparked a love affair between Russell Crowe and Meg Ryan," the disgruntled 55-year-old director lamented.

What worried Hackford the most was that everyone would be so sick of the Russell/Meg romance that they wouldn't want to see the movie that spawned it. "My biggest fear," he said, "is that there's been so much exposure, people will think they've already seen this movie. And they haven't." He argued at the London premiere of his film that Russell and Meg's off-screen relationship "had an indelible and very destructive effect on the release of the film in the US because the real-life story overpowered the film".

Russell's response was swift. He wasn't going to take the criticism lying down. "Taylor is being impolite, impolitic and imbecilic," he said in his and Meg's defence. "I think you will see that the *Proof Of Life* box office, when it's not such a family-oriented time as Christmas, will be much higher. What we know, personally, is that we put as much effort into the process as possible and are pleased with the outcome." Russell didn't say who, specifically, he was referring to by "we" but he had only kind things to say about Meg. He described her as "courageous" and "special".

"Meg's great. She's a gorgeous woman and a great actress," he said. Meg was equally glowing about him. "Russell's as good as it gets. He's a magnificent actor, a wonderful man and inspiring for the whole crew," she said, by way of returning the compliment. "All I know is that I've learned quite a bit. He's a very specific actor and he's so capable. Just the way he deals with props, the way he uses language."

David Caruso, the actor who played Russell's collaborator, was moved to say that the actor had got inside his role to such a degree that in his opinion Russell would be perfectly capable of carrying out kidnap negotiation in real life. Russell himself doubted he would have the patience, his mind going back to when he was an army cadet as a kid and there were four hundred young men lined up on the parade ground, all wearing the same uniform. Instead of seeing it as a moment where to conform was imperative and discipline essential, Russell saw it, he said, as a chance for comedy. His sense of mischief, marching right when everyone else went left, landed him many a solitary hour in the jailhouse while everyone else was pretending to be a soldier.

Hackford, after all the trials and tribulations he and his team had endured in the making of *Proof Of Life*, found some satisfaction in the end product. "I'm really proud of it, though when you're this close, you lack perspective. I know this was a life experience," he said tellingly.

But at the Sydney premiere of the movie on February 23 it was noticeable that during the scene where their local screen hero passionately kisses Meg, the Aussie audience laughed heartily. Russell's affair with Meg invested *Proof Of Life* with unintended irony and obliged the marketing strategy for the film to be altered to play down the love story.

On-set romances are not uncommon in the world of movies. It is discreetly accepted that many are just for the duration of the movie before both parties return to their respective partners. The intriguing question about Russell and Meg's liaison was whether it was an on-location fling or whether there was substance enough for the relationship to continue.

Meg was with Russell in London in July when he performed with his band Thirty Odd Foot Of Grunts at The Borderline, but then he was due to fly to Austin, Texas, to record a new album and play some live gigs in August. Meg had new filming commitments to consider and a young son to think about. She and Quaid were taking it in turns to stay at their Los Angeles home in Brentwood to look after Jack. She pined for Russell as he went on the road without her. He was desperately missing her too and his face would light up whenever she called him, which was sometimes eight or nine times a night.

Friends couldn't help but notice some changes in Russell after he and Meg had fallen for each other. In the Polo Lounge of the Beverly Hills Hotel he'd be at the bar nursing a lunchtime mineral water while waiting for Meg to call him on his mobile telephone. He'd cut back on drinking after Meg had teased him about getting a spare tyre. If it had been any other woman he wouldn't have cared less but when Meg said it, it touched a nerve. In Austin he took to having a female personal trainer help him work out and thought enough of her to fill a room full of balloons for her birthday and have her swept up by firemen for the surprise ride on a fire truck that she had always wanted.

By September Meg and Russell were able to snatch some time together in Australia, where they flew in to watch the Olympics and sample some of the wonderful Sydney festive atmosphere that pervaded what everybody acknowledged was the best Olympic Games ever. They watched some events and enjoyed lunch in Sydney on Tom Cruise's boat. Then their respective work commitments drove them apart once again.

For Russell, the previous six months on *Proof Of Life* had been thoroughly exhausting. On one of his promotional trips Russell listed his gruelling film itinerary. "We started off in England. We went to Poland, then to Ecuador, then back to England. But every time I had a break, when the character wasn't scheduled to be shooting, I had to go off and do *Gladiator* promotions. So I was pretty ragged actually. One jaunt lasted over eleven days. We left Ecuador, then went to Miami, Rome, New York, Los Angeles, Sydney, Auckland, Easter Island and back to Ecuador, where I was working at 3pm that day." It was estimated that he'd travelled forty thousand miles on his promotional duties and no one begrudged him the chance to rest. "I've got to try and get some time at home and sleep in my own bed and see my dogs and kiss my cows," he said.

By the time Russell was preparing to fly back to Australia for Christmas and to host his annual festive party in the grounds of his home, his affair with Meg had come to an end. The bottom line, he said, was that he had a big life in Australia. "When I'm off the hook with the schedules I have to come home. I can't sustain myself through the course of the year without filling up on home." He had kind words for Meg, however, adding: "I grieve the loss of her companionship, but I haven't lost her friendship. We're great friends. Meg and I talk all the time and we e-mail each other and stuff and she's an absolutely gorgeous person."

Shortly afterward Meg, speaking of the terrible beating she had taken from the public over the affair, said: "I found myself thinking all of a sudden, 'So this is what it feels like to be a scarlet woman'." But she was careful to avoid mention of Russell and said of her split from Dennis Quaid: "The reason we broke up had nothing to do with another person. My marriage was already broken. Nobody else broke it up. I know it to be true, Dennis knows it to be true." Meg told *W* magazine: "Neither of us, me nor Dennis, is cavalier about the break-up. We both behaved very honourably in our marriage and in our break-up."

Just when it appeared that Russell Crowe's life could hardly become more turbulent, America's Federal Bureau Of Investigation revealed on March 7, 2001, to a disbelieving world, that for much of the year Russell had been the focus of a kidnapping threat. Rumours had abounded in Hollywood and in California police circles for some time that a major Hollywood star had become a target for abduction. But such whispers tend to surface at regular intervals in Los Angeles, where large numbers of high-profile actors and actresses go about their business. It is one of the occupational hazards of international fame.

What made the threat to kidnap Russell so very out of the ordinary was that not only did the FBI publicly acknowledge that they were treating it all extremely seriously, but the world could see their agents were very obviously doing just that. Television film footage of Russell flanked by security men as he arrived at The Golden Globes awards was flashed to TV screens around the world. Newspapers and magazines carried similar pictures and Laura Bosley, spokeswoman for the FBI's Los Angeles bureau admitted, "We've confirmed an FBI investigation into a plot to kidnap the actor". She did add, however, that such threats were commonplace in that part of the world, but declined to name who made the threats or where they came from.

Two days later, on March 9, several security guards were in close attendance as Russell went through a question-and-answer session after two special screenings of *Gladiator* in Los Angeles. Two nights on found Russell again surrounded by guards as he chatted with Joaquin Phoenix and Kate Winslet at the Screen Actors Guild Awards after-party. The following day he was a guest at the annual Oscar lunch with the Academy's other nominees in an area that was roped off outside the ballroom at the Beverly Hilton hotel. By now it was very obvious to everyone that nobody was taking any chances.

Until the FBI's official confirmation, which in itself was unusual, initial reaction was that the story smacked of an outrageous publicity stunt – *Proof Of Life* was just hitting the cinemas. The story first broke in London – where Russell was promoting *Proof Of Life* – when the FBI alerted Scotland Yard's Criminal Intelligence Branch to its own investigation. News leaked out in the British press that Russell had been interviewed at some length by a female police officer. The FBI, in the light of the disclosure from another source, then went ahead and confirmed it.

Suggestions that the threat to Russell was just an artfully conceived hype were quickly discounted when Russell attended the Golden Globes awards ceremony on January 21, where he had been nominated as Best Actor for *Gladiator* – the award went to Tom Hanks.

It transpired that the threat to Russell had been made prior to that ceremony and the star subsequently appeared for the event with several tuxedoed agents around him. Although the presence of the security men was generally discreet, the FBI's true acceptance of the situation became apparent at the Golden Globes after-party held at Trader Vic's. Russell at one point went to the men's room to relieve himself and several male party-goers also heading for the same destination were astonished to find themselves stopped in the hall by a small army of men in tuxedoes. They thought they were merely being asked to wait in line until the bathroom was free. But moments later, they watched in astonishment as Russell emerged from the men's room and the tuxedoed contingent promptly fell in protectively around him.

"It's common knowledge the FBI was at the Golden Globes," an FBI source confirmed soon afterward, insisting it wasn't a stunt. "We wouldn't expend the resources unless we believed there was a credible threat."

Russell later revealed that when the FBI first approached him in January to advise him that he might be in jeopardy from an abduction threat, he regarded the situation a lot less seriously than they did. He was even able to make a joke about it all in front of the TV cameras at the Oscar nominees lunch on March 12 by imagining what it might be like for the kidnappers to be trapped in a room with him for any length of time. "If you want to spend that much time with me in a little room, I think you get into a very Hemingway situation where you're on the phone going, 'Look, we've passed the hat around, we've got a couple of hundred bucks. Can you take him off our hands?'"

However much Russell was able to make light of the situation in public, the reality was that agents in four different countries were alerted to the threat to Russell and the star himself was troubled by this extraordinary and unwanted development in his life. Although kidnaps in America were on the decline, the FBI's Laura Bosley said: "It's not unusual to have a threat like that when you're dealing with high profile people. It's not unusual, especially in Los Angeles, where most of them live or at least visit."

The start of the year had seen the actor embark on a hectic round of international promotional visits for both *Gladiator* and *Proof Of Life*, which had opened in America in December 2000. He would be jetting between three continents beating the drum for his two movies and security would be arranged wherever he went.

In Britain, Scotland Yard closely monitored Russell's movements

Chapter XVII

when he flew in for the February 21 London premiere of *Proof Of Life*. A high-ranking police source said: "Russell was taking these threats extremely seriously. He was genuinely worried."

The following month Russell was to be found in Australia. At the Melbourne and Sydney premieres of *Proof Of Life* he was protected by high-level security. Guests at the after-party in Melbourne were surprised and disappointed to find Russell was in not so splendid isolation in his own roped-off area. Security guards were employed to ensure that only a chosen few were allowed to rub shoulders with him. In Sydney, it was very much the same story. The protection organised for Russell was unobtrusive. But those who had received a much sought-after invitation to the event and who later tried to leave the cinema complex in George Street were told by security men that they would not be allowed to re-enter.

Soon Russell was on his travels again, this time back to England for the British Academy of Film and Television Arts (BAFTA) awards. In London two extra rooms were booked at the Athenaeum Hotel for Russell's minders. "It was the first time he'd ever had bodyguards with him," said a hotel employee. In the end, Russell opted to stay at the Dorchester Hotel overlooking Park Lane.

Three security guards escorted Russell to the BAFTA awards but again it was low-key protection and by now there was a strong body of opinion that the publicity that had been accorded to the kidnapping threat had made it much less likely that it would ever take place.

The FBI, which publicly acknowledged attending to Crowe just the once, at the Golden Globes awards, have never identified exactly who was behind the threats, nor precisely when they were made or why Russell was the target. Nor did the FBI care to reveal whether the danger from abduction came from any one individual, from a group or from one of the professionals involved in almost ninety per cent of all kidnappings.

Statistics for international kidnapping show that sixty per cent of those abducted are eventually released, twenty per cent are rescued, five per cent escape and nine per cent are killed. Russell was relieved that in the end he did not contribute to any of those figures.

Once the very real fear of kidnap began to recede, Russell could once again start to concentrate on his film career. Next up was a role as a circus performer in *Flora Plum*, to be directed by his good friend Jodie Foster. Ahead of him were twelve weeks filming in Orlando, Florida, and he was greatly looking forward to it. "I'm playing a beast in a freak show," he announced excitedly, adding jocularly, "I think it's incredibly appropriate!"

But his excitement proved to be embarrassingly short-lived. While rehearsing what in essence was not much more than an undemanding gymnastic training exercise, Russell unexpectedly injured himself, with the result that *Flora Plum* was hurriedly shut down.

"I was learning something called The Spanish Web," he explained, "which consists of two pieces of material hanging from the ceiling and you climb up them like a rope and knot them around your ankles and fall backward. But I tore off the laborum tissue which holds the bicep tendon on to the bone inside my left shoulder.

"I was five metres above the ground with no safety ropes and I suddenly went. I had no grip strength in my left hand so I then very slowly had to get myself back to the ground and tell the trainers, 'Excuse me, I'm going to the hospital'. There's no words to describe how embarrassed, humiliated and bereft I felt. They've had to shut the production down. How do you apologise for that?"

Despite his obvious embarrassment, Russell could, however, see the irony of the situation. "You go through the German front in *Gladiator*, or you battle crime in Los Angeles in the Fifties in *L.A. Confidential* and you get away with that. And I was hanging off helicopters in Poland in *Proof Of Life*. And then I'm doing something where basically I'm a gymnast and I end up in hospital.

"But I was in a massive amount of pain and I had surgery. They gave me the choice: you can either get knocked out completely or they give you the happy pill, so I took the happy pill. Then I took photographs of the operation and put them on the Internet!"

Ten days after the surgery Russell horrified his doctor by driving the twelve hundred miles from Melbourne to his home in northern New South Wales to recuperate. "I was in a right-hand-drive manual car. That means my left hand was changing gears. The doctor was a bit freaked out by the whole idea. But I said to him: 'As long as the movements are even, then it's got to have a physiotherapeutic effect.' He said: 'I can't disagree with you.' So I said: 'Well, bugger you then, I'm driving home.'

"I just needed the space, man, you know? And the one way that I can do that is in the car." As always, he was glad to be home.

XVIII

GRUNTS

*I can zero in on things that have happened in my life
and stuff like that. This is my version of therapy.*
Russell Crowe on his songwriting

It's August 4, 2000, and down at Stubb's Bar-B-Q, a popular open-air venue on 8th and Red River in America's famous music city of Austin, a crowd numbering over two thousand are in a state of high excitement and anticipation while they swelter in the blistering heat as the summer sun fries the Texas sky.

They are very predominantly female, it's standing room only, and they are all jostling for a better view, a closer look. The more determined of this swaying crowd of girls and young women have pushed, shoved and made judicious use of their elbows to manoeuvre themselves into the premier positions in front of the half-shell stage. From here, in the already unbearably steamy, heaving melee that makes for a sweat-soaked mosh pit, they will get an up-close-and-personal chance to scrutinise a singer-guitarist who cheerfully admits, "I suck as a singer, and I suck as a guitarist".

For many of these fans, it simply doesn't matter if that's the case. They've seen their hero unleashing hell at the cinema and now they've turned out at Stubb's in the hope that, on stage, musically, he'll do the same. One common factor unites the largest contingent in the crowd, the most devoted: they are ready to drool.

Nick Penn, the Australian comedian warming up the already over-heated gathering, gazes out over the crowd, notes the preponderance of women and announces: "We have two thousand three hundred people here. That's two thousand women and three hundred gay guys!"

They've mainly queued in person for several hours to buy their tickets. Some were queuing as early as 5:45 in the morning. They've paid good money – incredibly, some as much as $2,000 for what was originally a $15 ticket. The price has been pushed ever higher thanks to an on-line auction frenzy. Now, on a sweltering summer's day, they've been prepared to stand cheerfully in a line that stretches fully four blocks for several hours more in the blistering heat just waiting to get in. "I've never seen anything like this before," says Stubb's co-owner Charles Attall. "I knew it was going to be a hot show but I didn't think we'd sell four thousand five hundred tickets for these gigs in an hour and a half.

"There's certainly a lot of women coming," Attall later observed as he studied the throng clamouring for the doors to open. He estimated around eighty per cent of the ticket buyers were female. "A lot are fans of the music, but then there are some who are just curious to see what it's all about."

Yet, extraordinary to relate, the vast majority of the milling throng of girls would find it difficult to name a single song by Russell Crowe, the idol they have come to see and worship. Mostly they would be hard pressed even to recite correctly the name of the band he fronts with such unbridled enthusiasm.

But long before he hollers, "Hello Austin, how the fuck are ya?" – the tried and trusted live gig greeting beloved of rock groups on the road who struggle to remind themselves what town they are in each night. Russell has the audience champing feverishly at the bit. It's his first post-*Gladiator* gig with his band Thirty Odd Foot Of Grunts and his audience, almost to a woman, have recently seen him at the local movie theatre, up on the screen wrestling with tigers, wielding his sword against fearful odds in a marvellously constructed gladiatorial arena and fighting for good against evil.

By the time Russell takes the stage with his group Thirty Odd Foot Of Grunts, the big screen hero has the audience in the palm of his hand, cheering, stamping, whistling and screaming. The official slogan of the city of Austin, Texas, is "Live music capital of the world". But it's not every day in Austin that the man who's strongly fancied to walk off with the Best Actor Oscar is proficient enough with guitar licks and chord progressions on a Gibson guitar to be the day's main rock music attraction.

He may not be the best musician in the world but when he picks up a guitar Russell Crowe is a seriously serious musician. And when he makes a record, it is with earnest endeavour. "It's not William Shatner's Christmas album," he once remarked acidly to a critic who had dared to doubt the musical integrity of a track he was laying down in the studio.

The female squeals and screams of adulation reach a crescendo as Russell ambles on stage. Now, before their very eyes, is Maximus himself in the flesh, but this time he's dressed in black button-down shirt and blue jeans, and instead of a shield he slings a guitar strap over his shoulder, plugs his lead into an amp and strikes a snarling chord which reverberates at high decibels through the speakers. Then, with an Australian, a New Zealand and a Texas flag hanging limply overhead in the breezeless air, he proceeds to step up to the microphone to bare his soul to the worshipping females around him by singing of why he's such a loser in love.

Slugging back the local Shiner Bock beer from a bottle between numbers, Russell pours out his heart, his troubles, his thoughts on the perils of success and fame, and his memories, in a series of strikingly revealing personal lyrics and monologues.

In Austin, Russell and his Thirty Odd Foot Of Grunts are playing their first US gigs in eighteen months and much has changed for the band's lead singer-guitarist in that time. He's now one of the biggest movie stars in the world – thanks to *Gladiator* – and he can command around $15 million a movie. He's wealthy enough, if he had a mind to, to buy Arlyn Studios in Austin, where his band have been recording a new album called *Bastard Life Or Clarity*, and he'd still have change to purchase Stubb's Bar-B-Q many times over.

But Russell is up on stage with Thirty Odd Foot Of Grunts – he hates it being called Russell Crowe's Band – because he's passionate about his music. It remains, though, no more than a passionate hobby because, as he puts it, he's got a "day job" that takes up a lot of time and it prevents him from being a musician full time. His other TOFOG band members, some of whom have been with him for many years, accept the limitations of their lot and go off to their day jobs too. The drummer Dave Kelly is a cameraman who has his own editing studio, the bass player Garth Adam is a stockbroker, and long-time friend Dean Cochran, who has been a guitar partner with Russell since 1984, works for a charity in Sydney. They are very much a group, and any promoter who puts up a notice saying "Russell Crowe's Band" usually finds that particular venue ignored thereafter by TOFOG at Russell's own insistence.

They are, and always have been, in it together and in Austin Russell ensures the group mentality pervades by running the TOFOG operation, which includes documentary film of the gigs and a video, like a movie-set operation. There's even a caterer, so Russell and the band members can all sit down under the stars to eat dinner together every night and continue to share the bond they have kept down the years.

Russell resolved from the very beginning to steer clear of the corporate marketing hype and the demands that a major record company would impose upon him and his band if they signed up bigtime. "I know that with one turn down that corridor, I could make money for jam," he once explained, "but that's not what it's about. I'm sorry folks."

A six-figure recording contract deal would be a formality if the record companies thought for one moment that Russell would be prepared to sign a contract to allow them to market TOFOG in the way that other rock groups are launched in the music industry. Instead, to retain control and integrity, the band's relationship with their fans has been established via the Internet (www.gruntland.com) and the first album, *Gaslight*, was available only through mail order. Russell and the rest of TOFOG enjoy being answerable to just themselves and to their fans.

Russell is the first to concede he's hardly a worldbeater when it comes to either guitar or vocals. He's in it for the enjoyment and because to him it's another of life's adventures. He's realistic enough to know that he's never going to be Eric Clapton or regarded with reverential awe by other rock musicians in the way that Clapton is. "I'm a very mediocre guitarist, so I can't sit and jam with Eric Clapton with any level of competence," he says. "But I can jam with any actor that walks the planet. If I could sit with Eric Clapton and get him to give me a little wink, that would be perfect. I know it is not going to happen because the talent isn't there."

Nevertheless, his blazing desire to make good music has earned him enough respect within the rock world to attract the likes of Ian McLagen, for several years Rod Stewart's keyboards wizard in The Faces, to play on the band's *Bastard Life Or Clarity* album. After he had completed filming of *L.A. Confidential* in 1997 and was waiting for the movie to be released following a very favourable reception at the Cannes Film Festival, Russell was anxious not to rush straight into anything new. He opted to spend time helping out with the lighting for a girlfriend's band and it meant he came into contact with plenty of respected Los Angeles musicians. Ian McLagen was just one.

Russell does, however, happily tell the story against himself of how a fine musician by the name of Novi Novag came to play the viola on two tracks on the album. Russell had known Novi for a number of years and he was determined to persuade her to join him on a couple of tracks in the studio. He felt sure she wouldn't refuse since he had fond memories of a musical collaboration a few years back. "She'd played on a track on *Gaslight*, our previous album," he says, "and I always thought it was such a great session that she'd remember me. But she didn't!"

Russell could earn many millions of dollars if he chose to take his band on a major tour. In 1994 and 1995 his acting obligations were readjusted continuously to allow the band to perform and record in places as far apart as New Zealand, Los Angeles and Sydney. In

1996 he managed to squeeze in a ten-week tour of Australia, and more recently TOFOG have played in Italy – at the San Remo Music Festival and at an exclusive gig organised by Armani and attended by Sarah, Duchess of York and a host of luminaries from the world of fashion.

There have also been TOFOG appearances at dozens of Australian pubs, halls and hotels, and in the US at varying opportune moments. One memorable Los Angeles gig was at Johnny Depp's club The Viper Room. "The place was packed," Russell recalled with satisfaction. "A lot of my pals came along – Danny DeVito, Kim Basinger, who never goes anywhere, and her husband Alec Baldwin." Prior to the band's arrival in Austin they fitted in an appearance in London at The Borderline.

Inevitably, as his stature as a movie star has grown and movies have demanded more of his time, gigs have tended to be fitted in around Russell's "day job". It goes without saying that live performances by the band always attract packed audiences, even if many have come along merely out of curiosity. As programme host Kevin Connor told his radio audience on Austin's 107.1 KGSR the day before the first of TOFOG's four local gigs: "For some of us who have lived here for a while, we have never seen such an international frenzy over a show at a club."

The response has surprised everybody, not least Russell himself. Stubb's Bar-B-Q is a venue where some of the greatest rock stars in the world have played and at first the management weren't too sure about hosting a little-known band called Thirty Odd Foot Of Grunts. But each time Russell makes a popular movie, interest in his gigs and records moves up several notches. The downside is that the band have to fight that much harder for their credibility and to prove that they are not just flying on Russell's movie coat-tails.

Gladiator turned demand for tickets for his Austin gigs into a desperate scramble. A total of four and a half thousand were sold in less than two hours on May 26, forcing the organisers to move the concerts from the indoor venue to the much larger outdoor one behind Stubb's Bar-B-Q. It constituted a record for the venue and there were enquiries for tickets from a host of different countries, including Canada, New Zealand, Switzerland, England, Japan, Ireland, Taiwan, Italy, Germany, Brazil and even China. One woman sent Mike Hall, Stubb's director of operations, one dozen red roses in a bid to secure a ticket. But in vain. This time fans had to be there to purchase in person at the ticket office and five hours before it was open there were already long queues around the block. Suddenly Stubb's Bar-B-Q were looking at Thirty Odd Foot Of Grunts in a very different light. Perhaps Russell and the boys might like to play another show or two? Or maybe they'd like to stay there another week? In the end they played Stubb's Bar-B-Q on three successive Fridays. "It's been great for the venue," said Charles Attall. "People from all over the world know our name now."

Russell's remarkable fame as a movie star has pop promoters falling over themselves with offers to send the band out on tour. TOFOG could fill the big-seater venues of the world to the rafters night after night. But Russell has never been into his band for the money. Instead, he's at Stubb's in Austin for a series of gigs that will leave him out of pocket because he's agreed to donate all the proceeds from the ticket sales to the local People's Community Clinic, a charity which provides health care to families with low incomes. And because he likes to perform live.

Such is the gratitude of Rick Perry, the Lieutenant Governor of Austin, that he not only declared the following Friday, August 11, "Thirty Odd Foot Of Grunts Day", but he also made Russell an honorary Texan and bestowed upon him the certificate and flag which ratifies it. "Not bad for an Australian from New Zealand," chuckled Russell, although he was prepared to accept the accolade as a serious honour and in the spirit in which it was offered.

Local town dignitaries are never slow to seize upon a PR opportunity so up in the VIP balcony overlooking the swaying crowd of adoring females at the gig was Rick Perry along with actress Sandra Bullock, who lives near Austin, and Ron Howard, who is directing

Russell's next movie, *A Beautiful Mind*. Rick was not just there to be seen, he really enjoyed the music along with the rest.

The band opened up with a song called *Other Ways Of Speaking*, inspired, says Russell, by his friendship with actress Jodie Foster. By the end of his two-hour set, the crowd was baying for an encore, a heavily perspiring Russell was stripped down to a tank-top and he was shaking his pelvis behind his guitar, which reduced many of the girls to screaming delirium. Rock, country-tinged melodies, introspective folky ballads and rhythmic numbers that lead the crowd into a line-dance as per the steps displayed on the back of the gig tickets, Thirty Odd Foot Of Grunts had capably run through them all. The finish was a rousing version of the Johnny Cash classic *Folsom Prison Blues*.

During the concert Russell's shirt came off by public demand. "Take off the shirt!" shrieked one of the female fans at the most inappropriate moment, just when Russell was introducing *Memorial Day*, the song he wrote about his grandfather. He eventually removed it to screams of approval for the rock number *Somebody Else's Princess*.

After *She's Not Impressed*, a song about a woman who doesn't think he's a suitable bet to build a nest with in which to have children, Russell informed the crowd that he did indeed want babies. He said it not once but several times, which invited a hundred female hands to shoot up in the air amid cries of "Me! Me!".

"We'll make a list," he teased them and added, "now don't you be throwing your panties up here, either. I know some of you are planning on doing that. Just keep them on." The interplay with the girls continued as he asked them whether they'd like the beer can he'd been drinking from or the butt end of his cigarette. Again there were high-pitched squeals and a surge forward for the souvenirs.

For Russell, a rock concert gives him a completely different buzz from making movies. Working on a movie set, he has said, is about endurance and patience, but there's something feral and primal about playing in a rock 'n' roll band. There's an attacking performance energy, not used when acting in a movie. There's a power to playing live, a release as opposed to the control that's required on a film set, and an instant feedback from the crowd. He views the adulation from the fans at a live gig as a double-edged sword. On the one hand, and certainly before *Gladiator*, it was a pointer to how well his music was appreciated. But he's not flying on some rock star ego trip. Between numbers he likes to bring back down to earth any inflated opinion the fans may have of him by delivering a series of monologues explaining that he is just as human as the rest. "Burning the pedestal" is how he likes to describe it and he's often so open in his monologue song intros that he'll even talk about his father's struggle through a spell of unemployment.

He also likes to joke and tease his audience along. At The Borderline in London on July 23, shortly before moving on to Austin, he'd gently needled his British audience about their weather and the fact that the Brits had allowed France to win the football World Cup, a game the Brits had invented. They laughed along with him, as did Australian singer Kylie Minogue, who was in the audience, and Russell's then new love Meg Ryan. On a more serious note, he introduced *The Photograph Kills* by alluding to the publicity over Meg that he'd endured, making the last eight weeks "the worst of my life".

Russell's music is, above all, a means of self expression and for the Austin crowd there was a remarkable insight into his innermost feelings. He acknowledges that much of his introspective material, such as the newly recorded *Sail The Same Oceans*, came out of his relationship with Danielle Spencer. "She's got an album coming out soon, but I'll bet there aren't any songs about me," he joked in Austin.

If you want to find the real Russell Crowe, listen to his songs and look at the lyrics, say many of those close to him. He views a three-minute song as a perfectly legitimate and worthwhile means of creative expression and with Russell it's usually a song sung from the heart. "The thing is, I'm not doing it for other people," Russell says of his music. "I write songs for myself. For me, a three-minute pop song is a completely incredible medium for me to be expressive in. I'm not a musician's musician, I'm a storyteller. If a song doesn't have a narrative, it doesn't have a point."

The band's curious name – Thirty Odd Foot Of Grunts – has its origins in the fact that there are five males in the band, all roughly around six feet tall (give or take a few collective inches) and a grunt is a very masculine promulgation. So, the story goes, if all the band members were laid head to toe then it would equal thirty odd foot of grunts. Russell wanted a name that rolled trippingly off the tongue and that, he says, was it.

But he has also attributed the name to an analogue dialogue replacement session for the movie *Virtuosity* in which the band's first single, *The Photograph Kills*, was featured. Film is measured in feet and, for the purposes of a sequence of sound effects for *Virtuosity*, Russell was required to provide thirty odd foot of grunts. Afterward the phrase stuck in his head and when the band later went on tour, that was the name with which they billed themselves on the tour posters.

While the core personnel of the band has changed little over the years, when it comes to recording Russell is only too happy to encourage his mates to join in. Hence the appearance of actor Jack Thompson on blues harp on a track called *High Horse Honey* on TOFOG's debut three-track EP *The Photograph Kills*. Also roped in for back-up vocals were actress Kym Wilson, with whom Russell appeared in the TV series *The Brides Of Christ,* and actor Robert Mammone, his co-star in *The Crossing*.

Russell had gathered his other TOFOG band members around him in Austin in the summer of 2000 to record a host of new songs they hadn't tried out in the studio before. It proved a prolific and creative few weeks. They had taken thirty-eight songs in all to Texas and ended up recording twenty-eight of them, with just ten ending up on *Bastard Life Or Clarity*. A further eight were record-ed, mixed and completed but did not figure on the album merely because there was a collective spirit about the other ten which connected to the CD's title. Russell was anxious that the album should be straightforward rather than longwinded and deliberately chose a producer who would simply come in and record the band and their songs rather than inject extraneous musical flavours and embellishments.

The last time TOFOG toured Australia had been in 1998–99, and Austin also afforded Russell and the band the chance not just to record new numbers but to play to audiences who weren't principally turning up just to party. "When we tour in Australia, we play in pubs in front of one thousand to two thousand people and they've all been on the sauce," he explained. "They've all been on the joy juice. So you tend to sort of play to that audience at a certain point in the tour. And that simplifies a lot of the songs. What we've done for the last year and a half is write in the grooves that we want to move toward. What's tended to happen is that the songs are a little softer now, not as cranked as they used to be. But we still venture into that area when we too have been on the joy juice."

The reconfiguring of TOFOG's music and live gigs means that Russell can now encourage people to listen to his lyrics and he ensures there's no need to read between the lines. He lays his feelings bare. "I can zero in on things that have happened in my life and stuff like that," he says of his lyrics. "This is my version of therapy. Some blokes go and lie on a couch."

In Austin he took the time to introduce his songs with poignant recollections and observations and became extremely irritated at any chatter from the crowd when he was talking. At one of the gigs he stopped the show three times to castigate the guests chit-chatting in the VIP balcony with "Shut the f— up". He added: "This is what happens when you invite Hollywood bastards to the show." Close inspection of the sleeve notes of the *Bastard Life Or Clarity* CD gives a fascinating insight, not least that Russell deliberately keeps his own name low-key – he lists himself last among the members of TOFOG behind Garth Adam, Dean Cochran, Dave Kelly, Stewart Kirwan and Dave Wilkins.

But it is the words in his songs which provide real fascination. Russell's *forte* is that he's a born storyteller. He loves to write songs and he's been writing them since he was a young boy. *Sail The Same Oceans* has the following notification on the CD's sleeve notes: "This song is for Jack Thompson" – his good friend and co-star in the film *The Sum Of Us*. Jack was playing a commercial sea captain in the movie and it inspired Russell to write the number. "Jack made me think of those old salty sailors," he says.

But Russell, as he confessed openly in Austin, admits that the driving force behind the song was his frequent trips abroad, which contributed hugely to his split with Danielle Spencer. The lyrics emerge as an intensely personal lament; that the constant travelling overseas to go off and play a dozen different characters left them both wondering who he really was and spelled the destruction of their love. "I'd done a lot of travelling for the previous couple of years," he said of his inspiration for *Sail The Same Oceans*, "and it was getting really intense. It was getting to the point where I'd come home and all the stuff that I'd done, I'd just have to put aside. It coincided with breaking up with Danielle. I was trying to balance the travel and where home was at that time."

Significantly, *Sail The Same Oceans* is probably the standout track on *Bastard Life Or Clarity*, although there are no fancy guitar licks and the chord progression follows a familiar path from G to B minor to C to D. But it's a strong melody arranged with a jangling country music tinge and delivered with real depth of feeling in Russell's vocals. Falling apart, he wails, wasn't part of the plan when he became so involved with Danielle.

Sail The Same Oceans has emotional echoes of an earlier song of Russell's on the album *Gaslight*, called simply *Danielle*. Here he bemoaned the fact that Danielle was an invisible travelling companion for him – she's in his heart but not in the plane seat beside him as he jets away. There are outpourings of extreme angst as he recounts how he and Danielle tortured each other to the point of crying by his absences. In his lyrics, Russell doesn't hold back:

Four months now stretch out before me
No one in my heart is going to call
Me from the other room
Expecting me to move
Danielle, Danielle, Danny, I love you
(Copyright 1998 Gruntland PTY Ltd)

The album sleeve for *Gaslight*, too, is itself revelatory. It's an illustration of a dimly-lit room, empty save for a vacant director's chair in one corner. On the wall is the shadow of a man sitting in the chair while the light from the room's two huge windows are blocked by camera lenses focused inward, all prying. It's an illustration of the emptiness of fame, and one song on the album in particular, called *David*, takes up the theme of confusion when fame arrives. It's based on Russell's experiences of strangers coming up to him on planes or in the street having read in newspapers and magazines about people who are also called Russell Crowe. These Russell Crowes were a ballroom dancer and a snake trainer charged with abusing his snake. Bizarrely, the famous Russell Crowe gets asked: "That Russell Crowe I've been reading about, is that you?"

Another intensely personal offering on *Bastard Life Or Clarity* is *Memorial Day*, a moving memory of Russell's grandfather. "This song is for Stanley J. Wemyss MBE," says the sleeve note of the man who was a cinematographer in the Second World War. It was written as Russell's thoughts turned to ANZAC day, the annual day in May when those Australian and New Zealand troops who gave their lives in the war are remembered. Russell's lyrics intone that he now wears his grandfather's medals as a mark of the freedom gained from the war, whereas his grandfather would not wear them because to him they brought back painful memories – they represented death and destruction. "I know a lot more about him now that's he's dead than I ever knew when he was alive," Russell says of his grandfather. "He was a very reticent man and every year around ANZAC day I start thinking about him."

Russell's *Things Have Got To Change* is a road song inspired by his desire every now and then to get on his motorbike and ride into the outback for a week or two at a time and leave his troubles behind. A video which accompanied the song looked more like a soap opera being played out in a caravan park, but it's a cry from the heart that when high pressure situations become too much then the only way things are likely to be different is if there is a pro-active change to alter them.

Equally revelatory in its own very different way is *The Night That Davey Hit The Train*, which Russell dedicated to the late actor Daniel Pollock, who co-starred with Russell in *Romper Stomper*. Pollock battled drug addiction before dying aged twenty-three in tragic circumstances, throwing himself in front of a train at Newtown station in Sydney in 1992. For years Russell was so angry about his friend's death that he found it hard to talk about it without being vitriolic. He also didn't necessarily see it as suicide. He saw it as an accident, citing Pollock as being very accident prone.

But at his live TOFOG shows Russell usually recounts how Pollock's friends shut him out of their lives one by one and regrets that he himself was unable to help him more to prevent his suicide.

During the making of *Romper Stomper*, Pollock talked with Russell about suicide – one of only three people Russell says he's had significant conversations with on the subject of the taking of one's own life, the others being TOFOG bandmate Dean Cochran and actor Ben Mendelsohn. "I find myself thinking about Daniel every now and then," explained Russell, "and have that thing in my mind about 'there but for the grace of god go I' kind of thing.

"Some people don't think Daniel committed suicide, they think it was an accident. That's OK. But I did have conversations with Daniel about that subject so whether he intended it or not, that song is about three separate conversations on that subject matter."

The Legend Of Barry Kable is a collaboration between Dean Cochran and Russell, which tells the tale of a painter and docker in Australia called Barry, who ended up living on the street around

Sydney's Darlinghurst Post Office, surviving on cheap port and the kindness of people like TOFOG's guitarist Dean – or "the Reverend Billy Dean" as Russell occasionally introduces him on stage.

Dean drove a van for the Sydney City Mission for seven years and one of his tasks on his shift every day for five years was to go and collect Barry and try to convince him to sleep it off at a hostel. Russell is full of admiration for such selfless work. "I think Dean's a hero, spending his life devoted to people on that level of charity. I mean, there's very little to gain personally or financially out of doing that sort of stuff."

Russell was steeped in music from an early age. He wasn't the first teenager to grow up wishing he was Elvis Presley and, although born a decade after Presley's first hit, his interest in the king of rock 'n' roll led him to a general curiosity in, and eventually a thorough knowledge of, Fifties rock music, which now warrants almost connoisseur status. His musical tastes are, however, eclectic and his large record collection ranges from operetta to the complicated sounds and rhythms of Dead Can Dance as well as the simpler catchy tunes and rhythms of the group Travis, singer-songwriter David Gray and the heart-rending vocals of Sinead O'Connor.

When it comes to songwriting, Billy Bragg has been a major influence on Russell. A songwriter who, rather like Russell, accompanied himself on ragged but effective electric guitar, the Essex-born Bragg started off singing revolutionary songs in pubs before becoming aware of leftist folk singers like Leon Rosselson and Dick Gaughan when he shared a stage with them at political benefit concerts. Bragg later went on to introduce their work to younger audiences as his own following grew and he himself managed to re-establish the link between political movements and contemporary folk song that had been severed in the Seventies. Bragg's songs caught the mood of disaffected British youth in the early Eighties, but Bragg was also adept at writing love songs whose passionate realism matched that of his political lyrics. Russell has always considered them to be inspirational.

Russell's music is not, however, to everyone's tastes. Not long after he had finished filming *L.A. Confidential*, Russell was back in Australia rehearsing with his band when Danny DeVito flew in to Sydney to promote his film *Matilda*, which he had directed. Russell and Danny had struck up a firm friendship during the making of *L.A. Confidential* – in the film Russell had to punch him and stand over his dead body – and, when Danny called him up, Russell invited him along to the rehearsal, which was being held in a dingy little room. On his arrival, Russell offered Danny a drink, a sandwich and a cigarette, but he declined them all saying he'd prefer just to sit and watch and listen. But some time later, when the band took a short break, Danny decided he'd like a cigarette after all – much to Russell's surprise, because he didn't think he smoked. "Are you guys going to sing any more songs?" asked Danny, pulling two cigarettes out of the packet. When Russell enthusiastically told him that there was plenty more to come, Danny broke the filters off the two cigarettes and firmly plugged one into each ear.

EPILOGUE

According to a new survey, sixty per cent of married
women say they would rather take a shower with Russell
Crowe than take a shower with their own husband.
Apparently the remaining forty per cent of married
women couldn't be reached – because they were
showering with Russell Crowe.
Conan O'Brien, host of US TV show
"Late Night With Conan O'Brien".

As e-mails, cards, telephone calls and other messages of congratu-
lation were pouring in from various parts of the world for Russell
following his Best Actor Oscar win, Russell himself was on a plane
to New York studying the script for *A Beautiful Mind*. He was greet-
ed with a round of applause by cast and crew when he arrived on
the set. After first buying everyone a drink, Russell then settled
down to work. Paul Bettany, a handsome young British actor who
has a role in the film and who is destined for big things, couldn't
believe it. "That's dedication for you," he said.

Russell contented himself with the knowledge that there would
be other times to party, but now he had a new movie role to get
inside and it was going to be far from simple. He would be playing
the role of John Forbes Nash Junior, a man who went from boy
genius to paranoid schizophrenic but who emerged thirty years
later from his mental nightmare to win the Nobel Prize for work
completed before his breakdown. Russell had the formidable job of
portraying Nash from the time he entered Princeton University at
the age of nineteen, through his deterioration and on to his eventual recovery in his sixties.

The film's title and the inspiration for the movie comes from *A*
Beautiful Mind, a biography of John Forbes Nash Junior by former

New York Times reporter Sylvia Nasar, whose book chronicled Nash's whole incredible and tragic life story.

As a young man, Nash appeared to have it all. He was handsome and self-assured and had entered Princeton University with a one-line recommendation from his college tutor: "This man is a genius." In 1950, within fourteen months of arriving at the university, he produced the Nash Equilibrium, a formulated theorem that enabled the arcane field of game theory to become an important influence in modern economics and political science. It was to win him the Nobel Prize on October 11, 1994 – forty-four years later.

But the intervening years were extraordinary to say the least. Nash continued to use his incredible mind to solve problems that other mathematicians thought unsolvable. He seemed poised for further success. He married and he and his wife were blessed with a baby. But then he sank into paranoid schizophrenia and was repeatedly hospitalized against his will. His wife, Alicia, divorced him but then took him in when he pleaded with her to rescue him from the degradation of wandering around Princeton impoverished and the butt of jokes from the local children. Eventually, after a thirty-year nightmare, he re-surfaced to win the coveted Nobel Prize.

Ron Howard, the film's director, can trace his own interest in mental illness back to a childhood trauma he experienced when he was eight years of age. He was then a child star on the American TV sit-com *The Andy Griffith Show*, where he witnessed a guest actor suffering a complete mental collapse in front of the cameras. Howard watched in horrified fascination as the poor man started speaking in words that did not make sense. By the time everyone realised something was seriously wrong, he had crumpled to a heap on the floor in the fetal position. "It was one of the most extraordinary, intense, terrifying things I have ever witnessed," he said.

The incident stayed in Howard's mind and twice he came close to getting a movie project about mental illness off the ground. Both projects stalled at the script stage but Sylvia Nasar's biography gave him the inspiration to try to bring Nash's truly remarkable story to the screen. He picked Russell to star in the $40 million movie and once he was in place, Howard assembled a strong supporting cast, including Ed Harris, Judd Hirsch and Christopher Plummer, with Jennifer Connelly as Nash's long-suffering wife Alicia. "I think he can play roles other than a gladiator, which obviously I am not," was Nash's enigmatic comment on the casting.

Sylvia Nasar declared that the choice of Russell to play Nash was inspired. "Crowe isn't just beautiful, he's a superb actor who's got it all: emotional intensity, presence and brains," she said. "This is a drama about the mystery of the human mind in three acts: genius; madness; reawakening. Crowe will be totally convincing in all of Nash's incarnations. He'll convey Nash's raw mental power and confidence at the outset, his torment and terrible isolation during his illness and finally his incredibly moving triumph."

Nash is now seventy-two and Russell was introduced to him when he visited the set but avoided anything more than a brief chat with the mathematician. He was anxious not to pick up too closely on the post-trauma Nash as he had to assume so much of the man's physicality when he was so very much younger. He did, however, notice that he had beautiful hands and polished nails and resolved to let his own nails grow.

Instead of a searching conversation with his subject, Russell concentrated his research on early photos of Nash and listened to taped interviews with him and with patients with similar mental disorders. He knew *A Beautiful Mind* would stretch his acting powers to the limit. Not since *Romper Stomper* had Russell been able to take on a role that was so extreme.

After *Gladiator*, it would have been so easy for Russell to take up one of dozens of tough guy roles that were being offered for huge amounts of money. "People throw money at me to do things that aren't significant," he observed. "So I don't do them. It's funny, there's a correlation between the more money that they offer you and the shittier the script is."

While *A Beautiful Mind* was scheduled for a winter release in

2001, there was much discussion in film circles about Russell's suitability to play James Bond should Pierce Brosnan ever hand in his 007 screen mantle.

John Glen, who directed five Bond films including *Octopussy* and *A View To A Kill,* voiced the opinion that the Bond movies would continue for the next twenty years and, while Pierce Brosnan was doing an excellent job, he wouldn't play Bond for ever. "I can't think of anyone better than Russell to fill his shoes," he said. "To play Bond, you need a man who has great screen presence and is believable in the part. Looking at him you could easily believe Russell capable of savagely bumping off bad men with a wry comment." One thing is certain: Russell's choice of movie roles in the future will continue to surprise. He is eminently castable and Hollywood has come to terms with his ability to play the good guy as well as the bad.

As a film actor of eleven years experience and as a man in his thirty-eighth year, Russell has come a very long way since George Ogilvie cast him in *The Crossing* and fixed his missing front tooth for him. Russell Crowe has matured and grown up. These days he would be unlikely to pull a face very publicly behind Australia's Prime Minster as he once did after accepting an Australian Film Institute Award. Explaining away the petulant gesture afterward he said: "We shook hands and he wouldn't look me in the eye, and that really annoyed me."

He's still just as likely to party when the mood takes him but friends notice there is a temperance now that has replaced the hell-raising. He's learned that a four thousand-mile three-week motorbike trip around Australia with pals – where they say nothing to each other all day, but just ride before enjoying a convivial drink and discussion about what they've seen on their travels – is a far preferable way of letting off steam than the use of fists in a public bar.

Fame does not always sit easily on Russell Crowe's broad shoulders. Fans hand him good-luck charms or leave them outside his house – a silver dollar, Stars of David, Maltese and Greek Orthodox crosses. "They usually come with sincere letters about my on-going safety, so I feel obligated to carry them with me," he says, revealing his superstitious nature.

He can, however, comfortably cope with the fan mail and the autograph hunters most of the time. He understands the fervency of fans because he's a fan himself – he admired Jodie Foster's work as both an actress and as a director so much that, before he had even met her, he sent a little rugby shirt for her baby boy. But at other moments the burden of expectation that goes with his superstar status grates upon him, especially in Hollywood. For example, when *Virtuosity* was being launched in America, he found himself having to argue his way out of being ferried to a screening in an ostentatious limousine when he preferred to walk the block and a half to the cinema. "It's ridiculous," he said. "I kept saying, 'I do have my own legs, mate'. I mean, it's not just some frivolous form of rebelliousness for the sake of being cool or whatever. Aside from the practical consideration of it, that a block and a half is a block and a half, it's such a waste of money."

It's an honest statement, and it explains why some Hollywood movie personnel find him difficult and why Russell refuses to live there full time. He wants to act only between the words "Action" and "Cut". By living well away from Los Angeles, on green fields among his animals in northern New South Wales, he feels he can bring a different level of energy to Hollywood than he would if he was "living in the office", as he puts it.

"Some people say cinema's not a serious job," he says, "but I used to be the bloke lining up for the ticket and I want to make sure that person is getting their money's worth."

FILMOGRAPHY

Blood Oath, 1990

Also known as *Prisoners Of The Sun*

Harrowing drama based on the true story of the war crime trials of ninety-one Japanese officers and men conducted on the island of Ambon in 1946. Bryan Brown stars as Army prosecutor Captain Cooper, with Russell Crowe as his assistant counsel Lt Jack Corbett, who helps him in the trial investigations into the Japanese atrocities committed against Australian prisoners of war. Also featuring Jason Donovan.

Director: Steven Wallace

The Crossing, 1990

Love triangle set over a period of twenty-four hours in a country town on ANZAC day involving two young men, Johnny (Russell Crowe) and Sam (Robert Mammone), and a teenage girl called Meg (Danielle Spencer), whose childhood friendships are eclipsed by the overpowering chemistry of the love they share. Emotions reach boiling point when publican's son Sam unexpectedly returns to the town after a year in the city to seek out Meg, the girl he left behind. He is shocked to find that she has embarked on an affair with Johnny, who happens to have once been Sam's best friend. Meg is torn between the two lovers and the trio's lives are irreversibly changed and their fates decided at the town's railway crossing.

Director: George Ogilvie

Australian Film Institute nomination for Best Actor for Russell Crowe

Proof, 1991

Martin (Hugo Weaving) has been blind since birth and his distrust of humanity prompts him to take photographs to document his world. By taking photographs, Martin has proof that the world he senses is the same one that other people see. He develops a friendship with Andy (Russell Crowe), an amiable dishwasher at the local restaurant, whose honesty and kindness wins his trust and whose help he then enlists to describe the photographs for him. But their strong, genuine friendship is threatened by the cunning of Martin's lovelorn housekeeper Celia (Genevieve Picot). She is obsessed with Martin but, frustrated by his constant rejection of her, she sees seduction as a weapon with which to destroy Martin and Andy's friendship in a cold, cruel, calculating act of revenge.

Director: Jocelyn Moorhouse

Australian Film Institute Best Supporting Actor Award for Russell Crowe

Spotswood, 1991

Also known as *The Efficiency Expert*

No-nonsense time-and-motion efficiency expert Wallace (Anthony Hopkins) is brought in to analyse financially troubled Balls' moccasin factory, located in the quiet Melbourne suburb of Spotswood in 1960s Australia. His job is to turn the workers from a bunch of oddballs into a well-oiled working machine. But, while facing marital problems and questioning the ethics of his job, he learns to appreciate the laid-back atmosphere at the family-owned factory, as well as the eccentric workforce of whom only sales executive Kim (Russell Crowe) appears to have any ambition or grasp of how to run a business. Also starring Ben Mendelsohn and Toni Collette.

Director: Mark Joffe

Romper Stomper, 1992

Russell Crowe as skinhead leader Hando, a brutish leader of a gang of moronic neo-Nazi skinheads who regularly do battle with Melbourne's Vietnamese community. When the gang attacks a group of Vietnamese in the process of purchasing the skinheads' favourite bar, the "gooks" counter-attack with a large force, driving the skinheads from their warehouse base in a long drawn-out battle. Co-starring Daniel Pollock as Hando's right-hand man and Jacqueline McKenzie as a drug addict whose father (Alex Scott) has abused her in an incestuous relationship.

Director: Geoffrey Wright

Australian Film Institute Best Actor Award for Russell Crowe

Love In Limbo, 1993

Also known as *Just One Night*, and *The Great Pretender*

Coming-of-age comedy about a sex-obsessed teenage boy called Ken (Craig Adams), a handsome girl chaser called Barry (Aden Young) and featuring Russell Crowe as Arthur Baskin, a bureaucratic clothing factory warehouse supervisor and a virginal Welsh Baptist, who form a friendship in the 1950s. Sex is a mystery for the trio, who all work together. Anxious to lose their virginities, they head off on a road trip to a brothel on Kalgoorlie's infamous red-light street in a fumbling attempt to transform themselves collectively overnight from boys to men.

Director: David Elfick

Hammers Over The Anvil, 1993

Alan Marshall (Alexander Outhred) is a young boy who has suffered many hardships in life, but none so savage as being struck down by polio, which leaves him unable to walk without crutches. Despite his afflictions, Alan dreams of becoming a great horseman like the town's hero, East Driscoll (Russell Crowe). Handsome and skilful, Driscoll is the most popular man in town. But, as Alan discovers one summer, heroes can fall when horse broker Driscoll becomes entangled in an affair with Grace McAlister (Charlotte Rampling), the much older aristocratic English wife of a landowner.

Director: Ann Turner

The Silver Brumby, 1993

Also known as *The Silver Stallion*, and *King Of The Wild Brumbies*
Based on Elyne Mitchell's classic Australian children's tale of the same name, which is about Thowra, a stallion like no other, which roams in the unforgiving wilderness of the Australian mountains. Grand in stature and a beauty to behold, with a silvery mane and tail and striking cream coat, Thowra is king of all the Cascade Brumbies. Wise in the ways of the bush and courageous and daring in the face of danger, the Silver Brumby is revered by all, including his greatest enemy, man. For years men have tried to claim the elusive Brumby as their prize, but without success. Then a horseman, a high country loner known as The Man (Russell Crowe), sets out to capture the horse, which according to legend can never be tamed. Also starring Caroline Goodall as Elyne Mitchell, who relates the horse's story to her daughter.

Director: John Tatoulis

The Sum Of Us, 1994

Harry Mitchell (Jack Thompson) is a down-to-earth widower who willingly helps his gay football-playing plumber son Jeff (Russell Crowe) in his search for Mr Right. Harry has comfortably come to terms with his son's sexual preference and has long ago made up his mind to allow Jeff to be his own man. But there are complications in Jeff's search for Mr Right when Jeff falls for Greg (John Polson), a gardener who has not yet admitted to being a homosexual. Harry, meanwhile, finds a new love, Joyce (Deborah Kennedy), who expresses shock that he tolerates having a gay son living under his roof.

Director: Geoff Burton, Kevin Dowling

For The Moment, 1994

This film features the lives and loves of three airmen at a training school in Manitoba, Canada, in the 1940s. Aussie fighter pilot Lachlan (Russell Crowe) accompanies his friend Johnny (Peter Outerbridge) home to meet Johnny's fiancee, where he falls instantly for her older sister, Lill (Christianne Hirt), who has found it difficult to cope with loneliness since her husband went off to war. Drawn to dashing Lachlan, Lill and the airman embark on a clandestine romance.

Director: Aaron Kim Johnston

The Quick And The Dead, 1995

John Herod (Gene Hackman), the sadistic mayor of Redemption, rules ruthlessly and violently over the thugs and miscreants who make up his town, circa 1870. Each year, in order to weed out his rivals and to protect his power, he holds a shooting contest which attracts people from miles around, including his son The Kid (Leonardo DiCaprio). It is a quickdraw shoot-to-kill contest which Herod wins every year. Then into Redemption rides Ellen (Sharon Stone), a mysterious lady gunslinger who signs up for the contest. But it is not the prize money she is after. She is seeking revenge for the death of her father and her real target is Herod. In the running for Ellen's favours are The Kid and outlaw-turned-preacher Bud Cort (Russell Crowe), a former hotshot with a pistol who has renounced violence and found God. Pressed into picking up a gun once more, he sides with Ellen to bring Herod down.

Director: Sam Raimi

Virtuosity, 1995

Sci-fi action thriller starring Russell Crowe as SID 6.7 (short for Sadistic, Intelligent and Dangerous), a virtual reality super psychopath who has been programmed with a composite of the minds of 183 real life serial killers and psychopaths, ranging from Attila the Hun to Adolf Hitler. Primarily created to test the mettle of trainee police officers undertaking simulated criminal investigations, SID

6.7 suddenly breaks the bonds of cyberspace and explodes into unstoppable havoc-wreaking real-life mayhem and murder, able to take a beating but keep on kicking because he can regenerate his silicon-based body parts. Denzel Washington stars as cop-turned-convicted-murderer Parker Barnes, who is promised a full pardon and immediate release if he can shut SID 6.7 down.

Director: Brett Leonard

Rough Magic, 1995

Also known as *Miss Shumway*, *Jette*, and *Un Sort* (France)
Romantic comedy set in 1950 and based on the novel *Miss Shumway Waves A Wand* by James Hadley Chase. Ex-Marine Raider Alex Ross (Russell Crowe) is working in Mexico as a stringer for *The Los Angeles Times* when he falls in love with magician's assistant Myra Shumway (Bridget Fonda), who is running away from an arranged marriage.

Director: Clare Peploe

No Way Back, 1996

Shattered by the murder of his son, mobster Frank Serlano (Michael Lerner) kidnaps the young son of FBI agent Zack Grant (Russell Crowe) in revenge. Serlano's terms for release are for Grant to deliver the man responsible for the murder of his son.

Director: Frank Capello

L.A. Confidential, 1997

Film noir adaptation of the James Ellroy bestseller about the seamier side of 1950s Los Angeles. Three detectives, Kevin Spacey, Guy Pearce and Russell Crowe – as Officer Bud White – each use their own tactics and methods to investigate a coffee-shop massacre. Also starring Kim Basinger and Danny DeVito.

Director: Curtis Hanson

Heaven's Burning, 1997

Colin O'Brien (Russell Crowe) hits the small time as a petty criminal getaway driver who accidentally leaves a bank robbery scene without his partners in crime but with more than cash. Due to a chain of bizarre events, he finds himself speeding away from the bank across the sunburnt Australian countryside with a passionate bleach-blonde Japanese honeymooning wife (Youki Kudoh) who has faked her own kidnapping. On their way, the fleeing duo meet a number of oddball characters, including a crippled accordion player, a drug-addicted palm-reading hairdresser, a blind dress store owner and a blousy barmaid. On the trail of the fugitives are a bunch of mean hoods baying for blood, two droll Sydney detectives and a jilted, crazy kamikaze Japanese husband. With Ray Barrett as Colin's father.
Director: Craig Lahiff

Breaking Up, 1997

A photographer called Steve (Russell Crowe) has been dating a teacher, Monica (Salma Hayek), for two years but their relationship is going through a sticky patch and she feels that they should stop seeing each other. But a few days later they get back together only for the bickering to continue, which leads to a real separation and dates with other people. Then suddenly Steve asks Monica to marry him and she accepts, but the union is not harmonious.
Director: Robert Greenwald

Mystery, Alaska, 1999

Also known as *Pond Rules*

Mystery, a small town in Alaska obsessed with ice hockey, is turned upside down when the local team gets the unexpected opportunity to play a big NHL team, the New York Rangers, in a major televised event. The town sheriff, John Biebe (Russell Crowe), a former player, and the town judge, Walter Burns (Burt Reynolds), join forces to whip the team into shape for the game of their lives. Also starring Mary McCormack as Biebe's wife Donna.

Director: Jay Roach

The Insider, 1999

A film based on the real-life story of Dr Jeffrey Wigand, a former tobacco executive who in 1995 blew the whistle on chemical manipulation of tobacco by cigarette company Brown & Williamson. Wigand is persuaded to spill the beans about his company's findings on the addictive power of nicotine by Lowell Bergman (Al Pacino), producer of influential CBS current affairs TV programme *60 Minutes*. But Wigand becomes the target of a smear campaign and pays a heavy price for speaking out, including the loss of his home, his family and his trust in others.

Director: Michael Mann

Best Actor Oscar nomination for Russell Crowe

Gladiator, 2000

After a resounding victory in battle in Germany, loyal Roman general Maximus Decimus Meridius (Russell Crowe) is in line to succeed emperor Marcus Aurelius (Richard Harris). But the wise old man is murdered by his depraved, cowardly son Commodus (Joaquin Phoenix), who then orders the general's death and has his family massacred. Escaping from the soldiers despatched to kill him, Maximus is then captured by slavers and sold as a gladiator, where he is trained in the art of gladiatorial combat by Proximo (Oliver Reed). He distinguishes himself so well in the arenas that he gradually fights his way back to Rome and a final confrontation in the Colosseum with Commodus. Also starring Connie Neilsen, Derek Jacobi and David Hemmings, the film was nominated for eleven Academy Awards.

Director: Ridley Scott

Best Actor Oscar for Russell Crowe

Proof Of Life, 2001

Tense, romantic hostage thriller about American engineer Peter Bowman (David Morse), who has been kidnapped by a revolutionary group. His wife Alice (Meg Ryan) is relieved when Terry Thorne (Russell Crowe), an ex-SAS trooper now specializing in corporate ransom cases, arrives to take up the trail. But he leaves the day after when it becomes apparent that the company Bowman worked for had not kept up their insurance payments. Thorne eventually decides to take on the case anyway with the help of Dino (David Caruso), another equally tough negotiator. During their tense negotiations with the kidnappers, Alice and Thorne find themselves drawn ever closer together.

Director: Taylor Hackford

A Beautiful Mind, 2001

Bio-pic of schizophrenic mathematics genius John Forbes Nash Junior, who was awarded the Nobel Prize for economics in 1994 for a complex game theory he developed forty years earlier at the age of twenty-one. Nash suffered bouts of schizophrenia over a thirty-year period before reverting to normal. Co-starring Ed Harris, Judd Hirsch, Christopher Plummer and Jennifer Connelly.

Director: Ron Howard

MAJOR TELEVISION APPEARANCES

Neighbours, 1985
Four episodes as Kenny Larkin

Brides Of Christ, 1991
Major drama series about teachers and students at an Australian convent school in the 1960s, starring Brenda Fricker as Sister Agnes and Sandy Gore as Mother Ambrose. Kym Wilson plays Rosemary, a student starting to question the Catholic doctrines while exploring her blossoming sexuality and who soon earns a reputation as a sexually promiscuous rebel. Then, at a school dance, she meets Dominic (Russell Crowe), the sweet-natured brother of a classmate. They become friends and although Rosemary yearns for the relationship to become something more, the Vietnam War drives them apart.
Director: Ken Cameron

Police Rescue, 1992
One episode playing Senior Constable Tom "Bomber" Young, a football hero who allows his lost confidence to impair his work when he joins the Police Rescue Squad.

The Late Show, 1992
One appearance as "Shirty, the slightly aggressive bear".

DISCOGRAPHY

Thirty Odd Foot of Grunts
"What's Her Name." (EP) 1997
Gaslight 1998
"Inside Her Eyes/The Legend of Barry Kable" (single) 1999
Bastard Life of Clarity 2001

INDEX

Crowe, Russell: and Australian Film
Institute award 57, 236; and *A
Beautiful Mind* 189, 230-4, 243;
birth 13; and *Blood Brothers* 37;
and *Blood Oath* 38-40, 46, 235;
and *Breaking Up* 121-2, 241: and
Brides of Christ 244; busking 33-4;
character 7, 8-9, 10-12, 15, 79; and
Courtney Love 181-2; and *The
Crossing* 40-55, 235; and Danielle
Spencer 41-2, 47-8, 51-2, 54, 55,
57-8, 77, 78, 83, 91, 110, 122-3,
182, 184, 187, 225; and Dean
Cochran 27, 33, 34; early television appearances 15, 17; educa-
tion 17-18, 19-21; and *Flora Plum*
212; and *For the Moment* 82-3, 91-
2, 238-9; and *Gladiator* 7-8, 9, 10,
17, 153-77, 179-181, 197, 242; and
Hammers Over The Anvil 71, 74,
76, 237; and *Heaven's Burning* 55,
124-5, 240; in Hollywood 81-3;
and *The Insider* 9-10, 143-52, 158,
242; and Jodie Foster 151, 212,
221; kidnap threat 208-12; and
L.A. Confidential 125, 131-42, 240;
and *Love in Limbo* 59-60, 237; and
Meg Ryan 192-3, 199-208; move to
Australia 14, 33; music 19, 20-1,
22-8, 214-29; and *Mystery, Alaska*
141-2, 144-5, 241-2; and
Neighbours 38, 244; and *No Way
Back* 120-1, 240; and *The Official
Tribute to the Blues Brothers* 77-8;
Oscar nominations 151, 178-89;
and *Police Rescue* 244; and *The
Profile* 22; and *Proof* 56-7, 62, 79-
80, 235-6; and *Proof of Life* 152,
178, 190-213, 243; and *The Quick
and the Dead* 86, 88, 93-116, 239;

and *Red Rain* 87; and *Romper
Stomper* 8-9, 61-9, 82, 227, 236-7;
and *The Rocky Horror Picture
Show* 29-33, 240; and *Rough Magic*
116, 120-1, 240; as Russ le Roq 19,
23-6; and Sharon Stone 86, 88, 93-
116; and *The Silver Brumby* 70-8,
238; smoking 8, 143; sport 19-21;
and *Spotswood* 58-9, 236; and Stan
Wemyss 16-17, 37, 186, 226; and
The Sum of Us 78, 84-92, 101-2,
238; and Thirty Odd Foot of
Grunts 206, 214-29, 244; and Tom
Sharplin 22, 23; and *Virtuosity* 117-
25, 234, 239-40
Crowe, Terry 11, 13, 21
Cruise, Tom 158
Cunningham, Ira 13

D

Daemion, Ami 74
Danielle 225-6
Dave Deceit and the Interrogatives
22
Davis, Judy 36
Davis, Peter 29, 30
De Niro, Robert 182-3
DeVito, Danny 134-5, 140, 229, 240
DiCaprio, Leonardo 99, 102, 105,
106, 114, 239
Donen, Josh 100
Donovan, Jason 38, 39, 235
Douglas, Michael 95
Dowling, Kevin 238
Dunaway, Faye 96

E

Ecuador 190-2, 196, 198
Efficiency Expert, The see *Spotswood*
Elfick, David 237

ACKNOWLEDGEMENTS

The authors wish to thank for their help with this book, and for their support, encouragement and inspiration: Roy and Liz Addison, John Airey, Dave and Sue Batchelor, Ruth Berry, John Burmester, Rodney Collins, Tom and Mags Condon, Corinna Cowie, Roger Davis, John and Wendy Dickinson, Ian Dowell, Kenneth Eastaugh, Jane Ennis, Peter and Janet Garner, Rod and Joy Gilchrist, Richard and Jane Hall, Phil and Ann Hammond, Stuart Higgins, Kathryn Holcombe, Lorinda Holness, Ingrid Holtz, Mike Hope, Clive Jackson, Jerry Johns, Stan and Anna Johnston, Barry Kernon, Robert Kirby, David Knight, Fiona Knight, Frank Langan, Lisa Lane, Ray and Janet Lewis, Bryan Marshall, Sarita Martin, Aysen Mustafa, Andrew and Angela Noone, Helen and Peter Pasea, Garth and Davina Pearce, Dimity Perry, Jean Platts, Arethusa Plouidy, Marie Louise Pumfrey, Patrick and Wendy Sandner, Rachel Sharp, Victoria Supple, Gordon Webb, George and Lottie Wood. And a big thank you to Sarah Larter, Piers Murray Hill and all at the Carlton Publishing Group for their co-operation and kindness.

Tim would especially like to thank British Airways and Quantas for their comfort, care and courtesy, and Anthea Bastian and all at Sullivan's Hotel, 21 Oxford Street, Paddington, Sydney, Australia for such a pleasant and enjoyable stay during his research.

SOURCES

The authors have respected the wishes of many interview subjects to remain anonymous and accordingly they are not mentioned in the book. They also gratefully acknowledge the following sources who helped in the preparation of this book but they are by no means all-inclusive:

Adelaide Advertiser, *The Age*, *Auckland Star*, *Austin Chronicle*, *The Australian*, Australian Film Institute, *Brisbane Courier-Mail*, *Ballarat Courier*, Channel 7, *Detour*, *Empire*, Foxtel, GMTV, *GQ*, *Heat*, *Hello*, *Juice*, "Late Night With Conan O'Brien", "Late Show With David Letterman", *Los Angeles Times*, Maximum Russell Crowe (website), *New Idea*, *New York Times*, *New Zealand Herald*, *New Zealand Listener*, *New Zealand Woman' Weekly*, *Now*, Radio KGSR (Austin, Texas), *San Francisco Examiner*, *Sunday Mail* (Queensland), *Sydney Morning Telegraph*, *Sydney Sun-Herald*, "Tonight Show With Jay Leno", *TV Week*, *Vancouver Sun*, *Vogue Men*, *W* magazine, *Who Weekly*, Woman's Day, *Gladiator: The Making of the Ridley Scott Epic*, www.gruntland.com.

PICTURE CREDITS

The Quick and the Dead: Tristar; *LA Confidential*: Monarchy/Regency; *The Insider*: Touchstone pictures; *Gladiator*: Dreamworks/Universal; *Proof of Life*: Castle Rock; *Romper Stomper* /SeonFilms: all courtesy The Kobal Collection

Russell Crowe at Sydney Boys High school; Russell Crowe as Eddie in the *Rocky Horror Show;* in *Police Rescue*; with Danielle Spencer: Newspix.com.au/NewsLimited.

Russell Crowe as boy with cricket bat; Russ le Roq: Simon Runting/Rex Features.

Rough Magic/20th Century Fox; *The Crossing*/Enterprise Pictures; *Proof*/Artificial Eye; *Love in Limbo*/Beyond Film; *Hammers Over the Anvil*/Beyond Film; *The Sum of Us*/MALOFILM: all Ronald Grant Archive.

Russell Crowe with Academy Award; Russell Crowe with Jodie Foster; performing: Popperfoto/Reuters.

Russell Crowe in suit, smiling: CORBIS.